Traces of Gold

Studies in American Literary Realism and Naturalism

Traces of Gold

California's Natural Resources and the Claim to Realism in Western American Literature

NICOLAS S. WITSCHI

The University of Alabama Press
Tuscaloosa

Hardcover edition published 2001.
Paperback edition published 2012.
eBook edition published 2009.

Typeface: New Baskerville

Cover photograph: "Middle Fork at Kings River from South Fork of Cartridge Creek, Kings River Canyon," California, 1936, by Ansel Adams.
Courtesy of the National Archives.

∞

The paper on which this book is printed meets the minimum requirements of American National Standard for Information Science–Permanence of Paper for Printed Library Materials, ANSI Z39.48-1984.

Paperback ISBN: 978-0-8173-5741-2
eBook ISBN: 978-0-8173-1371-5

A previous edition of this book has been catalogued by the Library of Congress as follows:

Library of Congress Cataloging-in-Publication Data
Witschi, Nicolas S., 1966–
Traces of gold : California's natural resources and the claim to realism in western American literature / Nicolas S. Witschi.
p. cm. — (Studies in American literary realism and naturalism)
Includes bibliographical references (p. 195) and index.
ISBN 0-8173-1117-3 (cloth : alk. paper)
1. American literature—California—History and criticism. 2. Natural resources—California. 3. California—In literature. 4. Realism in literature. 5. Nature in literature. I. Title. II. Series.
PS283.C2 W58 2002
813.009'3278'09794—dc21
2001003184

British Library Cataloguing-in-Publication Data available

To Meg,
For the sheer joy of it.

Contents

Acknowledgments

A shorter version of chapter 2 appeared in the fall 1999 issue of *Western American Literature* (34.3), and I am grateful to Melody Graulich for permission to reprint it here. I also wish to thank Daryl Morrison of the Special Collections Department at the University of the Pacific for permission to quote from the John Muir Papers, Holt-Atherton Department of Special Collections, University of the Pacific Libraries, copyright 1984, Muir-Hanna Trust; and the Huntington Library, San Marino, California, for a Frank Hideo Kono Research Fellowship that afforded me time to study their Mary Austin Collection and for permission to publish excerpts from the extensive archive.

This book would be a greatly diminished thing without the input of the many wonderful friends and colleagues who, in some cases, read and commented upon this project during its various stages and, in other cases, challenged and inspired me with compelling conversations: Zeno Ackermann, Mike "Dutch" Arnzen, Lawrence Berkove, Juliane Bierschenk, Donna Campbell, Curtis Clark (of The University of Alabama Press), Matthew Dennis, Karsten Fitz, Udo Hebel, Sue Hodson, Arnie Johnston, Mike Kowalewski, Nat Lewis, Glen Love, the Mesa Verde Colloquium, Tara Penry, Susan Rosowski, Greg Rucka, Heike Schaefer, John Seelye, Andy Smith, Molly Westling, Christine and Hanspeter Witschi, Laurence Witschi, and Harry Wonham. I reserve special gratitude for Suzanne Clark, whose leadership, intellectual range, and scholarly integrity have provided a model of academic excellence to which I continually aspire; and for Gary Scharnhorst, the very model of a scholar and a gentleman, whose guidance and insights on matters relating to both realism and the West have been valuable beyond measure.

Traces of Gold is dedicated to my wife, Meg Dupuis, whose intellectual and critical contributions to this study are surpassed only by the friendship, partnership, wit, and love that touch everything in our lives with infinite beauty.

Traces of Gold

Introduction

The Genres of Realism

When W. D. Howells assumed the editorship of the staunchly New England–oriented *Atlantic Monthly* in 1871, one of his self-appointed goals was to "westernize" the magazine by increasing its attention to and publication of a rapidly growing crop of western American literary artists. By the turn of the century he had become an influential advocate of western American literature, in large part because he believed that the realism he so vigorously championed would have its genesis in the work of such nominally western authors as Mark Twain, Bret Harte, Hamlin Garland, Edward Eggleston, Stephen Crane, and Frank Norris, not to mention himself.[1] Writing about his friend Twain in 1901, for instance, Howells asserted:

> The West, when it began to put itself into literature, could do so without the sense, or the apparent sense, of any older or politer world outside of it; whereas the East was always looking fearfully over its shoulder at Europe, and anxious to account for itself as well as represent itself. . . . [I]t is not claiming too much for the Western influence upon American literature to say that the final liberation of the East from this anxiety is due to the West, and to its ignorant courage or its indifference to its difference from the rest of the world. ("Mark Twain, an Inquiry" 44)

Similarly, in his 1899 review of Norris's *McTeague,* Howells offered, "It ought not to be strange that the impulse in this direction [toward realism] should have come from California, where, as I am always affirming rather than proving, a continental American fiction began" ("A Case in

Point" 39). Howells never did endeavor to "prove" this contention in his criticism, and so the possibility of a connection between realism as Howells imagined it and literature from the late-nineteenth-century American West remains, at least as far as Howells is concerned, just a speculative one. However, his emphasis on California as the locus of western literary development suggestively points the way for an examination of claims to realism in relation to the American West.

Shortly before Howells's ascension at the *Atlantic*, one of his favorites, Bret Harte, offered a much more skeptical assessment about the possibility of achieving realistic representation in California writing. Reporting for the *Boston Christian Register* in 1867, Harte promised that the oft-heard accounts of extraordinary California weather were in fact true, that "April shower[s] of great violence, lasting some two or three days" and "snow thirty to forty feet deep" were no more than "common yearly meteorological" phenomena on the West Coast. He assured his readers, "You will say you have read something like this in Munchausen, but these are the facts." And he concluded by asking them to consider the daily life of the westerner and to "imagine what ought to be the fiction of such a people" (*Bret Harte's California* 122). Consistent with Harte's reputation as a writer of idealized romances, the injunction to "imagine the fiction" would appear to confirm the legends of the golden West that had drawn countless travelers around the Cape and across the plains in search of something akin to paradise. However, Harte also takes a moment to observe that "a few of the settlers build their houses on props raising them up as the snow falls. Of course there will be an uncomfortable revelation in the summer when the snow melts, and real estate falls" (122). This pun on the shifting of frames of reference (both material and linguistic) lends Harte's essay a satiric edge. As much as it would seem to support the stories of western abundance, Harte's weather report suggests quite strongly that realism in western literature would be difficult to accomplish, since even mere facts might easily be mistaken for fanciful exaggerations. That is, by 1867 enough people had already, through their received impressions of California, imagined what the West *should* be like that the frames of reference for the "facts" were no more reliable than were the "fictions."

Stewart Edward White, a California writer hailed in his day as a realist but now largely thought of as a genre adventure story writer, offers a further useful gloss on the idea of western American literary realism.[2] In his 1899 short story "The Saving Grace," a satire of both the Howellsian formula for fiction and the Owen Wister formula for success, White tells of an East Coast novelist named Severne who is told by his fiancée, Lucy, that his fictions are too pedantically realistic. She would prefer instead for him to write a thrilling romance. Refusing to compromise his craft, Severne agrees to break off the engagement and, in order to recover from the ensuing grief, seeks out the remedy for psychologically ailing men that Wister had famously taken several years earlier, namely, the "west cure" of S. Weir Mitchell.[3]

Once at a dude ranch in Colorado, where the vigorous life on display confirms his genre-derived preconceptions of the cowboy West, Severne decides to write a realistic account of this "true" West that he has encountered. In keeping with his realist methodology, he tries to manufacture an authentic experience about which he can write. In the story's central event, Severne hires several cowboys to chase him as if he had just stolen some cattle, thereby teaching him the thrill of a high-speed pursuit. Unfortunately, a separate group of wranglers, unaware of the arrangement, also gives chase, eventually catching the hapless writer and stringing him up by the neck from the nearest tree. Rescued by his hired pursuers, Severne lives to publish an ostensibly realistic best-seller about the West that he has experienced. This success brings Lucy back to him, but ironically she returns full of pride for the romance he has finally allowed himself to write. Through the depiction of a staged representation that is mistaken for the real thing and through both Severne's misreading of the reality he finds in Colorado and Lucy's misreading of the truth-value of his representation of that reality, White suggests that genre assumptions go a long way toward making the representation and apperception of a "real" West an extremely difficult and contingent thing. This is precisely the problem posed by Harte's implication that western writing will be hard pressed to move beyond Munchausen-like exaggerations and, considered more broadly, is also the problem of the American West in literature: as a region, the West has long been known chiefly through the often hackneyed-seeming representations of popular genres, from Gold Rush romances to cowboy Westerns, from hard-boiled detective thrillers to nature writing. Realism, both as a genre and as a set of aesthetic or ideological characteristics, is not a term familiar to this roster.[4]

Yet westerners wrote of realism and realists wrote of the West, with California standing more often than not at the very center of this intersection. Rather than serving as a relatively isolated or unique example, as some have argued, California was the figurative metonym by which Americans generally came to think of and about the West.[5] Bearing this in mind, a closer look at the late-nineteenth- and early-twentieth-century California literature about which Howells (among others) was so enthusiastic unmistakably reveals a number of writers who claimed, in one way or another and often through the available forms of genre, that their particular works accurately represented the "real" West, that their textual productions were realistic depictions of the region and its culture. Authors from this particular region of the West as different as Dame Shirley, Bret Harte, John Muir, Frank Norris, Mary Austin, and Raymond Chandler deployed a variety of claims to textual realism in order to engage, replicate, and often challenge commonly held assumptions about the West as a whole. At the same time, historically acknowledged realists such as Howells and Twain, in proffering their own claims to representational verity, also relied on genre-derived "western" impressions about California (even Henry James used California as a formative space of westernness in his early novel *The American*). This is not to say that any given representation of or from the West can necessarily be judged as an unequivocally realistic one, and this book will not attempt to make such judgments. However, the frequency with which western writers made their claims to realism, just when their compatriots Howells and James were doing the same in the East, suggests that the relationship between American literary realism and ideas about the West was much more than merely coincidental. Indeed, it was a relationship worth investigating further.

The American West may in fact be said to be a key late-nineteenth-century production of American realism. The most pervasive and perduring idea about the West is the assumption that commonly associates "West" with nature, an association that has in turn provided many readers and writers with a benchmark for the real (recall Harte's use of natural phenomena as examples of the fantastically real, a tactic Howells and Mary Austin will eventually adapt into their respective theories of realistic representation). A product of the generic imagination, the process by which cultural ideas become powerfully lodged in the public imagination via repeated genre representations, this association of the American West with the great outdoors maintains that life in the West affords an unambiguous relationship with an unalloyed, nonhuman, real nature. *Traces of Gold* identifies a tradition within the American realist movement, however, that complicates this notion. While known for its culturally based mythos of wide-open spaces, unfettered opportunity, and ostensibly boundless scenery, the West has also been the primary source of raw materials for American industrial and economic expansion, particularly in the years between the California Gold Rush and World War II (see Robbins). The writers mentioned above exist within the intersections of these two modes of production, the cultural and the material, and their various claims to realism reveal—or betray, depending on whose work is at issue—how ostensibly realistic depictions of the West must rely on the representation of some form of material resource extraction (mineral, water, and/or oil). Western narratives of nature prove, upon closer examination, to be narratives of natural resources, the result of an ideology of realism inextricably tied to the material unconscious of western American culture.[6] By writing about California's natural resources, western claimants to realism have been able to take on the largest, most fundamental genre association that readers in American culture have had concerning the West, by challenging the representability of the region as simply natural. This figurative engagement with the material, economic, and cultural value of natural resource industries thus reveals the West to be a significant but heretofore unrecognized component of the cultural and literary moment known as American realism.

A little more than two months after leading his troops in the brutal destruction of a Cheyenne village on the Washita River in present-day Oklahoma, Colonel George A. Custer paused to send his wife, Libby, a letter that in part extolled the beauties of the western landscape. Sent on 9 February 1869 "from Indian Territory" (actually Fort Sill), Custer's letter describes how "We are now in the Wichita Mountains. . . . Tom and I sat on our horses as the view spread out before us, worthy the brush of a Church, a Bierstadt, the structure of the mountains reminding one of paintings of the Yosemite Valley, in the blending of colors—sombre purple, deep blue, to rich crimson tinged with gold" (Merington 226). At the very height of their popularity at this time, Alfred Bierstadt's epic-sized romantic fantasies were providing most Americans with "a conventional iconography" that visually defined the West, and California's Yosemite Valley was among the most prominent of these images, serving as a metonym for the rest of the region.[7] In the case of Custer and his brother Tom, a further notable detail is the revelation of the generic imagination at work. The landscape before them has first and foremost the effect of verifying the already-seen and internalized representation: "tinged with gold," this West is real in part because it looks just like Bierstadt had promised it would.[8]

In the realm not of pictorial representation but rather of words, California in the form of Bret Harte's tales played very much the same role, and again Steward Edward White provides a telling example. In his 1901 novel *The Claim Jumpers,* White spins the story of yet another writer from the East who goes West armed with a fully formed (and informed) generic imagination:

> It may as well be remarked here that Bennington knew all about the West before he left home [for the gold camps in the Black Hills of South Dakota]. . . . He could close his eyes and see the cowboys scouring the plain. As a parenthesis it should be noted that cowboys always scour the plain, just as sailors always scan the horizon. He knew how the cowboys looked, because he had seen Buffalo Bill's show; and he knew how they talked, because he had read accurate authors of the school of Bret Harte. (27–28)

As White's narrative unfolds, Bennington's foreknowledge about the West does not significantly change, not until he is beset by crises quite late in the novel. Much like Custer before him, Bennington finds at first that the parameters of reality, so long as they do not stray too far from expectations, have been satisfactorily defined by genre.[9] White's stories about misinformed and misguided eastern writers thus demonstrate that what holds for images may also hold for written texts: they provide the imaginative material, the filters, by which subsequent encounters with both the real and representations of that real are recognized as true.[10]

In this regard, genre productions provide a window on what readers and writers (who of course were themselves readers as well) thought of as realistic about the West. As Nancy Glazener points out in her discussion of the development of American realism as a set of readerly expectations, "The special usefulness of genre as a vantage point on interpretive practices is that it is one of the most public registers of interpretation, requiring readers to consider their experience of a text in relation to frameworks of interpretation they share with others" (16). In making this assertion, Glazener relies on Jameson's definition of genres as "social contracts between a writer and a specific public" (*Political Unconscious* 106), which she usefully modifies by observing that Jameson "does not take up the possibility that the contract governing a text's reading might be inscribed somewhere other than within the text itself" (273 n. 30). Glazener's formulation describes precisely the principle of the generic imagination, wherein a whole range of texts, media, and representations serve as powerful enablers of future interpretation. Those who think they have found either in a book or in the world itself a confirming account of the "real" have thought so more often than not because of knowledge that was already internalized from other genre sources.[11] And as White implies, the fictional character of Bennington stands in for a long line of American readers who easily construed Harte as an "accurate author." They knew the West through Harte, which is another way of saying he came across to many as realistic.

For the vast majority of writers from the West, though, this influence was often the heart of the problem, as many appear to have felt compelled to position their apparently more realistic representations in direct opposition to the misleading picture drawn by Harte. Alluding specifically to the precedent set by Harte's mining tales, Frank Norris insisted that the fictionalized westerner must no longer "speak of his local habitation as 'These 'ere diggin's,' or to address us as 'pard,' or to speak of death as the passing in of checks, of the kicking of the bucket. He would not be true to Western life" ("Literature of the West" 105). Similarly, in describing the uninformed, disconnected "indifference" that miners have to the land around them, Mary Austin offered her own writings as realism by positing that "Bret Harte would have given you a tale. You see in me a mere recorder" (*Land of Little Rain* 71, 68). And John Muir's complex negotiations with Harte's legacy also stemmed from a desire to set the record straight about what nature in the California mining country should look like. Notably, even Harte himself opened his own first book with a similar tactic by professing a wish to correct the image of unbelievably moral and excessively dissolute miners proffered by an 1854 booklet of etchings called *The Idle and Industrious Miner*. In his preface to *The Luck of Roaring Camp and Other Sketches* (1870), Harte argues that the reason why the etchings failed "to produce the desired reform in mining morality may have been owing to the fact that the average miner refused to recognize himself" (*Selected Stories* 3). Harte may very well have been responding to a willful misreading by miners who saw no need to reform their profligate ways, and it is far from certain that Harte's own satiric tales fared any better at reform than had their predecessors (whether they had been designed to do so or not). However, in each of the instances enumerated above, a reader had decided that previous representations were no longer adequate and thus tried to offer a newer, more realistic generic production.

All claims to realism have their foundation in a crisis of representation.[12] Howells, for one, rebelled not only against romantic depictions of the American grain but also against the representation of authorship in the culture at large (Bell, *Problem* 21–22). Speaking directly to the issue of popular genres in the West, Frederick Remington lamented that "When I began to depict the men of the plains, white and red, this Western business was new to art and we had the dread background of the dime novel to live down" (qtd. in Teague 60). Remington's complaint is hardly original, though. Norris before him inveighed against "the wretched 'Deadwood Dicks' and Buffalo Bills of the yellow backs" ("Literature of the West" 107), and Dame Shirley (aka Louise Clappe), who wrote from California over half a century earlier, in 1851, also observed that the men in the Rich Bar mining camp had in their assumptions been led astray by "a sickening pile of 'yallow kivered' literature" (Clappe 18).[13] Shirley thus promised to do what those who followed her also claimed, namely, "to describe things exactly as I *see* them, hoping that thus you will obtain an idea of life in the mines, *as it is*" (Clappe 35; emphasis in original). And Raymond Chandler plainly—and seriously—described his California-based novels as the "realistic" products of a "realist in murder" who had become fed up with the generic liberties taken by British murder mystery writers ("Simple Art of Murder" 59).

Most recently, the perception of a crisis of representation has emerged in the genre of literary criticism, a crisis that bears directly on the representation of western spaces as nature. In the opening pages of *The Environmental Imagination,* his study of American nature writing in the Thoreauvian tradition, Lawrence Buell laments that

> American literary history thus presents the spectacle of having identified the representation of the natural environment as a major theme while marginalizing the literature devoted most specifically to it and reading the canonical books in ways that minimize their interest in representing the environment as such. To put this abstract point in an immediate context: the grove of second growth white pines that sway at this moment of writing, with their blue-yellow-green five-needle clusters above spiky circles of atrophied lower limbs, along a brown needle-strewn ridge of shale forty feet

> from my computer screen—this grove can be found in the pages of American literature also, but it is not the woods imagined by American criticism. (9–10)

Buell's answer to this professional crisis of representation, not surprisingly, is a realism wherein the "immediate" nature that can be "found" supersedes the "imagined." In a chapter on the claim to realism in American nature writing, Buell offers that this particular genre has the unique ability to refer to objects extratextually, beyond the field of effects generated by the print technologies used to represent them. Unlike other historical forms of realism (Buell mentions those of Howells, Flaubert, George Eliot, and even computer-generated virtual reality), nature writing defers "to the authority of external nonhuman reality as a criterion of accuracy and value" (*Imagination* 113). And although he offers to revive the critical category of realism not for its claims to mimetic fidelity but rather for its ability to spark, through inevitably inadequate representations, a contemplation of all things nontextual, Buell also pauses to praise Mary Austin for achieving a convincing mimesis in a passage on weeds from *The Land of Little Rain* in which the unwanted plants take over a plot of land while figuratively taking over a paragraph that began with notes about other flowers (*Imagination* 99–100).[14] Despite occasional qualifiers to the contrary, Buell's ultimate point is to ask readers, especially academic ones, to refresh both their environmental awareness and their reading habits by noticing that American nature writers have in fact achieved prose representations of nature that are equal in both content and substance to that which may be apprehended by glancing out through an open window.

If, as Buell suggests, the idea of realism should be trusted once again as a mode of representation, then the American West is being asked to play what is best described as an overdetermined but all-too-familiar role. As Michael Cohen has observed, popular and environmentalist discourses have long depended on the idea that "the West [is] another name for the Wild" ("Literary Theory" 1107). With the advent of ecological literary criticism, or ecocriticism, this idea has also crept back into academic discourse. Of the four extended sets of close reading that Buell offers in his chapter on realism, two are from authors identified as western (Barry Lopez and Austin; the other two are John Burroughs and Thoreau). More strikingly, fully half of the texts covered in *The Ecocriticism Reader*, a recent critical anthology edited by Cheryll Glotfelty and Harold Fromm, are in one way or another also associated with the West.[15] And when one considers that the Association for the Study of Literature and Environment (ASLE) originated as an offshoot of the Western Literature Association, that three of this organization's first four meetings have been held in the West, and that the two leading centers of ecocritical scholarship are the University of Oregon and the University of Nevada at Reno, it becomes quite clear that the West is once again playing the role of referent to claims about nature, realness, and the realness of nature.[16] Simply put, nature writing is at present the genre of choice for readers of realism, and western nature is the dominant referent.

The emergence of ecocriticism is but the latest instance of a discourse on realism that returns time and again to an American West that is generically understood as a privileged site of pure nature. Culturally and critically, the West has become what Michael McKeon, working in another context, defines as a "simple abstraction" (15–19): a deceptively uncomplicated word that describes a rationally understood, accepted, and internalized concept but which disguises the complex historical and material processes by which that concept has come into being ("novel" and "realism" are similar abstractions of this sort). The analytical task is to understand and elucidate the processes of the generic imagination by which such abstractions come about. In the case of the phrase "western nature," the two words as often as not stand as two halves of the same meaning, rather than modifying each other. The elisions that take place when these two abstractions coalesce into one, however, are rarely investigated. By recovering for western writing its rightful place within the late-nineteenth- and early-twentieth-century marketplace for literary realism, and by narrating a history counter to the more familiar versions of western literature as a series of "mere" genre intrusions into the otherwise literary life of a nation or as a concatenation of regional voices, this book offers the opportunity to reconsider both the genres of realism through which terms like "western" and "nature" have become mutually reinforcing and the related cultural processes by which these particular abstractions have thus far been perpetuated.[17] To this end, *Traces of Gold* offers three related propositions: first, that there exists a heretofore unrecognized commitment to realism among writers in the American West that crosses traditionally recognized generic lines and which bears directly on the canon of realism concurrently developing in New York and Boston; second, that this genealogy of late-nineteenth- and early-twentieth-century realism, ostensibly founded on the representation of the West's natural beauty, is in fact keenly engaged with the West's natural resource industries; and third, that this literary history of natural resources belies, or at the very least complicates, the possibility for realistic representations of an unalloyed nature.

To begin demonstrating the extent to which the Far West played a historically vital part in the debates over American realism, chapter 1 opens by showing how the widely read literature of the California Gold Rush—published letters, forty-niner diaries, short stories, and journalism—developed as a discourse of realism centered on the representation of physical hardship. A compelling mixture of brutally frank descriptions and exaggerated physical comedy, hoaxes, and satire, writing about the mines depended on a claim to realism that took the threat to the integrity of the human body as its key motivating component. Bret Harte's contribution to this literary history, discussed in the second half of the chapter, was to transform the narrative of physical hardship into a tale of times gone by. Responding to what he perceived to be earlier misrepresentations of the "real" West, Harte established what subsequent generations will take to be the definitive version of the West: a narrative space in which a material industry is more past than present and in which physical privation is surprisingly absent. And despite Harte's prevailing reputation as a "romancer," the claim to realism underlying this move provided a key formal innovation for western American literary realism. John Muir, the subject of chapter 2, was one such writer who borrowed extensively from Harte, even though he struggled against the generic imagination established by his contemporary's failure to represent accurately (as Muir would have it) the mountains of California. In the process, Muir continued the transformation, initiated by Harte's tales, away from corporeal physicality in prose, successfully evicting both the miner and all evidence of his industry from the surface of the scenery. Muir needed to move through the literary history of the Gold Rush in order to erase the material history of that event from the landscape and, more importantly, from how that landscape could be rendered in words. In this manner he set the standard for western nature writing's apperception of a pristine, real, and ostensibly human-free western landscape. Chapter 2 thus tracks Muir's assiduous anti-Harte efforts to transform one genre (the mining tale) into another (nature writing), locating the late-nineteenth-century beginnings of a canon of western nature writing within the context of the resource narrative claim to realism.

Chapter 3 takes up W. D. Howells's use of the West as the raw material for realism. As the research in this chapter makes clear, the idea of literary realism and the idea of the West evolved in American culture almost simultaneously, particularly in the pages of magazines such as the *Atlantic Monthly* and *Harper's*. These periodicals published not only Howells, Henry James, Mark Twain, Mary Wilkins Freeman, and Sarah Orne Jewett, but also Bret Harte, John Muir, Frederic Remington, Mary Hallock Foote, Owen Wister, and Mary Austin. As noted above, Howells was a key figure in this roster, bridging one side to the other. More to the point, the West mattered to Howells, both as a signifier for his own self-identification (he was from Indiana, the "West" for antebellum Americans) and as a vital signifier of "the simple, the natural, and the honest." The western presence in American realist discourse goes far beyond such things as favorable reviews in the *Atlantic* of Eggleston et al. What ideas about the West and turn-of-the-century realism shared is nothing less than the mutual exchange of genre forms, figures, and assumptions about the constitution of what is "natural." Drawing to a conclusion the first half of the book, this chapter confirms the heretofore unacknowledged place and function of the American West as a source of raw material for late-nineteenth-century ideas about realistic literary representation.

At the turn of the century, the generic imagination relating to the West shifted considerably, as did the grounds for western claims to realism. In the highly significant year 1902, for instance, Bret Harte and Frank Norris died, Owen Wister's *The Virginian* (among others) arrived to replace the mining tale as the representative western genre narrative, and the Newlands Reclamation Act inaugurated what has come to be known as the "hydraulic West"—that is to say, water became the privileged signifier of the American West, its defining resource. These changes in how the West saw itself provide the impetus for the next three chapters, which present a series of critical responses by California-based western writers to the very premise of an easily represented reality founded in nature. Beginning with a discussion of the 1894 Midwinter Exposition in San Francisco, which Norris re-created parodically in *The Octopus*, chapter 4 follows the process by which the name "Bret Harte" ceased to serve as a significant literary predecessor. Indeed, this chapter finds an entire cultural economy pondering the inadequacies of Gold Rush representations. With regard to western literary realism, questions arose during this period about what exactly is real, what is fake, and how the difference between the two is best represented. Norris's California fiction, and in particular its attention to imitation, parody, and the function of artifice in the construction of realistic representations, thus offers a perfectly emblematic instance of a generic imagination in transition, for Norris struggled to replicate and update the landscapes of the mining West even as he marked the waning of mining's usefulness as a narrative of the real. This struggle to find a representable real signals the beginning of a shift in western American literary realism. Subsequent claimants to realism, rather than seeking to challenge Harte's version of the Far West, would ask more carefully how one comes to know with certainty any given version. After 1902, the claim to realism in western literature increasingly interrogated the limits of how one knows and represents that which is real.

Mary Austin and Raymond Chandler, the subjects of chapters 5 and 6, respectively, both approached the claim to realism as a moment of epistemological uncertainty—for them, to claim that one's representation is real is to ask how one knows or recognizes the "realness" of the assumed referent—and they both did so through an understanding of nature as resource. As a novelist, essayist, and critic, Austin was perhaps the most expressly Howellsian of the realists discussed in this book, although her work significantly modifies the tenets of representation that inherited from Howells. With *The Land of Little Rain,* initially serialized in 1902 in the *Atlantic Monthly,* Austin challenged the assumptions of an earlier generation of *Atlantic* writers (such as Muir and Howells) by putting pressure on the idea that western nature as represented was first "nature" and second representable. Through her commitment to an ethically oriented approach to representation, evident in her many attempts to modify public (mis)perceptions and media (mis)representations of western water resource issues (i.e., "little rain"), she concluded that the twentieth-century West's most necessary and vital piece of nature cannot be separated from the human mechanisms of value by which it is controlled and distributed.

The hard-boiled noir fictions of Dashiell Hammett and Raymond Chandler go one step further, resituating the human *body* within the material economies of western nature: a surprising number of Hammett's and Chandler's corpses, the main resource for any detective story, turn up in mines, reservoirs, and oil fields. California noir thus provides a fitting conclusion to the corporeal elision of western claims to realism that had begun in the 1860s. There is no nature in Hammett and Chandler that can be known independently of human materialism, a critical formulation that *Traces of Gold* identifies as the lasting achievement and legacy of western American literary realism. Indeed, the various elements of western realism identified in the previous five chapters—an insistence on the representational accuracy of one's texts with respect to previous genre (mis)representations, the placement of that judgment in relation to one's depiction of nature and/or resource industries, attention to the economy of the human body, and an inquiry into realism's epistemological function—all dovetail in the works of Hammett and, more importantly, his successor Chandler. Returning the human figure to the representational matrix of natural resources, Chandler's self-described realism argues that nature can no longer be counted on to provide a reassuring measure of accuracy and value, that nature is far from being that "final court of appeals" posited by recent theories of realism in environmental writing (Buell, *Imagination* 94). Consequently, the "simple" and "natural" basis upon which both the idea of realism and the idea of the American West had been founded is called into question.

In a letter written on 10 April 1852 and sent from the northern California mining camp of Indian Bar on the Feather River, Dame Shirley waxed poetic for a moment about the smaller, tributary streams that coursed through the landscape around the mine. More to the point, her subject was a system of trenches dug for the express purpose of bringing water to the miners' gold-filtering assemblage of rockers and Long Toms. She wrote: "I wish that you could see this ditch. I never beheld a NATURAL streamlet more exquisitely beautiful. It undulates over the mossy roots, and the gray, old rocks, like a capricious snake, singing all the time a low song with the 'liquidest murmur,' and one might almost fancy it the airy and coquettish Undine herself" (Clappe 112). The artifice of western nature realism is not just textual, it can also be material, in that a man-made stream can easily rival, can be just as "exquisitely beautiful" as anything nature can conjure up. And if Dame Shirley had not chosen to alert her readers to the artifice of the scene, by what mechanisms would a reader have been able to tell the difference between a real stream and a miner's ditch? Shirley's use of the standard lexicon for appreciative nature writing draws attention to the fact that the difference between an unadulterated (read: natural) scene and a manufactured one may very well in the end be not only indecipherable but irrelevant.[18] There may very well be a difference between the sort of nature that is untouched by human enterprise and the sort that has been irreversibly affected (and effected) by industry and culture. But in evaluating the difference in terms of their respective representation in prose, how does one know for certain? This is the perduring question asked both by western realism and by this book.

1

Bret Harte and the Gold Rush Claim to Realism

In November 1872, just two months shy of the twenty-fifth anniversary of the discovery of gold in California, Bret Harte attempts in some measure to separate the facts about the Gold Rush experience from the narratives by which that experience might best be conveyed. Speaking before a packed house in the city hall of Springfield, Massachusetts, Harte begins his lecture on "The Argonauts of '49" with the following disclaimer: "It is not a pretty story; I do not know that it is even instructive; I do not know that it is strictly true. It is of a life of which perhaps the best that can be said is, that it exists no longer" ("Bret Harte's Lecture" 8).[1] Already famous for his humorous and moving sketches of the gold country, Harte holds a certain stake in maintaining himself as an authority on the story of the Gold Rush. Thus, for Harte the writer turned public speaker, the story, while it may not be very pretty, is nevertheless worth telling. That it may not be true is apparently irrelevant, all the more so since the life behind the story no longer exists (if, as Harte implies, it ever existed at all). In this curious interplay of the ideas of truth, historical existence, and narrative representation, "life" and "story" are two distinctly separate entities. To say the least, this is not a position one would necessarily recognize as that of a realist.

And yet, by questioning the truth-value of Gold Rush storytelling, Harte participates in an ongoing debate that had up to that point been a crucial component of the Gold Rush genre: the examination of the relationship between the reality and its representation, between "life" and "story." With his preface to the hugely successful *The Luck of Roaring Camp and Other Sketches* published less than three years earlier, Harte had positioned his own tales in part as a corrective to "a series of designs—

suggested, I think, by Hogarth's familiar cartoons"—that had in their own way failed to represent the Gold Rush to Harte's satisfaction (*Selected Stories* 3).[2] In thus calling attention to the representability of the Gold Rush experience in such a way that implicitly privileges the ironic and satiric "romances" for which he has become famous,[3] Harte provides a gloss on the Gold Rush story that has significant ramifications for the idea of realism in western American literature. The generic imagination regarding the realness of the American Far West receives one of its earliest, most significant, and most lasting contributions through the productions of Gold Rush authors (including, in a provisional sense, Harte), who saw the accuracy of representation as one of their key motivating concerns. In the case of Harte and his successors, the separation of "life" from "story" will prove to be a crucial move in western American literary realism.

The story of gold in the American West was at first, however, rather slow to develop. Beginning with James Marshall's discovery in January 1848, it took almost a full year before the massive exodus known as the California Gold Rush could get fully under way. But by June 1849, packed steamers were leaving East Coast ports by the dozens for the long trip around the Cape, while out in Missouri tens of thousands of people were gearing up for the overland journey across plains and mountains. In all, roughly 67,000 people headed West in 1849, a group that has collectively become known to us as the forty-niners.[4] On 26 June of this year, however, at least one tired, frustrated, and not very rich gold seeker arrived by steamer back in Philadelphia. Theodore Taylor Johnson had "seen the elephant," as the Gold Rush experience was called at the time, and he had decided that it was not worth the effort. Rather, at the precise historical moment when most Americans were just beginning to take seriously the prospects of finding gold in distant California, Johnson came back home to New Jersey. And by September he was finishing a book about his adventures. *Sights in the Gold Region, and Scenes by the Way* (1849) is generally regarded as the first notable published account of a California gold miner's experiences, and as such it offers a telling glimpse of a rapidly emerging literary feature in the West: the Gold Rush claim to realism.

The California Gold Rush narrative begins almost apologetically as a realistic form. It is realistic in the sense that typical Gold Rush authors usually expressed an interest in providing a documentary account of their time in California. For his own part, Theodore Johnson writes in his preface that he has "faithfully endeavored to give as succinct and correct an account as possible, of my experience and observation" (n.p.). And the Gold Rush narrative is apologetic to the extent that most of its authors felt compelled to caution their readers with disclaimers regarding the frank description of difficult or brutal conditions and a lack of "literary" qualities in the prose. Most importantly, Gold Rush authors relied on the realist's strategy of invoking a crisis of representation. Positioning their own works as much-needed correctives to earlier, ostensibly inaccurate written versions of what "seeing the elephant" had been like, they issued a claim to realism that hinged most basically on the idea that someone, themselves, had finally gotten it right. Indeed, the problem of a potentially misleading text was already apparent to Johnson in 1849. Motivated by "the public announcement of the wonderful and extensive gold discoveries" whereby the "wonders of the gold region were accordingly trumpeted to the world, with unabating, but by no means unforeseeing zeal," he rapidly discovered that "the inaccessibility of the *placeres,* the diseases, the hardships, and the very moderate remuneration resulting to the great mass of the miners, were quite forgotten or omitted, the communications and reports of a few only excepted" (225–26). For Johnson, as for the many who followed him in publishing their own stories, the project of providing a "succinct and correct" account necessarily involved a correction of press puffery and misrepresented conditions (even as Johnson's closing recommendation that the reader go "view for yourself" [278] constitutes itself a sort of puffery).

By such measures, the Gold Rush tale may not necessarily qualify as a literature of realism. Indeed, out of the events of 1849 comes a great deal of genre-oriented farce, slapstick, satire, and ribald humor, not to mention the "romances" of Bret Harte. However, the act of writing and publishing a Gold Rush tale was perceived by many of its initial practitioners to be something of a reality-documenting literary event. The documentary, reformist impulse that pervades an important precursor to realism such as Rebecca Harding Davis's "Life in the Iron Mills" (1861)[5] obtains equally a decade earlier in the disclaimers and prefaces of many Gold Rush texts. Daniel Woods writes rather eloquently in 1851:

> Having so long been a miner, and acquainted with all his privations and sufferings; having experienced his elation at success and his depression at failure; having passed through the trying season of acclimation, and lain once beneath a lone oak, expecting, as he

> looked up to the stars shining clear above him, there to end his days; having rocked the gold-digger's cradle, wielded his pick and spade, messed and slept with miners, he is prepared to present a correct view of his subject for those who have friends at the mines. (5–6)

Dame Shirley, perhaps more sensitive to the rhetorical limits of melodramatic prose (and sounding just a bit Howellsian), apologizes to her sister in 1852 for sending letters that are "dreadfully commonplace and severely utilitarian in [their] style and content" (Clappe 106). She has persistently done so, she writes, in order to convey convincingly "an idea of life in the mines, *as it is*" (35; emphasis in original). Alonzo Delano begins his 1853 *Pen-Knife Sketches* by noting a promise made "around our camp fires among the hills . . . that somebody would show up the other side" of misleading newspaper accounts, which had waxed far too optimistic about "big strikes, rich leads, lucky *hombres*" (3–4). And even John Rollin Ridge swears, perhaps somewhat disingenuously, that he has written the sensationally bloody and largely fictive *Life and Adventures of Joaquín Murieta* (1854) "not for the purpose of ministering to any depraved taste for the dark and horrible in human action, but rather to contribute my mite to those materials out of which the early history of California shall one day be composed" (7).[6]

Thus it is that Bret Harte, in his preface to *The Luck of Roaring Camp and Other Sketches,* also claims no "higher motive than to illustrate an era of . . . California history" (*Selected Stories* 3), a move seemingly consistent with the inherited form of the Gold Rush disclaimer. But there is a difference in this self-presentation, one that accords with Harte's differentiation of "story" from "life." In 1853, Alonzo Delano, who had given up a brief career as a forty-niner to become a merchant, Wells Fargo agent, and occasional sketch writer for San Francisco's various magazines and newspapers, had concluded that some Gold Rush tales are "still left untold, and always will be" (*Pen-Knife* 112). Harte, on the other hand, promises that the materials may finally be collected to tell the untellable, that the stories of the Gold Rush can now be told (since, to some extent, the tales do not fully correspond to "life" in the first place). Much as Ridge had done before him, Harte confesses that "I shall be quite content to have collected here the materials for the Iliad that is yet to be sung" (*Selected Stories* 4). The trick to Harte's position, however, lies in his use of the term "Iliad."

According to his preface, Harte sees himself as a "humble writer of romance" who can "illustrate" for his readers both the "prosaic recollections" and the "heroic Greek poetry" of the forty-niners (*Selected Stories* 3). Similarly, in his Springfield lecture he pledges to his audience that he will "discourse briefly on an episode of American life as quaint and typical as that of the Greek adventurers whose name I have borrowed" ("Argonauts" 261). These paired allusions to the classical analogy created by the name "Argonauts" operate quite ambiguously. On the one hand it appears that in Harte's opinion, California's mining legacy is worthy of the label "epic." However, the idea that California's "Greek adventurers" were little more than "quaint and typical" also suggests an ironic reading, that the title of Argonauts which the forty-niners almost immediately gave to themselves is ill-deserved, that the life which "exists no longer" was largely one of vulgar ignominy.[7] In either case, Harte makes plain in 1869 and again in 1872 that epic or otherwise, the story of the Gold Rush can be told with a relative degree of confidence, largely because it has become the stuff of myth. By emphasizing the pastness of the very name by which the first gold seekers identified themselves, Harte asserts that mining is no longer a present-tense activity.

But why this deflection? Why suggest that the Gold Rush narrative form should convey a story of the past that is not "strictly true"? To begin with, temporal distance offers a relatively direct and untroubled explanation, in that the passage of almost twenty years between the publication of Delano's *Pen-Knife Sketches* and Harte's *The Luck of Roaring Camp* accounts in some measure for the shift in perspective offered by their respective formulations of gold frontier history. The demographic complexity of California in general and of San Francisco in particular grew exponentially during these two decades, as did the size and scope of the region's economic base. In May of 1869, for instance, in the same year Harte writes the preface to his most famous collection of tales, the West Coast became connected in a certain figurative sense to the nonmining present of the East through the completion of the transcontinental railroad. Franklin Walker hails this moment as a significant one for literary history: "With the passing of two decades had come the perspective necessary for the setting up of a heroic tradition. Significantly, Bret Harte's *The Luck of Roaring Camp and Other Sketches,* Mark Twain's *Roughing It,* and Joaquin Miller's *Songs of the Sierras* all appeared within three years of the completion of the railroad" (*Literary Frontier* 261). Not directly concerned with the question of why the construction of a heroic past may be necessary, Walker nevertheless implies that reflection about the past has become a central component of California's literary life. Indeed, history writing was very much in the air in 1869 San Francisco. In the summer of this year, Hubert Howe Bancroft began construction of a building that would in less than two years become the home of his "Literary Industries" corporation. A former miner and founder of the largest book, stationery, and printing enterprise west of Chicago, Bancroft would direct dozens of clerks, abstractors, and "research assistants" in the production of one compendious history after another, beginning in 1874 with a five-volume history of the West Coast's indigenous people, *The Native Races*. Calling his business a "history factory," Bancroft would use a veritable assembly line of note takers and ghostwriters to produce an immense thirty-nine-volume documentary account of the past in the American West (Caughey; Walker, *Literary Frontier* 302–15).

The question of what made self-history telling so vital an enterprise for Californians at the beginning of the 1870s is in large part answered by an enthusiastic editorial published in the March 1874 issue of San Francisco's famed literary journal, the *Overland Monthly* (for which Harte served as editor prior to his departure for the East in 1871). Responding to a recent state report on California's economic activity for 1873, the lead editorial column for March 1874 (in the "Etc." section) announces that a "new era" is afoot in the state. Referring to the events that first initiated California's rise to economic prominence, the piece begins by noting that "twenty-five years ago, the missionary and pastoral era of California came to a sudden end with the rush of gold-seekers from all parts of the world." A quarter-century later, a "new era" is under way:

> The wilderness was reclaimed and peopled; the arid soil was made to yield luxuriantly products native to various climes; society was established; diversified industry took the place of exclusive devotion to gold-hunting on one hand and supplying the gold-hunters on the other. And at last, California, which used to import her breadstuffs and clothing, can now boast that in the year 1873 she produced 25,000,000 bushels of wheat, and exported more wheat and flour than any other State in the Union. She can point to a wool-clip of nearly 40,000,000 pounds, a good share of which is manufactured in her own mills. . . . Without any circulating medium but gold dust a few years ago, her home coinage, at the San Francisco Mint, was over $22,000,000 last year, and has been in 19 years

> $350,000,000. Her commercial port was the *entrepot,* in 1873, of a gold and silver yield of $82,000,000. Her savings banks held deposits to the amount of $55,000,000. ("New Era in California" 281)[8]

Armed with the proof of a prosperous diversification of industrial activity, the editorial writer feels confident that 1873, the first year in which the state's export figures apparently equaled or exceeded those for import, marks the beginning of a new period in California history.

Funded by prosperity and taking the form of library, university, and art museum grants from the city's wealthier residents, a new civic liberalism is providing "the ideas and institutions which are superseding the halcyon days of 'two-bit drinks' and ox-teaming across the plains." "It is a great comfort to know," the column concludes, that "the spirit of a new era is really abroad in the land" (282). This last point betrays a possibly inadvertent pun to the closing assertion about there being a new spirit "in the land," since mining is by 1874 no longer a placer activity but largely an industry of tunneling into and carving out entire mountainsides. As the editorial makes plain, this new spirit is still one that draws heavily on the mineral riches that are dug out of the hills of the Sierra, as well as out of the Washoe in Nevada, and sent on their way through San Francisco's bank vaults and dockyards. With continued economic growth still dependent to a degree on the products of the mines, the new "spirit" is indeed "in the land." The *Overland*'s editorial demonstrates that far more is at stake than the simple observation that industry and, hence, the people's focus have grown and diversified in the move away from the monoculture of forty-niner mining. In suggesting that the spirit of the Gold Rush is no longer present in California, the *Overland*'s editorial executes a gesture similar to Harte's assurance of a life that "exists no longer." No longer prologue, the past is dismissed as passed; any continuity with the present is disavowed.[9]

Moreover, in progressing effortlessly from the taming of wilderness to the numerical data of prosperity to the establishment of ennobling (and well-endowed) "ideas and institutions," the author of "The New Era in California" implies that the diversification and stabilization of value evident in the state's economic report will hold equally true for the state's cultural production: California can now hold its own economically, and it hopes to do so culturally as well. This general belief is further evident in the packaging of such texts as the successive editions of J. S. Hittell's enormously popular reference guide *Resources of California*. For instance, the subtitle to the 1866 second edition reads "Comprising Agriculture, Mining, Geography, Climate, Commerce, &c.," and the chapter on mining begins, "Mining is the chief industry of California" (238). These passages remain unchanged through the fifth edition in 1869. In a telling shift, the subtitle is changed, for the first time, in the 1877 sixth edition to "Comprising the Society, Climate, Salubrity, Scenery, Commerce, and Industry of the State," and the section on mining begins, "Mining was until 1860 the chief industry of the State, but it has now been surpassed by both agriculture and manufacture" (296). Hittell has added society and scenery to California's market base while lopping at least nine years off of mining's status as the state's "chief industry." Here too mining is retroactively reduced to past history. If anything, mining by the 1870s was much more fully a part of the economic and cultural landscape than it had been in 1848. Mineral extraction as an economic, industrial, earth- and people-moving activity in the American West is only just getting started at the time of Harte's lecture in 1872.[10] Yet, as a literary discourse it has been relegated by this time to the status of a "quaint and typical" past that bears little relation to the material present. In its place, cultural production, which includes the writing of one's own history, becomes a key component in the production of value.

From early disclaimers about authenticity, to J. S. Hittell, and finally to Bret Harte, thus does the framing of the Gold Rush story subtly shift over the course of two and a half decades. But this is still only the frame, and Harte's ultimate contribution to the generic imagination of the West is of course so much more than just a gloss on the truth-value of the claim to realism found in Gold Rush literature. Indeed, in order to appreciate the impact of Harte's rereading of the Gold Rush narrative form, and in order to assess fully the significance of that rereading to the idea of realism in western American literature, the following section will examine where Harte comes from; that is, it will look inside the frame and adduce just what it is that Gold Rush writers felt the need to be realistic about in their descriptions.

Mining and Bodies

For the Scottish journalist J. D. Borthwick, the relationship between something ostensibly true and its representation could on occasion be a matter of life and death, or at least a matter of physical well-being. Having come to the goldfields in 1851 to try his hand at placer mining,

Borthwick turned his experiences into an internationally popular book called *Three Years in California* (1857). In one passage he describes an unfortunate miner who has a well-informed passion for phrenology, the interpretation of the bumps on one's head as indicators of personality traits. One evening this "phrenologer" makes the mistake of telling a fellow miner with "something peculiar in the formation of his cranium" that he is "a liar, a cheat, and a thief . . . who would murder his father for five dollars." Needless to say, the hapless phrenologist is beaten to within inches of his life, "without consideration of the five dollars" (124–26). As Borthwick implies, had the phrenologist heeded his own interpretation of the representation at hand, he might have kept his mouth shut and saved himself a great amount of discomfort.

Not surprisingly, given the difficulties incumbent in coaxing gold from mountain rocks and ice-cold rivers, discomfort is a key theme addressed by Gold Rush writers. To recall, Theodore Johnson warns against "the diseases, the hardships, and the very moderate remuneration" that come with gold mining (226), while Alonzo Delano claims to speak for those who have "climbed the mountains in 1849, with a heavy load on thy back, exhausted with fatigue, worn out with labor, with scarcely a mouthful of the mere necessaries of life in thy wallet" (*Pen-Knife* 112). Similarly, Daniel Woods establishes his own authority on the premise that he too has suffered the "privations and sufferings" of mining, having once been even reduced to awaiting death as he lay abjectly "beneath a lone oak" (4–5). On these grounds Woods feels motivated "to induce all who are doing *well enough,* who are living within their means and laying by a little, to remain satisfied at home" (7; emphasis in original). And Dame Shirley, whose "letters" about the joys and hardships of gold country life are in many respects the most eloquent and compelling published account available, writes with a touch of whimsical irony that "Really, everybody ought to go to the mines, just to see how little it takes to make people comfortable in the world" (Clappe 177). By the time the reader has come to this statement in Shirley's twenty-third and last letter, it has become patently clear that for her, moments of genuine comfort have been few and far between.

"Dame Shirley" is actually the pseudonym of Louise Amelia Knapp Smith Clappe, a well-bred Massachusetts woman who came to the diggings in 1851 with her husband, Dr. Fayette Clappe.[11] Addressed to her sister Mary Jane back in Amherst but quite probably written with publication in mind, Clappe's letters range in date from 13 September 1851 to 21 November 1852 and were published serially in a San Francisco magazine called *The Pioneer* between January 1854 and December 1855. Taken as a whole, the twenty-three "Shirley Letters" tell eloquently of a woman's life in a mining camp during the height of the Gold Rush. Written by someone who lived at the heart of the Rush in a stretch of camps along the Feather River in the northern Sierras,[12] Clappe's letters provide more than just an in-depth account of the social environment of a mining camp (an achievement in realism for which Clappe is generally credited);[13] they also speak quite extensively to the "privations and sufferings" involved in the enterprise.

As many immigrants to California had already done and would continue to do for decades, the Clappes came West for their health. Not surprisingly, it seems that the generally ailing Dr. Fayette Clappe was also bitten by the gold bug, attracted to the West by the very press coverage that so troubled Delano and his campfire companions. Life in San Francisco only made matters worse for Louise Clappe's husband. In her first letter, written from the mining camp at Rich Bar on 13 September 1851, Clappe recalls that Fayette, "after suffering for an entire year, with fever and ague, bilious, remittent, and intermittent fevers—this delightful list, varied by an occasional attack of jaundice,—was advised as a *dernier resort* to go into the mountains." Perhaps it is telling that "F—— was just recovering from a brain fever, when he concluded to go to the mines" (2). The remainder of Clappe's first letter limns a series of episodes in her journey to the "East Branch of the North Fork of the Feather River," during which time she falls off her horse several times and her husband is compelled "by sickness" to make frequent stops.

In her next several letters, Clappe writes variously about a startling number of events that focus on the comfort level and ultimate fragility of the human body. On one occasion she notes the "successful amputation" of a miner's leg, an event "illustrative of the frightful accidents to which gold-seekers are constantly liable; and I can assure you that similar ones happen very often" (29); and on another she muses about her "hotel" being a former brothel and, consequently, about the difficult time a woman might have in giving birth in such an environment (17–21). Clappe's third letter, dated 20 September 1851, concludes by describing the extreme degree of starvation the camp had been reduced to just the winter before. By the second week of her stay in Rich Bar, Clappe has fully grasped the fundamental crisis of the mining life, namely, the threat to the physical body. In a separate letter written on the same day in which she reports on the amputation, she describes both the passing of one of Rich Bar's four women of "peritonitis, (a common disease in this place)" (34), and "the funeral train of a young man who was instantly killed, the evening before, by falling into one of those deep pits, sunk for mining purposes, which are scattered over the bar in almost every direction" (31). And on 30 September, a mere three weeks after the Clappes' arrival in camp, Louise describes for her sister the noises that prevail in a mining camp. Beginning with a discussion of the profanity that rings endlessly through camp at all hours, Clappe shifts with no warning to a description of "the dreadful flume, the machinery of which, keeps up the most dismal moaning and shrieking all the livelong night—painfully suggestive of a suffering child" (39). In one deft stroke, the reality of physical danger has become a metaphor for describing the technology of mining. In the terms offered many years later by Harte, "life" and "story" are at this moment intimately entwined.

Even writing in an ostensibly realistic vein begins at one point to affect Clappe physically (or so she tells us). In "Letter Fifteenth," the one in which she apologizes for being "dreadfully commonplace and severely utilitarian" in her writing, Clappe brags to her sister about having asked to be lowered into a mining pit, "to see with my own eyes the process of underground mining, thus enabling myself to be stupidly correct in all my statements thereupon" (107). Here, corporeal danger becomes almost a precursor to textual accuracy, or at least to authenticity and believability. A still more explicit connection to writing comes at the end of the letter, when Clappe concludes: "I have spun this letter out until my head aches dreadfully. How tiresome it is to write *sensible* (?) things! But I have one comfort—though my epistle may not be interesting, you will not deny, dear M——, that I have achieved my ambition of making it both commonplace and utilatory" (114; emphasis in original). If nothing else, as a document of one writer's experience "in the diggings" *The Shirley Letters* provides a glimpse into the manner in which a particular way of life insinuates itself into the rhetorical choices available to and made by a writer.[14]

Eventually Clappe becomes inured enough to the realities of physical danger that she can report, with striking matter-of-factness, that "in the short space of twenty-four days, we have had murders, fearful accidents, bloody deaths, a mob, whippings, a hanging, an attempt at suicide, and a fatal duel" (133). By the time she departs from the mining district, her use in the narrative of such figures as the moaning flume machinery has diminished. It is at this point that she writes that in the mines one may actually learn to appreciate "how little it takes to make people comfortable in the world" (177). Yet, although "comfort" has become a closing keynote, the apperception and, hence, representation of the mortification of the flesh having passed, Clappe still emphasizes the notion that a life in the mines is one that tests the physical limits of the human body. Her final sentence promises, "You would hardly recognize the feeble and half-dying invalid, who drooped languidly out of sight, as night shut down between your straining gaze and the good ship *Manilla,* as she wafted her far away from her Atlantic home, in the person of your *now* perfectly healthy sister" (178–79). Having begun with the sickness of her husband and her own relative discomfort, Clappe brings her epistolary narrative to a close on a progressive note of resurrection: *she* is the one whose health has been revivified in the mountains. In this manner does Dame Shirley's narrative counter the pervasive evidence of physical danger that it confronts: at least one body has come out stronger and intact.

With respect to the tally of Harte's antecedents in Gold Rush storytelling, the name of Dame Shirley comes up quite often. More than a few commentators have pointed out, with varying degrees of appreciation and outrage, that Harte owes a great debt to *The Shirley Letters*. Among such critics who have credited Harte with drawing inspiration (if not directly lifting descriptive passages) have been Hubert H. Bancroft, Van Wyck Brooks, and Wallace Stegner. Most recently, Blake Allmendinger has revived an explicit charge of plagiarism against Harte (65–78). The evidence is at best sketchy for Harte's having directly stolen his material, hinging on the fact that both he and Clappe write about the birth of an infant into an (almost) all-male mining camp.[15] Whatever the truth may once have been, these congruent scenes detailing a moment of great physical distress lend credence to the assertion advanced by this chapter that Harte's fictions are keenly sensitive to the antecedent form of the Gold Rush narrative. Indeed, long before Harte, the communication (in print) of the physical hardships of mining becomes more than simply a descriptive trope for those who would write from and about the mines. Narratives of physical stress rapidly become coded in the era's textual production as a kind of doctrine; the fact of physical difficulty is turned into the stuff of popular "literature."

And as the example of J. M. Hutchings would indicate, the rendering through narrative of the miners' hardships could, in 1854, be worth a fortune. Hutchings in fact was able to buy his way out of the mines and into the more lucrative proprietorship of a monthly magazine (*Hutchings' California Magazine,* 1856–61), largely on the merits of a single piece of paper, a best-selling lettersheet entitled *The Miner's Ten Commandments.*[16] Lettersheets were large pieces of paper, usually blue, that were blank on one side and inscribed with etchings or verse or some other representation of the mining country on the other side. When folded in a certain way, the sheet would make an envelope that allowed for a brief letter to its recipient to be written on the blank side, now folded inward. A miner could thus send to his (or her) family back East both a personal note and a postcard-like token of California. Selling over 100,000 copies in its first year alone, Hutchings's lettersheet provides a text even more insightful that Dame Shirley's regarding the extent to which miners worried over the integrity of their physical being.[17]

Of the ten (actually, eleven) commandments offered by Hutchings, more than half in some way or another draw specific attention to the miner as a physical object. After the simple, succinct, and straightforward advice of commandment I—"Thou shalt have no other claim than one"—commandment II threatens that if a miner should happen to err by jumping someone else's claim, he will find himself reduced to poverty, his original claim "worked out" by others, and "at last thou shalt hire thy body out to make thy board and save thy bacon." Such indirect hints of physical degradation also occur in commandment III, which warns that by losing all of one's earnings at the faro table, "thou shalt not hold thyself guiltless, but—insane," and in commandment X, which cautions, "Thou shalt not commit unsuitable matrimony, nor covet 'single blessedness.'" Commandment IV promises more explicit physical privation and pains if the Sabbath is not observed: "Six days thou mayest dig or pick all that thy body can stand under. . . . For in six days' labor only thou canst not work enough to wear out thy body in two years; but if thou workest hard on Sunday also, thou canst do it in six months." In other words, a day of rest goes a long way toward preserving one both spiritually and physically from premature decay.

Hutchings's commandment VI is the most explicit in its discussion of physical trauma, and as it ultimately concerns the very real destructive force of liquor, it is also the longest. It begins, "Thou shalt not kill thy body by working in the rain, even though thou shalt make enough to buy physic and attendance with. Neither shalt thou kill thy neighbor's body in a duel; for, by 'keeping cool,' thou canst save his life and thy conscience. Neither shalt thou destroy thyself by getting 'tight,' nor 'slewed,' nor 'high,' nor 'corned,' nor 'half-seas-over,' nor 'three sheets to the wind.'" Following this catalog of euphemisms for "drunk" with a lengthy list of the names miners had for their favorite cocktails, this commandment warns of "crooked walkings and hiccuping talkings, of lodgings in the gutter, of broilings in the sun, of prospect-holes full of water, and of the shafts and ditches, from which thou hast emerged like a drowning rat." This commandment then concludes with the assurance that if the intemperate miner refuses to forswear the bottle, he will be "forever" plagued with the "headaches, tremblings, heart burnings, blue-devils, and all the unholy catalogue that follow." Beginning with death from overwork and murder, and running through an extraordinary catalog of mining vocabulary, commandment VI closes with a picture of a sort of perpetual delirium tremens. By implied association, this condition is as good as self-murder.

The dangers of creating some form of narrative misrepresentation (i.e., of telling a lie) are covered in commandment IX. Warning the miner not to "tell any false tales about 'good diggings in the mountains,'" this commandment promises that once the person lied to returns "with naught save his rifle, he [shall] present thee with the contents thereof, and like a dog, thou shalt fall down and die." That "false tales" should result in a condition very much like the one wrought by overwork and alcohol is suggestive of the connection a miner might make between the value of his life and the value of telling a story about that life. To put it a bit more accurately, Hutchings's lettersheet posits that California's community of miners clearly recognizes the representational economy into which the enterprise of gold hunting routinely places the physical body. To be a miner is not only to suffer physically but also to have that suffering recorded on paper. In both its content and its production and sales aspects, then, Hutchings's amusing but cautionary lettersheet affirms that the *story* of the miner's body can be quite valuable.

For confirmation that this idea becomes a central tenet of the Gold Rush narrative, we need look no further than Alonzo Delano. In 1854, the same year that saw the publication of *The Miner's Ten Commandments,* Delano published an account of his overland journey, *Life on the Plains and Among the Diggings,* doing so not under his California pseudonym, "Old Block," but rather under his own name and with a New York firm. In recalling his experiences in a distinctly serious tone, Delano shares his own thoughts on what the "elephant" looks like. And in one particular scene, he describes coming face-to-face in the Sierras with a very different sort of apparition: "I was attracted to the ruins of a shanty, by observing the effigy of a man standing upright in an old, torn shirt, a pair of ragged pantaloons, and boots which looked as if they had been clambering over rocks since they were made—in short, the image represented a lean, meagre, worn-out and woe-begone miner, such as might daily be seen at almost every point in the upper mines" (*Life on the Plains* 348). Delano has encountered here what Michael Kowalewski notes was a literary type commonly found during the Gold Rush, namely, the emaciated, worn-out miner ("Imagining" 62).[18] The connection between Delano's encounter and the notion of a literary trope is initially suggested by the fact that Delano encounters not a man but an "effigy"—a representation. However, Delano does not leave the textual connection hanging on so thin a thread, for this effigy is in fact an author and a bit of a poet. Delano continues in the next sentence:

> On the shirt was inscribed, in a good business hand, "My claim failed—will you pay the taxes?" (an allusion to the tax on foreigners). Appended to the figure was a paper, bearing the following words: "Californians—Oh, Californians, look at me! once fat and saucy as a privateersman, but now—look ye—a miserable skeleton. In a word, I am a used up man. Never mind, I can sing, notwithstanding,
>
> 'O California! this is the land for me;
> A pick and a shovel, and lots of bones!
> Who would not come the sight to see,—
> The golden land of dross and stones.
> O Susannah, don't you cry for me
> I'm living *dead* in Califor-*nee*.'" (*Life on the Plains* 348–49)

Parodying the tune that, according to legend, forty-niners sang out in unison as they disembarked in San Francisco, the "skeleton's" version of "O Susannah" offers the startling, paradoxical representation of a singing corpse that asks to be understood as "living," that is, as *not* a representation, but yet still only a representation, a "dead" effigy. The text of the note, which describes privation and a hint of death, becomes equivalent to the text of the effigy, which suggests visually the very same premise. And by making this case for understanding the "living *dead*" figure as having the ability to communicate actively, Delano suggests what has come to be known in more current terminology as the body-as-text formulation. More particularly, lines such as "living *dead*" and the "bones"-"stones" rhyme, an implied analogy between the miner and those gold nuggets he has searched for in vain, once again demonstrate that Gold Rush literature concerns itself quite keenly with affirming the value of the story of the miner's physical being.[19]

Of Human Value

The story of one apparently unfortunate miner turns out to have been greatly amusing to Bret Harte. In 1866, Josiah Whitney, director of the State Geological Survey and a professor at Harvard, acquired a human skull that had reportedly been found during the excavation of a new mining shaft in Angel's Camp, Calaveras County. Whitney believed the skull to be of Pliocene origin. Harte, however, joined the majority of local commentators in denouncing the skull as a hoax. In an essay "From Our Special Correspondent" dated 5 August and published in the *Springfield Republican* in Massachusetts, Harte pokes fun at the legitimacy of this apparent recovery of evidence from "the oldest portion of the earth's surface": "It appears that an honest miner, named James Matson . . . came across this osseous fragment at the depth of two hundred and fifty feet. The relic passed into the hand of Scribner, merchant, who transferred it to Jones, doctor, who, in turn, handed it over to the state geological survey, where it exactly fitted a theory promulgated by the survey of the extreme antiquity of man on this coast" (*Bret Harte's California* 62). Harte objects here to the convenience by which the skull confirms an existing theory, as well as to the daisy chain of handoffs that is supposed to serve as the object's provenance of authenticity. He also expresses doubt that a human being could have existed in a landscape dominated, as Whitney's Pliocene theory held, by "Huge Saurians" and volcanoes: "He [the erstwhile owner of the skull] must have passed a remarkably active existence in dodging the scoria and volcanic stones—those unrefreshing showers of the period" (63).

In a poem on this same topic published in San Francisco a week earlier than the letter (and in the *Springfield Republican* in late September), Harte makes even plainer his skepticism about the authenticity of the Calaveras Skull. Nine of the twelve stanzas of "To the Pliocene Skull" record the exhortations of a Whitney-like geologist who bids the skull to speak its ancient secrets. In the final stanzas, however, the narrator of the poem himself addresses the skull, and to him the relic does eventually speak:

> And, from that imperfect dental exhibition,
> Stained with expressed juices of the weed Nicotian,
> Came these hollow accents, blent with softer murmurs
> Of expectoration;
>
> "Which my name is Bowers, and my crust was busted
> Falling down a shaft in Calaveras County,
> But I'd take it kindly if you'd send the pieces
> Home to old Missouri!" (ll. 41–48)[20]

Unambiguously, Harte believes the skull to be that of an unfortunate forty-niner. Moreover, as Lois Rather has suggested, most locals thought the well-considered placement of the skull to be nothing more than a hoax, perpetrated by a fraternal organization of alcohol-inclined miners known as the "Ancient and Honorable Order of E. Clampus Vitus" (47–48).[21]

Harte's response to the Calaveras Skull highlights, for one, his sensitivity to the dangers posed by mining. By way of contrast, Harte concludes his letter with a more serious warning about the reality of those dangers. With a tone of regret, he reports that "the casualties which are incident to mining are so frequent that the eye scarcely rests upon their record in the daily press, unless the accident is fatal or involves life and limb or more than one fellow creature" (*Bret Harte's California* 65). This lament leads to one final recollection of a newspaper story Harte has found about a miner on the Comstock in Nevada whose leg was horribly broken, twisted, and subjected to the worst forms of (unsuccessful) traction that medical technology could inflict at the time. Offering his own warning of the sort once put forth by Woods and Johnson, Harte cautions that "Eastern folks, who are enamored with the idea of a miner's life, should remember that the injury spoken of was incidental to labors that are compensated at the rate of two dollars per day and board" (65). This final contrasting moment serves, then, to highlight the extent to which a hoax carries with it the potential to disrupt the accurate representation of physical danger. Harte implies as much a month later in another letter to the *Republican*, in which he laments that "since the discovery of the 'Pliocene skull' we have had several 'vestiges of creation' fished up in different parts of the state to tax our credulity" (*Bret Harte's California* 86). The very idea of representability is at issue: if a clearly false representation can be misread as "real" (as Whitney is accused of doing), then the genuine "real" (Harte's Comstock example) stands to be diminished in both accuracy and believability.

Such were the stakes regarding value and representation that predominated in both the California gold country and the neighboring silver fields of Nevada's Comstock Lode. Harte's colleague and, at the time, friend Samuel Clemens, who in the early 1860s worked as a writer in both regions, knew this well and addressed it often in his journalism.[22] In September 1864, for instance, staff members of the San Francisco Coroner's Office contrived a hoax against the city's local news reporters, a group that included Clemens, by planting a fictitious notice of a dead body found floating in the bay. All but one of the papers reported the incident and, when they discovered that it was not true, were compelled to print retractions. The coroner's office then used the incident as a pretense for denying the press access to its daily logs. In a piece for the *San Francisco Daily Morning Call* titled "A Small Piece of Spite," Clemens railed against what he saw as an egregious breach of the public trust by officials who by definition should work to ensure that trust: "If the Coroner permits his servants to close the door against reporters, many a man may lose a friend in the Bay, or by assassination, or suicide, and never hear of it, or know anything about it. . . . Who are the sufferers by this contemptible contumacy—we [reporters] or the hundred thousand citizens of San Francisco?" (235–36).[23] In this article, Clemens reacts angrily to a hoax and offers, in part, a defense of the right and ability of a journalist to put into words something approaching truth and accuracy. But he also wrote hoaxes himself, most famously from late 1862 to early 1864 as a Comstock journalist named Mark Twain. He was as interested in questioning the interplay of truth, value, and representation as he was in defending it.

To say the least, Twain knew how to work a hoax. On 28 October 1863 he shocked and sickened his Comstock-area readers in the *Virginia City Territorial Enterprise* with a story called "A Bloody Massacre Near Carson," in which he described a multiple ax murder in astonishingly gory detail. The murderer, distraught by the discovery that his investments in San Francisco's Spring Valley Water Company were worthless, expressed his rage by slaughtering his wife and children. According to the reception history of this little item, Twain's piece disgusted his readers so strongly that very few if any recognized that it was in fact a complete fabrication, a fiction. The key to the hoax, according to the apology Twain published the next day, lay in the story's description of a great pine forest in an area "near Carson" that local readers should have recognized as mere scrub desert. And, again according to Twain's apology, the apparent purpose of the hoax was to trick San Francisco's newspapers, who were always on the lookout for the sensational, into publishing an exposé of the undeniably nonfictional misprisions of that city's Spring Valley Water Company. Indeed, the *Gold Hill News*, the *Sacramento Union*, and the *San Francisco Evening Bulletin* all printed "A Bloody Massacre" verbatim.[24]

Twain's self-confessed reason aside, why might he concoct and publish such a story? Recent interpretations of "A Bloody Massacre" present only part of the answer, since the hoax has thus far been examined predominantly as a literary artifact. One usually finds one of two arguments made about it: either it is placed in the context of the literary style pioneered by the Old Southwest humorists, or it is read as being roughly autobiographical, in that it reveals an undisciplined Samuel Clemens attempting to work out the conflicting poses, gestures, and attitudes that would eventually coalesce in the persona of Mark Twain.[25] Moreover, criticism has shown that by mixing apparent fact with the gory sensationalism of a fiction, and also by testing his audience's geographic acumen by describing a phony landscape and turning one place with two known names ("Empire City" and "Dutch Nick's") into two places, Twain crafts a hoax that tests the idea that newspaper journalism deals in stable, reliable meaning. Thus is "A Bloody Massacre" understood largely in terms of the concurrent instabilities of meaning and identity. While these readings have much to say about the hoax as text and about "Mark Twain" as nascent persona, they still do not answer the question of why "A Bloody Massacre Near Carson" happened in 1863 Virginia City, Nevada, on the Comstock Lode. What, in other words, is at stake in such a literary performance for both reporter and reader of the *Territorial Enterprise*? The genre of the journalistic hoax as practiced on the Comstock provides a means of addressing, and perhaps mitigating through attempted humor, the anxieties generated by a culture wherein the value of material goods is constantly at issue and, as a result, terribly unstable. With respect to Clappe, Delano, and Harte, the hoax depicts both the physical trauma of mining *and* the beginnings of the erasure of that trauma from narratives of value.

The points on which the social, political, aesthetic, cultural, and economic relations of Twain's real-world setting are founded are also those on which Twain hangs his story. To wit: water, in the form of the Spring Valley Company; timber, in the form of the "great pine forest near Carson"; and mineral ore, in the form of the Comstock locale and the murderer's stockholdings in some of "the best mines." Natural resources, it may thus be said, determine both the core of Twain's hoax and the heart of life on the Comstock. In his twenty months as a reporter for the *Territorial Enterprise,* Twain joined his colleague and mentor Dan De Quille in writing almost daily columns on various aspects of the silver industry.[26] In this capacity Twain and De Quille would quite obviously incorporate the representation of natural resources as a key strategy in silver region journalism. Remarkably, a number of both Twain's and De Quille's pieces from this period are hoaxes or burlesques of some sort. One year before the resource-rich "Massacre" and after only three weeks on the job, Twain reported with full seriousness that a "Petrified Man" made entirely of calcified rock had been found in a cave in the eastern Sierra foothills; working off of Twain, De Quille would later create a similar hoax, debunking the "Petrified Man" by arguing in convincing pseudo-scientific detail that it was actually "A Silver Man" that had been found.[27] De Quille would, in fact, continue crafting believable, scientifically precise hoaxes well into the 1890s.[28]

In these instances of parodic journalism, as well as in numerous others by Twain and De Quille, a natural resource operates as the central ingredient in the elaboration of the hoax. Such a literary characteristic may strike one as simply attributable to the fact that being in residence in the Nevada Territory during its flush times would put mineral resources on anyone's mind, and that in the hands of men given to humor such material would inevitably result in literary joking around (Florence 36). However, the resource-based hoax also provides evidence of a cultural setting in which the material value of things seemingly factual and natural exists in a constant state of speculative uncertainty. Consider, for example, the following 1863 letter from Clemens to his mother, in which he explains the source of the apparent wealth he has been writing home about but never sending:

> Why, I sold "wildcat" mining ground that was given me, & my credit was always good at the bank for two or three thousand dollars, & is yet. . . . I have stock in my possession, which, if I had sold when it was first given me, from time to time, in the last months, would

> have brought me $10,000—but I have carelessly let it go down to nothing again. . . . Now, I raised the price of "North Ophir" from $13 a foot to $45 a foot, to-day, & and they gave me five feet. That will go the way of all the rest. I shall probably mislay it or throw it in my trunk & never get a dollar out of it. (*Letters* 1: 259–60)

Clemens's possession of numerous mine "feet" provides the credit that makes him a relatively rich man, despite the fact that he has not yet taken the time to cash in on any of his stockholdings. Despite its likely exaggerations and rather cavalier tone, Clemens's letter rather accurately indicates the degree to which Comstock fortunes were paper fortunes, banked on the speculative promise of soon-to-be-realized material wealth. As Twain would later recall in *Roughing It,* the wildcat spirit made for a "city with not one solitary poor man in it!" (286). This, then, is the paradox of a resource-based economy, in which the perceived value of an often worthless, ore-free mine is determined by the scraps of paper that represent shares, or "feet," in that mine.

When a mining operation was not paying its stockholders dividends on the profits, it was usually charging them cash assessments, in an attempt to raise capital. Which is to say, in the highly speculative and highly exploitative economy of the Comstock, a stockholder was more likely to have to pay cash in excess of his stocks' value then he was to collect profits.[29] Russell Elliot, historian of Nevada, notes that in 1867 "of some 400 companies organized, only 3—the Ophir, the Gould and Curry, and the Savage—were paying dividends." One mine, the Bullion, is famous for having collected (in 1870s dollars) over $3.8 million in assessments without ever producing a single penny's worth of ore (Elliot 134–35). Marion Goldman has called the Bullion Mine "a spectacular fraud" (19), and while such a comment might not be entirely accurate,[30] it nonetheless suggests the extent to which the uncertainty of the Comstock situation can lead one to think of paper mine shares as fraudulent indicators of value or, in a word, hoaxes.

Thus exists on the Comstock a context of unstable material value and possibly fraudulent representation, all focused by the production, as it were, of a natural resource. Recall, then, that Twain's infamous "Massacre" hinges each of its key points on a natural resource: the murderous motivation within the story, not to mention Twain's stated authorial agenda, arises out of unscrupulous water distribution and stock valuations, while the insider cues to the hoax depend on the locals' recognizing the nonexistence of a forest. A forest, it might also be noted, was as valuable a local resource as gold or silver, as hewn timbers were indispensable for the maintenance of mine shafts.[31] Finally, the murderer, a man identified as "P. Hopkins," had been not only a stockholder in the water company but also "a heavy owner in the best mines" in the region. This little detail places "P. Hopkins" in the company of most Comstock residents, laborers and capitalists alike. Whether the tale was believed or the hoax was spotted, or whether the sensationalized account simply came across as an entertaining read, "A Bloody Massacre Near Carson" provides a telling example of a local, unstable economy played out in that cultural economy's attendant journalism—its textual, as opposed to material, production. It also expresses a particular form of anxiety felt within the boom-to-bust context, an anxiety most clearly demonstrated in the fact that the loser of "feet" has made known his frustration over the loss of value by lashing out at his wife and children.

De Quille's "The Baby Crop," published in 1865, perhaps best sums up the case for the value of human bodies on the Comstock, in that De Quille draws remarkably clear lines between human figures, material resources, their value, and their representation on paper. He begins: "Nearly every day we find a little slip of paper in our drawer headed in big letters: 'BORN: To the wife of Mr. John Henry So-and-so, a son,' generally follows. One day we went to our drawer and to our unspeakable astonishment found three sons in it, all brand new" (230). De Quille continues this piece of satire by deliberately confusing those slips of paper crumpled in his drawer and vest pocket with actual children. At one point he regrets that "one night, in a fit of abstraction, we lighted our pipe with an infant but one day old" (231). He concludes his ruminations by assuring the reader that he has straightened out his reporter's priorities, asserting, "Send along your babies. We are now fully satisfied of their importance, and will see that they are properly cared for. They are fast becoming the great staple productions of Washoe" (231). The equation here is finally between written text and material resources, between slips of paper and the "great staple productions of Washoe," that is, children.[32] This formulation is highly reminiscent of the relationship between shares in a mine and solid rock, which is expressed in "feet." Taking note of the massive population explosion experienced by the Comstock region between 1860 and 1865, De Quille makes all too plain that the "production" of human beings is far outpacing the production of silver.

Thus, the value of the human figure was even more unstable than were mineral prices. In her study of prostitution on the Comstock in the 1860s and 1870s, Goldman notes that "the organization of the mines combined with the Lode's urban characteristics to create an atmosphere in which human life was generally devalued" (35). With the high premium placed on the speculative potential of silver-laced rock, the human labor required to exploit such a resource is concurrently devalued. Unsafe and neglectful working conditions, the extraordinarily high market for sex, and the culture of impermanence fostered by a boom-to-bust economy—all of these factors contribute to the ways in which value is placed on human beings.[33] It should therefore come as no surprise that both Twain's and De Quille's hoaxes rely finally on the representation of devalued human material for their jokes. Both "A Petrified Man" and "A Silver Man" turn human figures into display case objects. In the instance of Twain's "Massacre," the loss of stock value can only be recompensed through the elimination of family members, and in the "The Baby Crop" the breakdown of the distinction between a material resource and its representation on paper is made quite clear when De Quille's narrator tells us that he has stuffed a handful of children, not paper, into his pocket in order to put off thinking about them. Finally, it should be noted that Twain's hasty departure from both the *Territorial Enterprise* and Nevada was due in part to the angry public reaction generated by yet another one of his hoaxes. In his report on the Carson Fancy Dress Ball, Twain wrote that proceeds from the event, ostensibly earmarked for the Sanitary Fund (which F. L. Olmsted managed in Washington, D.C., before coming West), were in fact destined for the coffers of an East Coast miscegenation society.[34] Twain's suggestion that the charity funds were to support efforts of racial mixing proved to be too much for even his closest supporters. Clearly, bodies mattered to Virginia City's residents, who appear to have labored extensively under an anxiety about the unfixed material value of a human being. In the years after the initial rush in 1849, an overwhelming majority of writers in the far western mining regions saw that the material of the mines and the material of the miners had become inextricably entwined, confused, and combined.[35]

Ensconced in Buffalo, New York, with a successful first book to his name and a new bride, Twain reflected in 1870 on his *Territorial Enterprise* experience in a column for the *Galaxy* magazine. Recalling the "Bloody Massacre" brouhaha and his several other hoaxes, he notes that "to write a burlesque so wild that its pretended facts will not be accepted in perfect good faith by somebody, is very nearly an impossible thing to do" (*Contributions to* The Galaxy 47). This statement is commonly read as a wistful, knowing wink to an East Coast magazine audience about the gullibility of less-sophisticated newspaper readers out West.[36] However, it also hints at the lingering frustration of a former resident of a community wherein someone conditioned by the omnipresent but unreliable potential for instant and genuine riches might readily accept "in perfect good faith" whatever is presented as fact and, hence, as valuable. As reporters for the *Territorial Enterprise,* Twain and De Quille thus participated in what might be called a literary version of the instability of value sketched out above, configuring a textual dimension to the cultural dynamic playing itself out in mine shafts, assayers' offices, and stock-trading venues. By framing natural and human resources not just in terms of an ambiguously referential language but also in terms of both epistemological and material value, these hoaxing reporters brought to the forefront the perpetual negotiations of value that mark the silver-mining industry. The attempt to do so through humor indicates a need to defuse the antinomies, ironies, and contradictions inherent in a resource economy.

"Tell the Boys"

Narratives of corporeal threat in which the value of the human body stands in direct relation to the material products of mining, and humorous hoaxes that question the representability of such narratives—these, then, are the literary-cultural movements that Bret Harte brings together in his belittlement of the scientific claims made regarding the Calaveras Skull. More central to the argument of this chapter, they also finally provide the discursive context for Harte's immensely popular and influential "The Luck of Roaring Camp," written and first published in 1868. Surveying the genealogy of western American literature, Kate Chopin avows in 1900, "That was the beginning—that 'Luck of Roaring Camp'—so we have all come to acknowledge" ("Development" 70). On this point literary historians generally agree; as one recent anthologizer put it, Harte's "justly famous" tales "established the formulas and conventions for much Western fiction written thereafter" (Seelye 3).[37] However, with respect to an inherited tradition of Gold Rush writing, Harte also stands very much as the end of something. Simply put, Harte's particular version of the Gold Rush narrative puts an end to the genre's representation of physical privation, and "The Luck of Roaring Camp" provides the keynote example.

To be sure, there are plenty of injured or dead bodies in "Luck." Given Californians' cultural concern for the representation of value and the literary form he has inherited, Harte is almost required to attend to the privations of the physical being. Thus, "Luck" begins and ends with a corpse, opening with the death in childbirth of Cherokee Sal and closing with the bodies of both Luck (Sal's infant) and Kentuck, the latter two being victims of a springtime flash flood that rips through the center of Roaring Camp. Harte's representations of mining and value, however, differ significantly from those of his predecessors. Most notably, by floating what are arguably the tale's two most important bodies out of camp and out of life in that concluding flood, Harte figuratively washes the body out of the mining tale. As he bears the dead infant in his arms and "drift[s] away into the shadowy river that flows forever to the unknown sea," the character of Kentuck utters these final words: "tell the boys I've got the Luck with me now" (*Selected Stories* 17). The difference in Harte's version of mining mortification lies in his subtle emphasis not on death itself but rather on the ensuing account of that death. What Harte's washing away of both mine and body figuratively suggests is that the story now counts most. Kentuck does not appear to mind at all that he is going to die—he responds to the news with "a smile [that] lit the eyes of the expiring Kentuck" (17). What matters instead, it appears, is that his *story* of the child's passage down "the shadowy river . . . to the unknown sea" of death will be repeated, preserved, and (presumably) of some value to those who would pass it along by "tell[ing] the boys." In a manner foreseen by a text such as De Quille's "Baby Crop," Harte's narrative shifts the textual side of mineral extraction toward a discourse in which the primary locus of value is no longer the body or even gold but rather tale-telling, history, narrative. That is, Harte avoids the problematic representation of physical misfortune by refocusing the question of value onto the tale itself—in a textual sense, "story" has become much more valuable than "life." The ending to "The Luck of Roaring Camp" thus anticipates Harte's assurance in the 1870 preface that an accurate account of the Gold Rush "is yet to be sung," and thus does Harte convert a genre begun as realism into one in which the idea of truth supersedes the goal of a materially faithful representation.

Admittedly, this reading of just one Bret Harte story, even of an extraordinarily influential story, offers a figurative interpretation of Harte's narrative design that takes its model from the allegorical structure of that very narrative. As such it might hold as a valid reading for just that one story and nothing more. However, a few years later Harte will explore these issues of representation and mortification in his novella "The Story of a Mine," in which a man is murdered at the site of a newly discovered mine and the murderer, years later, comes across a painting of the mine site that, uncannily, has a body painted onto the very spot where his victim had lain. Harte's playful twist here is that the painter, Carmen de Haro, has had no idea of the murder, she had merely been attempting to paint the scene of the since-developed mine in its preindustrial idyllic state and in doing so imagined a resting figure supine on the ground. But in the "romance" of her imagination she has inadvertently created realism, a point Harte uses to underscore the slippery interplay of truth and representation ("Story" 49–51, 59, 116).[38]

Which is to say, in terms of realism Harte on this question sounds very much like his friend Mark Twain. In turn, a final glimpse at one more pivotal text from this period, the dissection of truth and representation in the West that Twain called *Roughing It,* will further confirm the leading role played by Harte's historicizing approach to the mining narrative. As many readers and critics have noted, Twain's 1872 pastiche of frontier adventures and western revelations offers a number of insights into the nature of words, particularly as they relate to identity, truth, market value, and representation.[39] In one telling instance in chapter 4, Twain quips about the material impact of language, as well as its status as commodity, by describing his encounter with a dictionary on the journey across the high plains. Tossed about in the bowels of an uncomfortable stagecoach filled with mailbags, Twain and his brother are with every lurch and jolt mercilessly beaten and pummeled and pounded about their bodies (19) by "six pounds of Unabridged Dictionary, for we did not know . . . that such things could be bought in San Francisco" (4–5). In a more complex example, Twain's recollection in chapter 20 of an oft-heard anecdote about Horace Greeley's equally bruising stage ride to Placerville, California, in the care of the legendary driver Hank Monk further emphasizes the exchange value of a story. What proves infuriating to Twain, and hence hilarious to his readers, is the fact that Twain hears the tale verbatim—not a word is ever changed—from a succession of tale-tellers encountered first in Julesburg, Nebraska; several days later "at the crossroads"; in Fort Bridger, Wyoming; in Salt Lake City, Utah; and finally in Ragtown, Nevada (131–36). The first nineteen chapters of *Roughing It* cover the details of Twain's overland journey. By rehearsing virtually the entire trek a second time with the recurring anecdote as his focus, Twain marks his journey westward with something like a passport story. It designates the stations of his progress, is a tale that many passersby before him had both taken with them and left behind, and his passage across the plains is not complete until he has paid the price of listening to this particular form of commodity exchange. Chapter 21 begins with Twain's arrival at his ultimate destination, Carson City, Nevada; listening to the Hank Monk–Horace Greeley anecdote thus serves as exchange currency, as the final price of passage along the road and of eventual admission into the western mining region.[40]

Twain maintains this emphasis on tale-telling as commodity throughout much of *Roughing It,* eventually drawing the book to a close on a note strikingly similar to that suggested by the ending of "The Luck of Roaring Camp." Having run the full gamut of rags to riches to rags as both a miner and speculator in "feet," Twain's narrator turns first to writing and then to lecturing about his experiences. The latter proves to be particularly lucrative, since "public lectures were almost an unknown commodity in the Pacific market" (537). The success of his very first such performance prompts Twain to close the book's penultimate chapter by exclaiming, "All the papers were kind in the morning; my appetite returned; I had an abundance of money. All's well that ends well" (536). His first-ever lecture had taken place in San Francisco (on 2 October 1866), and for the event Twain had even contracted for "three chief allies, with three auxiliaries" to sit in the front row and laugh, hoot, and applaud at the appropriate moments (535–36). In effect, Twain draws the penultimate chapter of *Roughing It* to a close by "tell[ing] the boys."

Consistent with its relentless dialectic of success and failure, the final chapter of *Roughing It* also allows for one more injection of the traditional mining tale topos, one more textual instance of the body's suffering. After a lecture in the Comstock town of Gold Hill, one month after his premiere in San Francisco, an unsuspecting Twain is subject to a nighttime hoax robbery perpetrated by his friends (another set of "boys"). As an unintended consequence of their late-night activities, the holdup men became "so chilled that it took them a couple of weeks to get warm again," while for Twain himself "the chilly exposure on the 'divide' while I was in a perspiration gave me a cold which developed itself into a troublesome disease and kept my hands idle for some three months" (541–42). Though the narrator's idle hands presumably kept him from writing for those three months, the evidence of this story's appearance in the last chapter of a "Mark Twain" book suggests that the narrator makes a full recovery.[41] This closing metatale in *Roughing It* affirms that the persona of Mark Twain has at last found decent employment. For Twain, as well as for Harte, "tell the boys" has become the operative paradigm with which to earn a living in the mining country, thereby replacing the narrative of bodily suffering, even the exaggerated, humorous narrative of physical hardship. In short, writing about mining has become the primary subject for those who would write about mining,[42] a literary adaptation that falls directly out of a genre deeply concerned with telling it right.

Subsequent prose writers in the resource West will thus inherit a discourse of mining and people that, on a fundamental level, substitutes a "quaint and typical" past for a difficult, physically demanding present. Popular writing about the mining industry becomes a matter of addressing not physical labor but history, a production of value that is textual rather than material. This is what Harte in a sense begins, in that he helps to put an end to a particular set of representational issues. Speaking of Harte, Twain, and a number of other early California writers, Patrick Morrow argues that "more satirically humorous or sentimentally mythic than what a modern audience would like to consider realistic, the Western local color movement, with its origins in a maverick, untutored journalism, did play a part in the nineteenth century movement from romance to realism" (16). Morrow suggests that in developing the idea of local "texture," Gold Rush writers contribute a descriptive mode to the literature that eventually becomes realism. Harte's move is finally not realism, though, in the descriptive or even stylistic sense—his satire of the generic disclaimer form, his questioning of the truth-value of the Argonaut narrative, and his somewhat allegorical fictions are textual acts that clearly indicate this. However, his (re)stabilization of value in the narrative, that is, his shift of the form away from the body and toward the narrative itself, creates an important precursor to the discourses of value—social, racial, gendered, class, as well as literary—that characterize American realism. After Harte, the idea of realistic representation, a crucial component of the Gold Rush narrative, also continues to inform western genres, particularly those interested in depicting nature, which, once the Gold Rush is "past," takes center stage as a representational concern in western American literature.

2

John of the Mines

Muir's Picturesque Rewrite of the Gold Rush

John Muir, for one, certainly knew the value of a Bret Harte tale. Hiking through the northern California woods late one afternoon in October 1874, Muir lost all track of time and was still without shelter as night began to fall. Luckily, he soon encountered a teamster who directed him to a place nearby that offered both "food and a bed." As Muir recalled in a newspaper article, this teamster proved to be a man "into whose good graces I found my way by telling a Bret Harte story" ("Salmon-Breeding" 21). Muir had arrived in San Francisco six years earlier in 1868, just as Harte's tales were giving rise to their author's initially meteoric career, and he was very much in a position to witness and appreciate Harte's widespread appeal to westerners. Strange as it may seem, though, Harte and Muir also shared a predilection for the same material and an inclination to move their respective literary productions toward a discussion of the "natural," and hence "real," that elides the presence of human bodies in a material economy. That is to say, while Muir was by no stretch of the imagination a Gold Rush writer, he nevertheless had quite a lot to say about this key event and its impact on California's scenery, so much so that his prose was greatly affected by the effort. When Muir himself becomes a widely read California author, his engagement with and reliance on a western genre—the Gold Rush narrative he inherits from Harte—begins to have a profound effect on his own chosen topic, the realistic representation of western nature.

In the early fall of 1874, Muir left San Francisco and headed for the very same hills that had not too long ago played host to a rush of gold seekers. Having spent "a period of three hundred days" immersed in what he called "the processes and vicissitudes of civilization," Muir rejoiced that "at the close of this season of fog and refinement I fortunately made good my escape to the mountains" ("Salmon-Breeding" 21, 20–21). Earning over the course of a lifetime such monikers as "John o' Mountains," "The California Thoreau," and "The Psalmist of the Sierra," Muir would of course create a magnificent career of wilderness advocacy.[1] Founded in part on the idea that mountains could help clear the fog generated by a crowded urban existence, Muir's nature ethos would lead to a number of significant contributions to the canon of American nature writing.[2] However, in 1874 he is only just getting started. Since his arrival in California, Muir had worked primarily as an itinerant shepherd, sawyer, and guide who also strove to publish his observations on botany and geology in newspapers such as the *New York Tribune,* the *Boston Weekly Herald,* and, by 1872, San Francisco's prestigious *Overland Monthly.*[3] During those "three hundred days" in 1874, though, Muir succeeded in transforming himself into one of San Francisco's most prolific and noted journalists. At the time of his "escape," his radically revisionary geological studies of the glacial formation of Yosemite Valley were appearing serially in the *Overland Monthly.*[4] And toward the end of the summer of 1874 Muir entered into a contract with the *San Francisco Daily Evening Bulletin* as a field reporter, assigned to submit, at his leisure, descriptive essays about his wanderings in the mountains. These essays, in which their author appeared with the byline "Special Correspondent of the Bulletin," made for front-page copy. Thus, in 1874 Muir could expect his readers to appreciate his status as a mountain enthusiast when publicly announcing his "escape to the mountains." Moreover, he could make his announcement while thinking of himself not only as a geologist and a botanist, but also as the relatively well known author of "Rambles of a Botanist" and "A Geologist's Winter Walk"; he could leave town cloaked in the mantle of professional writer.[5]

As a newly named "special correspondent" with an established reputation for writing well about his beloved mountains, Muir enters into a relationship with a discourse that had heretofore been ancillary to his previous publications. That is, he begins to confront much more directly that substantial body of popular writing that had long served as the primary textual link between San Franciscans and the nearby Sierra Nevadas, namely, the narratives about gold mining and the once ubiquitous forty-niner. In fact, Muir's very first article for the *Bulletin* reveals the beginnings of a professional awareness of the popular strengths of that discourse. Having begun with the celebratory note on the end of those "three hundred days" of fogbound human company, Muir's simply titled "Salmon-Breeding" essay proceeds to describe for the *Bulletin*'s readership a journey to the McCloud River near Mount Shasta in northern California, where the U.S. Fish Commission was trying to establish a salmon hatchery. But before he arrives, he loses himself in the dark, and it is here that Muir encounters the teamster who will trade him information for Bret Harte. That a tale of Harte's could prove useful to Muir not only as entertainment but, more significantly, as currency for successfully arranging for a decent place to stay is certainly a measure of Harte's popularity. Muir's benign, perhaps even respectful reference to Harte indicates that, at the very least, he recognized Harte's tremendous cultural value. More importantly, this brief episode demonstrates that Muir is indeed thinking about the textual aspects of an industry that had both literally and figuratively left its mark on the land. The fallout of this awareness will have tremendous consequences for the genre of western nature writing.

In the 1870s, the Gold Rush still provided the dominant narrative filter through which Californians viewed their mountains, and Muir, who effectively began his career as an environmental writer and journalist in 1871 San Francisco, was very much framed by this context. However, while the critical literature on Muir's achievements as an environmental advocate is quite vast, none of it even begins to address Muir's writerly engagement with the history of mineral extraction in the Sierra Nevadas.[6] The problem with this critical blind spot is that it fails to render a fully historicized account of Muir and his work. Consider, for example, the publication circumstances of Muir's "The New Sequoia Forests of California," an early, foundational essay that would become the centerpiece of the chapter "The Forests" in his memorable first book, *The Mountains of California* (1894). Published in the November 1878 issue of *Harper's* (813–27), this essay appeared alongside "The Valley of the Yomouri" (828–29), an idyllic poem about the sultry jungle pleasures of Cuba; "Wild Babies" (829–38), an anthropological study of how native people around the world raise their children; and "The Sea Islands" (839–61), a report on Georgia's Gullah communities, which closes with an etching of an old black man playing a fiddle, for which the caption reads, "Music hath charms" (861). One might easily argue from its placement that Muir's article on the sequoia participates in the exotification of the strange, of the other. A quick read through the essay itself, however, makes this interpretation hard to sustain (though one might still attribute such a motive to the magazine's editors).

The point is that a contextualized Muir begins to look like a very different writer. As will be discussed below, while it does not deal with racial othering, "The New Sequoia Forests" does reflect significantly on the discourse of the Gold Rush, in that it offers a picturesque and aging forty-niner turned harmless forest hermit. Moreover, this hermit disappears altogether from the landscape once Muir adapts this essay for book publication. If, as Simon Schama recently hinted, Muir's ecological agenda required that he "carefully and forcibly" edit "the mining companies . . . out of the idyll" (7–8), then attention must be paid to the editing as it happens. Historicizing Muir's environmentalist writings compels us to revise our understanding not only of his ecological vision but also the current state of what Lawrence Buell calls the American "environmental imagination."

The rhetoric of American environmentalism—which, as Buell affirms, depends crucially on the claim to realism (*Imagination* 83–114) and which develops to a great extent in the wake of Muir's literary achievements—relies quite intimately on the representational framework provided by the literary history of the Gold Rush. Just as in that now famous first summer, during which Muir had to pass through the Sierra foothills on his way to the mountains proper, so too does he find that he must work through the Gold Rush of literature in order to render textually his own vision of California scenery. More importantly, as Muir's professional writing career progresses from its beginnings in the early 1870s, his engagement with the written legacy of mineral extraction in the foothills increases. In 1874 Muir swaps a Bret Harte tale for lodging; by 1911 and the publication of *My First Summer in the Sierra,* a memoir about his landmark first encounter with California's mountains, Muir has developed a rhetorical approach to the depiction of natural spaces that couches a great deal of its ecological argument in a figurative language that maintains a foothold in the discourse of 1849.

My First Summer, which concludes significantly with the avowal, "I have crossed the Range of Light . . . [and] I gladly, gratefully, hopefully pray I may *see* it again" (354; emphasis added), at an earlier point assures, "Thundering underground blasting is still going on to feed the pounding quartz mills, but their influence on the landscape is light as compared with that of the pick-and-shovel storms waged a few years ago.

Fortunately for Sierra scenery the gold-bearing slates are mostly restricted to the foothills. The region about our camp is still wild, and higher lies the snow about as trackless as the sky" (74–75). Gradually, over the course of a career, Muir will bring himself to this point where he can dismiss mining as a superfluous dimension of the scene (and seen). With respect to attempting a realistic depiction of natural landscapes, of nature, Muir picks up where Harte left off, by eliding the "quaint and typical" past of mining (Harte, "Argonauts" 261) and eliminating the human body. As a consequence of the eco-aesthetic that Muir develops along the way, the human figure, as well as the material economics imbricated with the person, is dropped out of the scene altogether. Muir's eventual erasure of the evidence of an entire industry from the face of the land is thus achieved by his subsuming the industry within a discourse about scenery and value that predominantly concerns itself with the visual apperception of a landscape. In other words, Muir buries the mines within his particular version of the picturesque, a definition for which, as will become clear, he in fact derives from mining narratives themselves.

Of Books and Forty-Niners

Although Muir was quite unambiguous in his contempt for the methods and consequences of mineral extraction, his initial California writings, those composed and published before his assumption of a contractual commitment to professional writing, make little reference to California's Gold Rush past. This apparent omission is all the more remarkable given the fact that well-known pieces such as "Rambles of a Botanist" (June 1872) and "Twenty Hill Hollow" (July 1872) focus on the flora and scenery of an area located in the gold-rich foothills between the Merced and Tuolumne Rivers. This is not to fault Muir for being oblivious, willfully or otherwise, to the history around him, for these earliest publications do in fact demonstrate an oblique rhetorical engagement with the legacy of 1849. In "Rambles," for instance, the word "gold" appears as a modifier no less than six times, although each such reference is made not to the mineral but rather to the "lake" of yellow *Compositae* blossoms that surround the narrator. Muir describes this scene as being "one flower-bed, nearly four hundred miles in length by thirty in width" into whose "flower-gems" he has been "nestling deep in a goldy-way of vegetable suns" (769–70). And in "Twenty Hill Hollow" he further reconceptualizes the familiar California adjective in his discussion of the *Compositae,* describing them again as a "goldy-way" and offering the neologism "con-golded" to describe the effect of sunshine meeting yellow flower head (85). In this latter piece, Muir draws explicit attention to the valence of the term "gold" by situating it in a trinity of value and aesthetics that strives to advance the term from one set of associations to another, from the "red shirt" to the flower, from the industry of humans to the industry of nature. He writes: "Truly, said I, is California the Golden State—in metallic gold, in sun gold, and in plant gold" (86). Taken as a progression across time, this figure is fairly suggestive of Muir's wish for the conceptual and economic replacement of the mineral gold phase with an appreciation of the resources offered by vegetal gold.

Thus do Muir's earliest renditions of California landscape show their author working to shift a familiar figurative (and economic) signifier from mining to another, more aesthetically determined set of values. But such challenges hardly amount to a full engagement with the textual history of a landscape. Prior to his contract with the *Bulletin,* Muir wrote as a self-proclaimed glaciologist and mountaineer in order to take issue, through his *Overland* series, with Josiah Whitney's and Clarence King's theories of the catastrophic formation of Yosemite Valley.[7] But as a journalist hired to describe the people and places of his chosen subject, the mountains of California, he must now engage a subtly different audience and, hence, a different set of texts. Thus it is that Muir, who was already known to most readers as someone well read in the book of nature,[8] in 1874 signals to them that he is also quite familiar with popular literature. This is the moment at which he barters for lodging with a Harte tale, and here he begins to write about the mining country as something more than just a "goldy-way" of flowers and hills. Becoming a widely read critic of mining's impact on Sierra scenery, Muir would whenever the opportunity presented itself decry what he calls the "pick-and-shovel storms" that had raged across the landscape, and on occasion he would also direct his scorn at the nameless, brainless, gold-fevered masses who in their rush for wealth "cover[ed] the ground like grasshoppers" ("Nevada's Dead Towns" 201). However, Muir's descriptive handling of individual people reveals a kinder, gentler critic, for he seems quite plainly to enjoy the company of those old Argonauts he occasionally comes across in his jaunts through the hills. Moreover, the figure of the old and weary ex-miner would serve another purpose for Muir as well, a purpose of a distinctly textual nature. By writing favorably about the individual but vilifying his activity, Muir *separates* the person from the industry, thereby reconceptualizing not only the historical and the figurative landscape of California's mountains but also that of the figures who populate that history. Eventually, Muir evicts the miner from the textual landscape, but for the time being, as he continues to develop a voice and subject matter that will shortly garner him a national readership, he works to render the forty-niner as a harmless, picturesque remnant of a bygone era.

On this count, literary history had already done much of the work for Muir, for by the mid-1870s the figure of the weary, broken, and often aged miner has long been a familiar literary type. In a development virtually concurrent with the discovery of gold at Sutter's Mill in January 1848, diarists, journalists, and writers of humorous sketches begin to develop a body of writing that both chronicles and retroactively defines the Gold Rush as historical experience. In the process, the decaying, forlorn miner rapidly becomes a key component in their lexicon. He appears in print as early as 1851, in the published diaries of the argonaut Daniel Woods, who recalls an encounter with "an old man of three-score and ten years. . . . He says when he is home-sick he can not cry, but it makes him sick at his stomach. He is an old industrious man, but has not made enough to buy his provisions" (63). Two years later, the merchant, sketch writer, and occasional prospector Alonzo Delano further capitalizes on this figure when he writes of having encountered, in 1850, the rag-doll effigy of "a lean, meagre, worn-out and woe-begone miner, such as might daily be seen at almost every point in the upper mines" (*Life on the Plains* 348). And journalist J. D. Borthwick, in his widely read book of 1857, similarly describes this figure, noting that in a mining camp one would occasionally see "the live carcass of some wretched, woebegone man, clad in the worn-out greasy habiliments of quondam gentility; the glassy unintelligent eye looking as if no focus could be found for it" (48).[9] With the passage of years, this noble, decrepit figure becomes a traditional fixture in the literary and historical landscape by which California's origins are remembered.

Bret Harte, whose name serves for Muir (as it does for many others) as the key signifier of gold camp literary history, does surprisingly little during this time with the old and weary miner, although he does employ a number of familiar characteristics in order to sketch characters such as the catatonic ex-forty-niner in "Miggles," the Old Man in "How Santa Claus Came to Simpson's Bar," and the D.T.-suffering Johnson in "Mrs.

Skagg's Husband."[10] However, while these representations are by no means fully developed characters, neither do they come across, through Harte's selective use of traits, as entirely stereotypical miners. Harte's friend Mark Twain, on the other hand, who appears perhaps more interested than Harte in adding a voice to this budding tradition, very plainly invokes the aging miner in his 1872 book *Roughing It,* where he tells of his mid-1860s sojourn among the "decayed mining camps of Tuolumne, California":[11] "The mere handful of miners still remaining, had seen the town spring up, spread, grow and flourish in its pride; and they had seen it sicken and die, and pass away like a dream. With it their hopes had died, and their zest of life. They had long ago resigned themselves to their exile. . . . [T]hey stood, as it were, in a living grave, dead to the events that stirred the globe's great populations" (412). Twain describes one particular man there as someone "who had had a university education; but now for eighteen years he had decayed there by inches, a bearded, rough-clad, clay-stained miner." Never one to miss a joke that challenges the limits of representational language, Twain extends the logic of the living-in-death analogy to include the so-called dead languages: "At times, among his sighings and soliloquizings, he unconsciously interjected vaguely remembered Latin and Greek sentences —dead and musty tongues, meet vehicles for the thoughts of one whose dreams were all of the past, whose life was a failure" (412–13). Twain concludes by noting that this "tired man" spends his hopeless, futureless days "waiting for rest and the end" (413).[12] First encountered as a sick, demoralized, and impoverished miner in Daniel Woods's account, this literary figure has become by 1872 a slowly wasting specter of death.

This characterization proves quite useful to Muir, for it is the very one he takes up when he too begins to write about miners and the mines. Predominantly, but not exclusively, Muir does so by writing, and then rewriting, about John Nelder, a forest hermit he first describes in an article on "The Royal Sequoia" ("Summering . . . Royal Sequoia") published in the *Bulletin* on 21 September 1875. Muir tells his readers that while sauntering through a redwood grove in the mountains east of Fresno, he comes across an "old, gray-haired man" sitting quietly by the door of his "quaint, old-fashioned" cottage and wearing a "weary-eyed and unspeculative" look on his face.[13] Stopping to chat, Muir "bit by bit" learns this hermit's story. Unfortunately, the tale proves to be "only a sad illustration of early California life during the gold period, full of intense experiences, now up in exciting success, now down in crushing reverses, the day of life waning meanwhile far into the afternoon, and long shadows turning to the east; health gone and gold; the game played and lost; and now, creeping into this solitude, where he may at least maintain independence, he awaits the coming of night" ("Summering . . . Royal Sequioa" 129). Written for a San Francisco newspaper, this account no doubt expects on some level to remind its readers of the familiar figure from the once rich goldfields, for Muir has here described a man who embodies both the deathwatch characteristics of Twain's scholar-cum-miner and Borthwick's glassy-eyed "live carcass." Upon concluding his recollection of the hermit's life story, Muir finally gives the man's name—John Nelder. More importantly, and in order to emphasize how much both the man and his value as a literary figure have changed, Muir also chooses this moment to inform his readers of that which he finds most interesting about the hermit: Nelder, it seems, has become something of a naturalist. In waiting out his days in pastoral tranquility, Nelder has nevertheless stayed relatively active and vital, becoming "a keen intuitive observer of nature. Birds, squirrels, plants all receive loving attention. . . . [H]ow tenderly he strokes the sapling sequoias, hoping that they will yet reach the full stature of their race" (129). These nurturing, almost Wordsworthian habits of observation seem very much to recommend him to Muir, despite—or perhaps because of—his past.

At this point Muir leaves Nelder behind and continues to explore for his readers the sequoia grove. However, this would not be his last visit, so to speak, with the ex-miner-turned-hermit, for later in his career Muir will significantly rewrite this encounter on two other occasions. In any event, by having appropriated the familiar literary type of the old, graying miner, in order to suggest that he has in his dotage begun making rudimentary but eye-opening observations about the natural world, Muir has once again attempted, as with his earlier use of "goldy-way," to reconfigure a trope familiar to the literary history of the mining country. What makes the introduction of Nelder significant is the extent to which it shows Muir interested in and engaged with the human dimension of the figurative language derived from the Gold Rush.

Muir continues to work through and revise the literary history of the Sierra foothills in the following year, 1876, describing in another article for the *Bulletin* his encounter with a group of "pioneers" very much like John Nelder. In describing a visit to the glacial riverbeds and ancient caves near the mining town of Murphy's Camp, Muir steps directly and deliberately into the literary history of the Gold Rush, into the very heart of the mother lode country of Calaveras County. Harte's "Mrs. Skagg's Husband," for instance, takes place in Angel's Camp, which stands only a few miles downriver from Murphy's. Angel's Camp was also the location to which Twain had gone during his sojourn in the mining country and where he first heard the tale that would become "The Notorious Jumping Frog of Calaveras County." Murphy's Camp itself was believed by many to be the point of origin for the legendary Gold Rush bandit Joaquín Murieta, and enthusiastic locals also claimed that Harte's "A Night in Wingdam" (*Golden Era,* Nov. 1860) was in fact about their town. Most significantly, though, in 1852 a miner from Murphy's Camp named A. T. Dowd became the first white man to see what would soon become famous as the Calaveras Grove of giant sequoia trees, a grove for which Muir had a profound fondness.[14] The discovery of the grove and its marvels were amply reported in *Hutchings' California Magazine;* considering that Muir at one time worked at Hutchings's Yosemite sawmill, it is not too great a leap to assume that Muir would have been very much aware of the literary significance of Murphy's Camp.

In any event, Muir uses his visit to this region to revise further the image of the forty-niner. Declaring that the town and its environs have been "placed invitingly open before the student like a book," Muir avers that "the people and the region furnish mines of study of never-failing interest and variety" ("Summering . . . Discourses" 1). In offering a pun that combines his favorite figure of nature as book with the idea that study equals mining, Muir hints at something he will increasingly do as his career as a writer progresses: he will collapse the human figure into the processes of a nonhuman nature, a move that ultimately manifests itself in a rhetorical attempt to work the mines—and miners—off the face of the scenic Sierra landscape. Murphy's Camp provides the opportunity to begin this process in earnest.

Muir opens this article by situating his "discovery" of the old mining town in the context of an inquisitive search for the long-dry "channels of the ancient pre-glacial rivers" that once flowed through the hills. After a brief discussion of these river channels and their enduring value as gold beds, he segues to a discussion of the current social conditions of this once booming region. Reminiscent of Twain's recollection of a similar scene, Muir notes that "many a brave fellow has recorded a most eventful chapter of life on these Calaveras rocks. But most of the pioneer miners are sleeping now, their wild day done, while the few survivors linger languidly in the washed-out gulches or sleepy village" ("Summering . . . Discourses" 1). Additionally, Muir unmistakably invokes Harte, who had fancied himself as something of an American Dickens, by noting that the miners' "Micawber-like waiting" has reduced them to an "exaggerated form of dotage" in which they "play in the streets with children." Drawn from the lexicon of mining narratives, these are clearly men who no longer pose any threat: "As dead as the rivers, they are yet a rare and interesting set of men, with much gold mixed with the rough, rocky gravel of their characters." The easily achieved analogy between the vestigial traces of long-dry riverbeds and the "lingering" survivors of the "grand old gold-days" allows Muir to position the forty-niner as a mere trace on the land, "more exhausted than the mines" (1).

By collapsing the once active miner into geologic history, Muir recreates him as a benign facet of a more complex *natural* system; and it is along these lines that Muir completes his thumbnail sketch of the worn-down forty-niner by picturing him as one who, in waiting quietly for sleep to come, has by virtue of his "contact with Nature" become, like John Nelder, quite the amateur naturalist. An ex-miner who shows Muir about "the diggings" near Murphy's Camp takes care along the way to point out a weed favored by the local Indians and to offer his speculations about dragonflies: "Well, their jaws work sidewise, instead of up and down, and grasshoppers' jaws work the same way, and therefore I think they are the same species. I always notice everything like that, and just because I do, they say I'm eccentric" ("Summering . . . Discourses" 1). Far from "eccentric," this figure appeals to Muir precisely because he has replaced the hunt for metallic wealth with the Muir-like pleasures of nature observed. In a sense, the only ravaging of a landscape now possible is that of the eye, and in this respect Muir is quite correct when he unabashedly assures his readers that "the sketches of Bret Harte, Hayes, and Miller have not exhausted this field by any means" (1).[15] Indeed, in 1876 the "field" of scenic landscape description as Muir would pioneer it is far from exhausted. And in chronicling a small "chapter of life," as he puts it, in the waning lives of the miners, Muir begins his efforts to collapse the human figure into the landscape (into the book of nature, as it were), thereby effecting a subtle but definitive shift in the apperception of scenery.

In November 1878 Muir introduces John Nelder to a national audience by revising his *Bulletin* article on the Fresno Grove and (as noted at the head of this chapter) publishing it in *Harper's New Monthly Magazine* as "The New Sequoia Forests of California." Notably, this new version contains several additions and one key deletion. Much more descriptive and detailed than the tourism-oriented *Bulletin* version had been, this account of how a sequoia forest propagates, creates water channels for itself, and so forth presents Muir's answer to the question of whether the big trees are on the verge of extinction. In short, Muir argues that in fact many young and vigorous trees are on their way, that the forest is vital, thriving, and in no danger beyond that posed by the ax and saw. Nelder, whose loving hand had symbolically helped to nurture along those sequoia saplings in the earlier version, is also still around. His story is the same, and Muir retains both it and the comment about the hermit's experience being a "sad illustration of early California life during the gold period" (818). However, this figure no longer has a name, nor does he dote lovingly on the young trees in the grove. In this *Harper's* version, Muir reconfigures Nelder as a nameless hermit who sits by his cottage reading the book in his hands while remaining woefully oblivious to the book of nature that surrounds him. Muir no longer claims for him the role of observer, no longer allows him to function as an element of forest vitality. The argonaut once named John Nelder now merely sits and "awaits the coming of night." This return to the forty-niner once described by Delano and Twain, a return to a man who is no longer a budding naturalist and can only stoically anticipate death, signals the beginning of Muir's effort to be rid of him altogether.

The closing months of 1878 prove to be a significant time in Muir's writing about mining. At roughly the same time as the appearance in print of his *Harper's* revision of Nelder, Muir can be found trekking eastward through Nevada in the company of a U.S. Coast and Geodetic Survey crew and sending his usual dispatches to the *Bulletin*. He writes about the mountains, the trees, the possibility of glacial activity in the Great Basin's distant past; and on 15 January 1879 the *Bulletin* publishes Muir's essay on "Nevada's Dead Towns." With its title alone this piece reflects a striking departure for the young journalist, for rarely had Muir submitted for print a piece that by its very title indicated that it was to be solely and explicitly about human activity and habitation. Moreover, this piece, in which Muir's reliance on the picturesque begins to crystallize, provides a further and ultimately definitive instance of Muir's developing efforts to remove the miner from the context of the scenery. Beginning with a condemnation of the boom-to-bust mentality of past mineral rushes, Muir once again situates the remnants of those "mining storms" in both literary and geologic history: "Wander where you may throughout the length and breadth of this mountain-barred wilderness, you everywhere come upon these dead mining towns, with their tall chimney-stacks, standing forlorn amid broken walls and furnaces, and machinery half buried in sand, the very names of many of them already forgotten amid the excitements of later discoveries, and now known only through tradition—tradition ten years old" (195). As Muir sketches the scene, the apparatus of early efforts at mineral extraction is literally being reclaimed by the ground into which it once probed. The more telling detail of this opening passage, however, is the mention of the forgotten place-names that are "now known only through tradition—tradition ten years old." The two major silver strikes and subsequent boom rushes in Nevada at the time had occurred in 1860 and again in 1873, neither of which provides a ten-year differential with respect to Muir's visit in 1878.[16] However, 1868 coincides precisely with the publication of "The Luck of Roaring Camp," the first significant event in Harte's rise to fame. This potentially suggestive reference to the force with which *literary* history has made itself felt in the shaping of a mining legacy at the very least hints at Muir's increase in thinking about that tradition since the moment four years earlier when he had bartered a Harte tale for lodging information.

Moving beyond Harte signifies, for Muir, a move into the picturesque.[17] Later in this report from the field, Muir tells his San Francisco readers that, compared with the senseless and brutal devastation evident in Nevada, California's Gold Rush relics are downright scenic. He begins by praising "the dim old ruins of Europe," noting that in their dilapidated state they "have something pleasing about them, whatever their historical associations; for they at least lend some beauty to the landscape. . . . They have served their time, and like the weather-beaten mountains are wasting harmoniously. . . . The same is in some degree true of the dead mining towns of California" (202). Nowhere else in his descriptions of a mining zone does Muir attempt an analogy even remotely similar to this comparison to picturesque ruins.[18] In all probability the figure worked for him in the context of "Nevada's Dead Towns" but ultimately was not an assertion he was comfortable with, and so he refrained from using it again. However, it does finally hint at the direction Muir's thinking about mining and miners was headed in 1878—toward the primary appreciation of the visual dimension of the Sierra, toward the scenic. Muir's thoughts about the mining history of the Sierra have slowly and subtly shifted since his engagement with the imagery of the "goldy-way," and in his report from Nevada we see his most concerted and deliberate effort to date to contrive a vision of scenery that in some sense both includes and occludes the material evidence of a once thriving industry.

And what of the figure of the miner? Through a careful shift in diction, Muir has the person known as "miner" also disappear into the picturesque mists of the past. Noting that "the fever period is fortunately passing away," Muir assures that "the prospector is no longer the raving, wandering ghoul of ten years ago" (203). In fact, the prospectors for mineral wealth whom Muir encounters do not appear to be miners at all. "In marked contrast" to the "destructive unrest" caused by the manic miner of old, Muir finds much to praise in "the orderly deliberation into which miners settle in developing a truly valuable mine. At Eureka we were kindly led through the treasure chambers of the Richmond and Eureka Consolidated, our guides leisurely leading the way from level to level, calling attention to the precious ore-masses which the workmen were slowly breaking to pieces with their picks, like navvies wearing away the day in a railroad cutting; while down at the smelting works the bars of bullion were handled with less eager haste than the farmer shows in gathering his sheaves" (201). The "wandering ghoul" of the prospector phase has in this passage been deftly replaced with an altogether different, and again much safer, being: the workman. Whereas "all kinds of people—shoemakers, tailors, farmers" once threw everything away to become miners (201), the man who works underground for the orderly profit margin of the Richmond and Eureka Consolidated behaves more prudently than even the farmer (who is of course famous for foolishly rushing to get his hands on the harvest). The rabid, ore-crazy miners have thus transmogrified into responsible, careful, and yet unskilled laborers ("navvies") who know their place in the process and obligingly perform only those tasks to which they are assigned. Even allowing for a degree of irony in this strangely complimentary portrait of a resource industry, the figurative language Muir employs in describing his descent into the heart of a working mine clearly suggests that the industry, miners and all, has gone underground, that the scenery is safe.[19]

First Book . . .

Beginning with his early 1870s self-transformation from amateur outdoorsman to professional writer (and, one might argue, professional outdoorsman), Muir consistently crafts his texts in such a way as to render California's remnant miner as either reverting to or already a part of nature. This attempt to naturalize (and neutralize) a familiar figure becomes yet more evident when Muir begins to elide the miner by shunting him underground as a "workman" and, in the case of the revised John Nelder, by rendering him more passive than active and disconnecting him from his name. Thus, as might be expected, when in relation to his reading public Muir undergoes a second pivotal transformation—that is, once he reenters the public sphere in the 1890s after a decade-long hiatus from professional writing and activism—his textual approach to both the Gold Rush and the human figures associated with it shift once again as well, this time quite decisively.[20] Largely the product of his association with Robert Underwood Johnson, an editor at *Century* who in 1889 undertook to renew his publisher's ties with the California writer, Muir's reemergence in the 1890s is dominated by his assumption of the now-familiar mantles of national conscience for wilderness preservation and public voice of the forests.[21] And in this final and most public phase of his career, a phase that includes the publication of both Muir's first book and his philosophically significant memoir of his first encounter with the mountains, Muir naturalizes not only the figures and relics of the Gold Rush but the Gold Rush itself. In a move that further extends the logic of representation he had begun with his discussions of the scenery around Murphy's Camp and of the workmen of the Richmond and Eureka Consolidated, Muir tells a history of resource exploitation and human activity that finds itself inevitably reverting to a state of post-human nature. In becoming the wilderness advocate who not only could read nature's book but also write books himself, Muir completes the figurative process by which mines and mining are erased from the land. However, in insisting that the mines and miners are no longer in the scenery, Muir paradoxically gives them a greater presence in his texts than they had previously enjoyed. This presence, which will eventually become manifest in *My First Summer in the Sierra* (1911), is most immediately demonstrated by the revisions Muir makes in collecting many of his earlier *Bulletin, Harper's,* and *Scribner's* pieces and shaping them into his first book, *The Mountains of California* (1894).

In April 1894, Muir wrote to Johnson that the manuscript for *Mountains* was "finished and out of me, therefore hurrah." In describing the process by which he had revised the fourteen previously published essays collected for the book, Muir averred, "I have worked very hard on every one of them, leaning them against each other, adding lots of new stuff, and killing adjectives and adverbs of redundant growth—the *verys, intenses, gloriouses, ands,* and *buts,* by the score."[22] This characterization of revision suggests a process of addition ("adding lots of new stuff") that was balanced with a frugal but arguably minor correction of style ("killing adjectives and adverbs"). Outright deletions, it seems, were not needed. In truth, Muir's revisions are much more complex. For instance, while an 1875 *Overland Monthly* piece on flooding in the Sierras appears in the book as chapter 9,[23] Muir omits fully one-third of the article, a detailed description of the town of Knoxville. In a related move, to create chapter 13 Muir appends his Murphy's Camp piece onto another detailing a visit to some nearby caves, a combination that has the effect of stressing not a perduring, albeit dried-up, human community but rather a progressive passage to a nonhuman space. And in the immense chapter 8, "The Forests," in which material borrowed from Muir's *Bulletin* and *Harper's* sequoia essays serves as the centerpiece, the hermit of the Fresno Grove finally, figuratively speaking, has his night descend upon him. Much of the prose about the trees remains unchanged, but all mention of an ex-miner-turned-forest-dweller has been removed. In a revision that signals the extent to which Muir now hopes to diminish the importance of human activity in the mountains of California, John Nelder is simply, and completely, eliminated.

But the mines themselves are still present, notably in a highly picturesque form. No doubt aware of the extent to which his editing had altered the tone and shape of his earlier writings, Muir tells Johnson that "six of the sixteen chapters are new" when in fact only two chapters in *The Mountains of California* consist of entirely new material. And appropriately enough, the aforementioned letter to Johnson provides a key to understanding how Muir thought of his editorial process, which in turn provides the key to understanding his placement of the mines in this book. In presenting his text as having "redundant growth," Muir offers a subtle reversal of his favorite metaphor of the book of nature; in this case, instead of nature being the book the intrepid naturalist may read, it is the book that is described as nature, at least with respect to a language that can be weeded and killed. Thus, as Muir shifts the emphasis from human to nature in the refocusing of certain sections, he also thinks of his narrative as naturalized, insomuch as he implies that his words might be considered emblematic of material phenomena in nature. Not surprisingly, this editorial principle describes fairly well those few portions of the book that arise not from revision but are newly composed in 1894. Through what he calls his "new stuff," Muir most clearly demonstrates the direction in which he presumes to take the material evidence of an industry stuck amidst the scenery.

In his letter, Muir specifically requests that Johnson carefully read the first chapter, and indeed it is in this important opening piece, framing as it does the rest of the book, that Muir most dramatically reconceives his earlier textual formulations regarding mining narratives. As the inclusion of his Murphy's Camp article as chapter 15 reminds us, Muir could at one time write quite directly about the history of the foothills. In chapter 1, however, Muir deploys a rhetorical "growing" and "killing" that presents itself as being explicitly *not* about the mines, a sort of preterition through which the process of rhetorically naturalizing a narrative appears most clearly, and which keeps the mines present despite their ostensible erasure. Consider, for example, the structural movement of the following paragraph, quoted in full from approximately the midpoint of the chapter:

> The rose-purple zone along the base of the range comprehends nearly all the famous gold region of California. And here it was that miners from every country under the sun assembled in a wild, torrent-like rush to seek their fortunes. On the banks of every river, ravine, and gully they have left their marks. Every gravel- and boulder-bed has been desperately riddled over and over again. But in this region the pick and shovel, once wielded with savage enthusiasm, have been laid away, and only quartz-mining is now being carried on to any considerable extent. The zone in general is made up of low, tawny, waving foot-hills, roughened here and there with brush and trees, and outcropping masses of slate, colored gray and red with lichens. The smaller masses of slate, rising abruptly from the dry, grassy sod in leaning slabs, look like ancient tombstones in a deserted burying-ground. In early spring, say from February to April, the whole of this foot-hill belt is a paradise of bees and flowers. Refreshing rains then fall freely, birds are busy building their nests, and the sunshine is balmy and delightful. But by the end of May the soil, plants, and sky seem to have been baked in an oven. Most of the plants crumble to dust beneath the foot, and the

> ground is full of cracks; while the thirsty traveler gazes with eager longing through the burning glare to the snowy summits looming like hazy clouds in the distance. (7–8)

Subtly shifting its subject after the fifth sentence, this paragraph becomes not about the mining region per se but rather about seasonal growth in the foothills, faintly suggesting that even mining is but a seasonal phenomenon. A second paragraph after this one brings the foothills through the reawakening of both flora and fauna in autumn, a movement that ultimately serves to celebrate the "abundance of life" and the "delightfully pure and tranquil music" offered by the scene (8, 9). A few extant traces of mining "occur at long intervals along the belt, and cottages covered with climbing roses" by now "make scarce any mark in general views" (9). Mark Twain quips in *Roughing It* that California's scenery is best viewed from a distance (385). With respect to the traces of a resource industry, Muir very much achieves this perspective, preferring the tableau to the details and letting the detritus of industry become overgrown by "a paradise of bees and flowers" in the middle of a paragraph that quickly forgets all human incursion into the scenery.

. . . AND *FIRST SUMMER*

And so it is that John Muir has become the writer who in 1911 offers the following assessment of the history of Sierra mining: "Thundering underground blasting is still going on to feed the pounding quartz mills, but their influence on the landscape is light as compared with that of the pick-and-shovel storms waged a few years ago" (*My First Summer* 74). Although *My First Summer in the Sierra* is presented as the diary account of a young man who experiences the "Range of Light" and its "goldy-way" for the first time in 1869, the figurative language suggests otherwise.[24] Highly reminiscent of the first chapter of *Mountains*, where the remnants of the "pick and shovel" period "make scarce any mark in general views," this brief observation, ostensibly made by a young shepherd on the way to higher ground, is in fact that of an older, different writer who has refined and revised his stance on the literary representation of an extractive industry.[25] To be sure, by this time the visually and ecologically destructive practice of hydraulic mining, first introduced in 1852, had been outlawed by the 1884 *Woodruff v. North Bloomfield* decision (Kelley 21–28, 229–42). With respect to Muir, then, the shift in his representation of the terrain is in part historically determined. However, recall that as early as 1876 Muir was applying a picturesque aesthetic to such mining remnants as Murphy's Camp, revising literary history as much as he was describing the world. By 1911 these revisions in Muir's Gold Rush lexicon have reached the point where the gradual removal of the human figure from the site of transgression—that is, from the face of the mountains he once mined—has also enabled the erasure of (at least) the visual impact of mineral extraction. Muir's textual elision may be a matter of historically shifting mining practices, but his rhetoric was headed in that direction well before the industry went fully underground.

However, while insisting that the mines and miners are no longer a part of the scenery, Muir paradoxically gives them a greater presence in his texts than they had previously enjoyed. In *My First Summer,* Muir has now fully appropriated the language previously associated with mines and miners for the description of the mountains themselves. Simply put, Muir transposes the suffering and privation once embodied in the person of the forty-niner onto the land itself. As early as 1878, while on his way to Nevada, Muir had commented in his journal (but not, significantly, in any publication) that the hills around Placerville, California, in the heart of the gold country, looked as if they had been "scalped," the result of hydraulic mining practices (qtd. in Wolfe 198). And in the late 1880s, in transcribing his 1869 journals for *My First Summer,* Muir had written that "every gully + valley + flat + bar [has been] shoveled + riddled + made raw + bare as if fairly skinned alive."[26] Revised in the published version to state that mining activities had "wash[ed] away hills and miles of the skin of the mountain's face, riddling, stripping every gold gully and flat," this passage shows Muir trying a variety of formulations through which to represent a humanlike suffering imposed by the mining industry not on the men but rather on the mountains (74). Indeed, the ultimate removal of the qualifier "as if" suggests just how emphatically Muir may wish to convey the injury done to the hills. The effect of this move is to humanize the land even as the human is removed from its context. Michael Cohen has suggested that *The Mountains of California* represents Muir's "anatomy of California's spiritual watershed" (*Pathless Way* 286). Thought of in similar terms, *My First Summer* offers what might be called a corporeal anatomy of the Sierras.

In the case of mining, Muir anatomizes disfigurement and pain; elsewhere in *My First Summer* he presents a different but nevertheless equally embodied vision of the land. To be sure, he has not altogether abandoned his oft-employed figure of nature as book—he describes one vista as "a grand page of mountain manuscript" and another as bearing "divine symbols crowded together on [a] wondrous page" (135, 200). However, the range of figurative language in *My First Summer* shows Muir trying to yoke together a great many approaches to the representation of mountains, among them the spiritual, the textual, and the physical. In the following description of a thunderstorm, Muir deftly moves across a variety of these formulations: "Now comes the rain, with corresponding extravagant grandeur, covering the ground high and low with a sheet of flowing water, a transparent film fitted like a skin upon the rugged anatomy of the landscape, making the rocks glitter and glow, gathering in the ravines, flooding the streams, and making them shout and boom in reply to the thunder" (166–67). Although the association of water with skin stands merely as a suggestive simile ("like a skin"), this membrane or, in faintly textual terms, "sheet" nevertheless stretches to cover a landscape that, without grammatical qualification, displays a "rugged anatomy." Moreover, the effect of the skinlike water is to make the rocks "reply" to the thunder. In this rush of metaphor, the notion of a humanized landscape asserts itself over and above the hesitation that the water is only "like a skin."

Muir also reverses the metaphor, at times describing humans by using the elements of the scenery. In a passage highly reminiscent of his account of Murphy's Camp, Muir describes his employer, Patrick Delaney, as "one of those remarkable California men who have been overflowed and denuded and remodeled by the excitements of the gold fields, like the Sierra landscapes by grinding ice, bringing the harder bosses and ridges of character into relief" (288). However, unlike the men in Murphy's Camp, Delaney, who rides up to the sheep camp only occasionally to bring provisions for his shepherds, has lost whatever ties to the woods he may once have had—he carries "a heavy rifle over his shoulder intended for bears and wolves," and when that does not work he readily turns to the use of strychnine (15). Needless to say, this glacier-worn ex-miner devotes none of his time to empirical observation. Just as John Nelder had been first disconnected and then eliminated from the mountains, so too is the forty-niner Delaney no longer a fixture in the hills.

Delaney's lead shepherd, Billy, is no better. Completely unresponsive to the elements around him, Billy lands on Muir's bad side when he exclaims, "What is Yosemite but a cañon—a lot of rocks—a hole in the ground—a place dangerous about falling into—a d——d good place to keep away from" (197). In a complete reversal of the formulation he gave in 1874 when leaving for Mount Shasta, Muir now presents the man who has spent all his time outdoors as being "smothered and befogged" (198). Earlier in the book Muir admits that Billy is in fact "hard to place in this wilderness" (171), by which he suggests that despite his insensitivity to nature (born as it is by his servitude to the vile chore of sheepherding), the lead shepherd nevertheless bears some slight connection to the world around him. Indeed, Muir offers this possibility through an extended joke he makes in describing, of all things, Billy's pants. The combined product of sleeping on the forest floor and wearing a hip pouch out of which oozes perpetually the grease of his lunch, Billy's

> trousers . . . have become so adhesive with the mixed fat and resin that pine needles, thin flakes and fibres of bark, hair, mica scales and minute grains of quartz, horblende, etc., feathers, seed wings, moth and butterfly wings, legs and antennae of innumerable insects, or even whole insects such as the small beetles, moths and mosquitoes, with flower petals, pollen dust and indeed bits of all plants, animals, and minerals of the region adhere to them and are safely imbedded, so that though far from being a naturalist he collects fragmentary specimens of everything and becomes richer than he knows. . . . Instead of wearing thin they wear thick, and in their stratification have no small geological significance. (172–73)

Concluding that "man is a microcosm, at least our shepherd is, or rather his trousers," Muir jokingly offers the possibility that one may even inadvertently develop into the sort of naturalist Muir admired in John Nelder and the Murphy's Camp remnants (173).

But the crucial point is that Billy is not, nor has he ever been, a miner. He may spend his days in the woods, and he may adorn his body with the habiliments of an accidental naturalist, and he may eke out an existence fraught with the privations suffered by the forty-niner in working himself "stupidly weary" and eating "whatever comes handy," but he is in no sense connected with the Gold Rush (31). Muir has succeeded in disassociating altogether the literary type of the mountain rustic from the discourse of the Gold Rush and has returned him to the strictly pastoral dimension of the shepherd. As Paul Alpers has recently shown, the shepherd's life signifies the primary conduit through which the pastoral mode attempts to explore issues of human community (8–28, 79–93). Muir, who strictly speaking is no pastoralist, revises this formulation further by implying that even the shepherd's life is not adequate, that the nature-sensitive *observer* is perhaps best suited to addressing the issues inherent in the literary representation of human community in relation to the outdoors. Thus does Muir completely remove the forty-niner while retaining much of this figure's representational force as inherited from Harte, Twain, and Delano. Muir's encounter with John Nelder eventually helps him to conceive of mining as having injured the body of the mountains. In reproducing this impression in print, however, he has to evict the forty-niner and bury the mines.

Dr. Clara Barrus, the personal physician, literary executrix, and eventual biographer to naturalist John Burroughs, published in 1910 an article in the *Century* in which she detailed a series of meetings, in Arizona and in the Sierras, between her charge and Muir. Dubbing the latter "John o' Mountains" in order to offer a parallel name to Burroughs's more widely known moniker of "John o' Birds," Barrus concludes her almost hagiographic account with a visit to Yosemite. After being guided to sights such as Nevada Falls and Half Dome, Barrus notes how one in their party expressed to Muir "the gratitude we felt at the inestimable privilege of seeing all this wondrous beauty under his guidance" (528). Seeing—perhaps simply a term by which a turn-of-the-century ecotourist would describe an encounter with Muir's Yosemite. And yet, Muir's treatment of the foothills regions of the "Range of Light" in *The Mountains of California* and *My First Summer in the Sierra* clearly limn a gradual turn toward the scenic at the expense of the material. This pattern manifests itself even in the closing words of *My First Summer:* in both the transcription notebooks of 1887 and the 1910 typescript draft, Muir ends by praising the Yosemite once more and saying, "I humbly pray I may see it again and again and learn something from its sacred pages, God grant I may be allowed to study this book."[27] In the final published version, however, Muir has pared this wish down to read, "I gladly, gratefully, hopefully pray I may see it again" (354).

The crucial claim of all nature writing is that the text can in some way offer access to the realness of a nontextual, nonhistorical nature. Indeed, Lawrence Buell posits that the claim to realism implicit in nature writing depends on a "dual accountability to matter and to discursive mentation" (*Imagination* 92). According to this argument, whereas textual representations of the outdoors may refer to their own constructions as discourse, they can also "put the reader in touch with the environment," with matter that is not constructed but rather natural, nonhuman (97). In such a rhetorical strategy, as Buell describes it, the human figure counts only minimally, if at all, in a text's presentation of ideas (7). Indeed, as Christine Oravec notes in her examination of the political impact of Muir's rhetoric, "Whenever Muir introduced a human presence into his descriptions [of the Sierra], he consistently subordinated it to the surrounding elements" (249).[28] However, as Muir's revision of the mining past reveals, this subordination is less an ecologically conscientious act of rhetoric than it is a deferral of literary and economic history, founded on the driving of a material industry and its attendant discourse into the unseen (and un-scene). The now familiar environmentalist call to arms that says "when we try to pick out anything by itself, we find it hitched to everything else in the universe" (*My First Summer* 211) is built upon the insistence that human and material economies maintain little, if any, relation to the real. Muir's crucial shift from "reading" to "seeing" signifies an unhitching of nature from history—nature can be counted on, nature is real. Muir thus offers a claim to realism that enables, among other things, the majority of twentieth-century environmentalist expressions, including Buell's contention that any textual reference to matter may be accurately and confidently gauged independently of history, that "nature is the court of appeal" wherein references to matter may somehow be separated from the material forces that inevitably give shape and meaning to any landscape (*Imagination* 94). In short, Muir's ecological realism depends on the very economic and literary history it presumes to do without.

3

"Why, Have You Got the Atlantic Monthly *Out Here*?"

W. D. Howells, Realism, and the Idea of the West

Writing for a relatively young nation, Ralph Waldo Emerson advised his readers in 1836 that if they desired "an original relation to the universe," they should look not to the "retrospective" traditions of religion and philosophy, not to the writers of "biographies, histories, and criticism." Rather, they should look, plainly and simply, to "Nature" (9). A little over half a century later, W. D. Howells, while not so fully concerned as Emerson had been with the ontological and epistemological ramifications of his argument, offers a strikingly similar rationale in his defense of literary realism: "The time is coming, I hope, when each new author, each new artist, will be considered, not in his proportion to any other author or artist, but in his relation to the human nature, known to us all, which it is his privilege, his high duty, to interpret." He continued, "Now we are beginning to see and to say that no author is an authority except in those moments when he held his ear close to Nature's lips and caught her very accents" (*Criticism and Fiction* 300, 302). Armed with this hope for the future of literature, Howells advises writers of realism to heed the now-famous dictum that a good novel should concern itself—indeed, should "verify" itself—only through the selective depiction of what Howells calls "the simple, the natural, and the honest" (302). Here, as in Emerson, past forms and writers represent an unoriginal and hence tainted relation to the real, while something called "Nature" serves as the gateway through which an unalloyed truth may be achieved. The difference between Emerson and Howells, of course, is that the latter is not interested in a transcendental identity built on romantic idealism but rather in something called realism, the representation of the real.

In this respect, Howells's allusive revision of Emerson places his claim to realism in a distinct relation to that of his contemporary John Muir. The persistence of a generic imagination inherited from Bret Harte's Gold Rush notwithstanding, Muir's approach to and revision of Emersonian idealism argued not only for the spiritual dimension of western nature but also, more importantly, for its material immanence as a pure and untouched entity.[1] That he should develop this realist aesthetic of landscape representation by writing for such magazines as the *Atlantic Monthly, Scribner's,* the *Century,* and *Harper's* is hardly surprising. As Nancy Glazener has argued quite comprehensively, the genre debates and designations promoted by this relatively tight circle of East Coast literary periodicals were extremely influential in promulgating a literary form and ideology now fully recognized as American realism (20–50 passim). Muir's writings have their most obvious predecessor in American romanticism; similarly, as a literary form realism too saw itself as an engagement with and, ultimately, a rejection of something called romance. As writers, both Muir and Howells clearly sought to verify something ostensibly real by appealing to prevailing ideas about the "natural." And they both employ the West as a source of that "natural." Muir, it could be said, does so largely by force of geographic necessity—he happens to be living in California when he fully inaugurates his writing career. For Howells, though, the choice to use the West signifies a far greater understanding of the function that the idea of the American West had in the culture of his day.

Muir did not publish with the *Atlantic* until the 1890s, well after Howells had given up the editorship of this magazine. That is, Howells himself appears never to have selected a Muir essay for publication, and so the only tangible connection between the two writers, aside from their common approach to Emersonian idealism, is simply their affiliation with the *Atlantic* group of magazines (as Glazener calls it). However, if we are to judge more broadly the relationship of Howellsian realism to ideas about nature and the West, such congruities that do exist within the pages of the influential *Atlantic* group are quite telling. In February 1888, for instance, a retired U.S. army general by the name of Randolph B. Marcy published in *Harper's* an essay recalling the western American landscapes he had seen while working toward the eradication of the Indian from the plains. Marcy claimed that his interest lay in offering to both travelers and potential farmers a "more accurate knowledge" of the western regions (402). One month later, *Harper's* began a series by

Charles Dudley Warner on western American cities which, again, attempted to add to and correct readers' knowledge about the ostensibly real West: "It is a common remark at the West that 'Eastern people know nothing about us; they think us half civilized'" (557). Meanwhile, in the December 1887 issue of this same magazine, just two months prior to Marcy's article, Howells issued from "The Editor's Study" his credo about "the simple, the natural, and the honest" (*Criticism and Fiction* 302). The almost simultaneous publication of the two movements represented here—the elucidation of a "real" West and the now-acknowledged manifesto moment for American realism—may only be a coincidence, yet this apparent coincidence points rather tellingly to the fact that culturally dominant ideas about the realist novel and about the American West developed at roughly the same time and in the same literary venues.

The example of Mary Hallock Foote, a native of New York's Hudson River Valley who relocated to the West in 1876 with her mining engineer husband, can further illuminate this point. Foote established a reputation early as an illustrator, providing etchings for popular works by both Longfellow ("Hanging of the Crane") and Hawthorne (a reprint of *The Scarlet Letter*).[2] And as her husband's career took them first to California, then to Leadville, Colorado, and eventually to Coeur d'Alene, Idaho, Foote's own writings began to appear in venues such as *Scribner's* and the *Atlantic*. Her very first essay for *Scribner's*, entitled "A California Mining Camp" and published in 1878, describes in fairly picturesque terms the Hispanic workers of the New Almaden quicksilver mine near Santa Cruz. New Almaden was the ostensible site of Harte's "The Story of a Mine," and in her largely romanticized and self-illustrated rendition Foote revises the pastness of Harte's depiction (published just one year earlier) with a picture of ongoing, present-tense mining activity. In 1881, Howells accepted for publication in the *Atlantic* "In Exile," Foote's tale of courtship between an eastern schoolteacher and a mining engineer who meet in California. Ironically, Howells suggested, in the interest of believability, that Foote revise the sad ending into a happy one (L. A. Johnson 32–33), an episode that hints at a crucial tension in Foote's career: the desire to meet readers' expectations about the West while still providing a believable sense of the not-so-pleasant realness of the region. As Foote's career progressed through the 1880s and 1890s, such novels as *The Led-Horse Claim* (set in Leadville, Colorado, serialized in the *Century*) and *The Chosen Valley* (set in Coeur d'Alene, Idaho, also serialized in the *Century*) offer what has long been taken as increasingly realistic renditions of mining and, later, irrigation in the West. By the publication in 1899 of her richly evocative California-based mining story "How the Pump Stopped at the Morning Watch," Foote had developed a mature style that had already prompted the essayist and travel writer Kate Field to observe that "the chaotic period which followed the discovery of Gold in California will be described in history, but not as Bret Harte has described it, and the later evolution of the new society may be traced by some philosopher, but hardly so vividly as it has already been done in the stories of Mary Hallock Foote" (69).[3] Later critics would agree: Arthur Hobson Quinn argues that Foote was "more of a realist than either Harte or Clemens in portraying the life of the mining areas" (645), and Wallace Stegner concurs that her mining camps "are almost the only real ones in local color fiction—very much more real than those of Bret Harte" (xi). In a very practical and definitive way, Foote's development as an early and important voice in western American literary realism can be directly tied to the very publications that, by virtue of their editorial processes, set the terms for realism as a whole.[4]

What appears fairly obvious in magazines of the 1880s, though, is not so evident in critical writing about those magazines, for the cultural and historical ties between the West and the movement known as literary realism have thus far gone largely unexamined. In a study similar to Glazener's in its focus on magazines but concerned with an ostensibly unrelated aspect of late-nineteenth-century literary culture, David Teague has recently shown how the same publications leading the development of a realist ideology were also largely responsible for the crafting of a vision of the fabled Far West founded on middle-class consumer tourism, accessible nature, and rugged but noble cowboys. These magazines thus crafted for readers an influential and realistic picture of the West: "By the early 1890s, when large numbers of Americans from the East had gained access to desert land by train, it was, in a way, a familiar landscape even to those who had never seen it, simply because people had seen so many Arizona cowboys in so many deserts in so many *Harper's Monthly* and *Harper's Weekly* stories and illustrations" (Teague 53).[5] As it turns out, the magazines in the *Atlantic* group published not only the works of Howells, James, Freeman, and Jewett; they also published Harte, Muir, Remington, and Wister, as well as Foote, Mary Austin, and Richard Harding Davis's *The West from a Car-Window*. But these western writers were guilty of being realists by more than simply association. Their tales, firsthand accounts, and naturist essays from the late nineteenth century, as the previous two chapters have begun to demonstrate, abounded in claims to representational verity. The same holds true for novelistic fiction of the period. Glazener's study, however, is only the latest on realism that neglects to mention the West as a key representational concern of those writers affiliated with the *Atlantic* group. Thus, the connection between the claims to western realism and those made specifically for fiction by, say, the Dean of American Letters still remains to be established.

Howells stands at the very intersection of the debates over both realism as a distinct genre and the depiction of the West as America's "real" nature. Stephen Fender has observed in his study of Gold Rush literature that Howells was "himself a westerner who saw the West as a likely source for the new realism in American letters" (5). And Kenneth Lynn's biography of Howells documents not only Howells's well-known advocacy of western writers (among them Harte, Twain, Hamlin Garland, and Frank Norris) but also the editorial acumen he demonstrated in choosing, for instance, to review positively Edward Eggleston's *The Hoosier Schoolmaster* in the *Atlantic* at a time when such a move might easily have "risk[ed] the displeasure of influential readers" in Boston (*Howells* 167–68). In large part, though, Howells was and is very much a writer of the genteel, urbanized East. Alluding in 1887 to the Ohio-born Howells's allegiance to eastern literary tastes, the Indiana poet Maurice Thompson sarcastically asked, "Who thinks of Howells in connection with Western literature?" (qtd. in Scharnhorst, "At War over Realism?" 294). The answer for Thompson, of course, is nobody, since by this time the name of Howells is firmly fixed in the literary firmament of Boston and New York. And yet, revisiting the grounds upon which Howells has at times been identified with the West will show that the concepts underlying realism are, in the few decades leading up to the turn of the century, intimately tied to the development of the West as both a material and a cultural resource. Howells very deliberately builds a definition of realism by using the idea of the West, with all of its associations with a thing called "Nature," as one of his key touchstones for the real.

Realism or Romance?

In June 1886, Maurice Thompson and a number of other Indiana writers, including James Whitcomb Riley, gathered to inaugurate the American Association of Writers, which within a year was renamed the Western Association of Writers in order to reflect the specifically regional makeup of its membership.[6] Concerned for the reception of (mid)western fiction in the nation's literary culture as a whole, Thompson, as the organization's first elected president, singled out Howells as a target. In a series of articles, public lectures, and private communications, he accused the frontier-born Howells of having abandoned his native West in favor of a "worship of the vulgar, the commonplace and the insignificant" (qtd. in Scharnhorst, "At War over Realism?" 294). The Western Association of Writers is of course not alone in making such charges. Frank Norris, in his "Plea for Romantic Fiction," will echo the charge of realism's interest in the insignificant when he labels Howells's fiction as "minute" and only interested in "the drama of a broken teacup" (76). However, Norris does not so easily escape being associated with Howells and realism when the *Boston Evening Transcript,* in repeating the idea of realism's vulgarity in its review of Norris's California novel *McTeague,* laments that "the equipment for a modern realistic novel writer is the knowledge of some particularly seamy places in life, a power of detailed description of sordid or nasty things, an intense desire to make them real to the reader—and a few words of praise from Mr. Howells. The theory seems to be that culture is acquired in order to revert perversely to a morbid contemplation of those things from which culture ought to have enfranchised us" ("A Rough Novel" 38).[7]

Little more than a year after his initial public attack on Howells, Thompson had an apparent change of heart about the man who had mentored several of his poems into the *Atlantic.* He did not, however, relent in his critique of realism. In a review of Howells's *The Rise of Silas Lapham,* Thompson wrote of the author, "He has tried to be purely and simply realistic, but in failing he has made his very strongest romance" (qtd. in Scharnhorst, "At War over Realism?" 294). Glazener's chapter on "The Romantic Revival" amply demonstrates how the terms "realism" and "romance" signified for most late-nineteenth-century writers, critics, and readers the battle lines across which were argued questions about proper and adequate representation in fiction (147–88).[8] But as Gary Scharnhorst has suggested, as often as not genre distinctions served merely as the pretext for hashing out regional differences.[9] Thus it is precisely the idea of regional difference that allows for a glimpse into the function of the West in its relation to realism. By no means do these first few examples represent the full extent of the debate over realism as it transpired in the late nineteenth century, but they do provide a sense of the terms involved.[10] They are, in short, "realism," "romance," and as this chapter will demonstrate, the less visible but no less significant "West."

The turn-of-the-century novelist whose claims to representational accuracy most directly engage the ostensibly competing claims of western romance and western realism is Frank Norris.[11] Writing in 1901 for the *Boston Evening Transcript,* the very same newspaper which in its review of *McTeague* two years earlier had impugned Howells of sanctioning a literature "of sordid or nasty things" ("A Rough Novel" 38), Norris lays out his own assessment of realistic representation and of how Howells fits into the equation. In "A Plea for Romantic Fiction," Norris argues that by definition it is romance that "treat[s] of the sordid, the unlovely," what he calls "variations from the type of normal life" (76).[12] Accordingly, realism "confines itself to the type of normal life," a definition to which Norris adds a further clarification that answers quite directly the accusations of impropriety made by his reviewer in Boston. He writes: "Also, Realism, used as it sometimes is as a term of reproach, need not be in the remotest sense or degree offensive, but on the other hand respectable as a church and proper as a deacon—as, for instance, the novels of Mr. Howells" (76). Distancing himself and his work from a genre signified by the name Howells, Norris concludes with the assertion that "Realism is minute; it is the drama of a broken teacup, the tragedy of a walk down the block, the excitement of an afternoon call, the adventure of an invitation to dinner" (76). Realism thus emerges in this definition as the complete opposite of what the Boston reviewer of *McTeague* reproachfully claimed it was. Notably, Norris offers no challenge to the idea that "sordid or nasty things" have no place in literature—this to him is simply unthinkable. Where realism entertains, romance teaches (78); found "sitting among the rags and wretchedness, the dirt and despair of the tenements of the East Side of New York" (77), romance charts "the unplumbed depths of the human heart, and the mystery of sex, and the problems of life, and the black, unsearched penetralia of the soul of man" (78). And so Norris uses Howells and the idea of a tame, prim realism as a foil for his own writerly preferences: Norris writes that which Howells does not, even as they both work to convey something essentially real and true. In this regard Norris is hardly alone, and his fuzzy distinctions between romance and realism are indicative of a generic uncertainty.

In the canon of American realism, a figure of no less significance than Henry James provides one of the earliest demonstrable attempts by realism to work itself out against romance as both genre and style, and he does so, long before Norris, in a novel that is not exactly "western" but which nevertheless contains a significant western component. In James's *The American,* first serialized in 1876 in the *Atlantic* (edited at the time by Howells), the lead character Christopher Newman hails from San Francisco, where he was "successful in copper . . . only so-so in railroads, and a hopeless fizzle in oil" (41), a provenance that marks Newman as a "typical" western tycoon whose money comes in large part from the resources of the land.[13] As a novel, *The American* moves unsteadily toward an explication of Newman's growing awareness of his insurmountable status as an outsider in Parisian society, with James working through a variety of generic modes in his search for the literary form that will soon be called realism (see Brooks). As John Carlos Rowe has recently summed up the case, "*The American* is generally treated as a formally divided work, which begins realistically enough and ends in a flurry of events drawn from the popular romance and supernatural thriller" (57). In the process, though, the representational distinctions raised by such labels as "romance" and "realism" become hopelessly but tellingly confused.

Before *The American* had even finished its serial run, long before its appearance in book form, James felt compelled to defend the accuracy of the novel's representations. Responding to a letter from Howells that had acknowledged receipt of the final installment of the novel, James takes up the charge that a happy ending would have better served the readers of the *Atlantic:*

> I can quite understand that as an editor you should go in for "cheerful endings"; but I am sorry that as a private reader you are not struck with the inevitability of the American dénouement. I fancied that most folks would feel that Mme de Cintré *couldn't,* when the finish came, marry Mr. Newman . . . it would have been impossible: they would have been an impossible couple, with an impossible problem before them. For instance—to speak very materially—where would they have lived? (Edel 104)

Continuing his defense of the novel's representational and dramatic accuracy, James confesses to Howells that to have shown Mme de Cintré crossing the lines of French decorum for the sake of a happy marriage would have meant that "I should have felt as if I were throwing a rather vulgar sop to readers who don't really know the world and who don't measure the merit of a novel by its correspondence to the same" (Edel 105). Ultimately, James tries to affirm that his ostensibly accurate knowledge of the world should predominate over his readers' mistaken impressions of it. Hence, in 1877 he favorably measures the accuracy of his fiction against the world it presumes to represent.

In his 1907 preface to the New York Edition version of this novel, James famously reverses this judgment, using *The American* as an illustrative example of the differences between true realism and what he calls "romance": "I had been plotting arch-romance without knowing it" (*Art* 26), he confesses. Regarding the craft of accurate, honest, and above all realistic representation, James puts forth the oft-quoted figure of "the balloon of experience [which] is in fact of course tied to the earth" (*Art* 33). Simply put, whereas the writer of realism always keeps a hand on that tether, the writer of romance "insidiously" cuts it, thereby disconnecting textual representation from anything known to readers grounded in the material, experiential world. Regarding his own novel, James explains, "What I have recognised then in 'The American,' much to my surprise and after long years, is that the experience here represented is the disconnected and uncontrolled—uncontrolled by our general sense of 'the way things happen'—which romance alone more or less successfully palms off on us" (*Art* 34). In his letter to Howells, James had affirmed that his novel was very much true to "the ways things happen," even if his readers did not expect or could not accept such representations. However, thirty years later, James overrules his qualification to Howells about "where would they have lived" (one ostensible measure of realism) by offering another rationale for accuracy, namely, by observing that "they would positively have jumped then, the Bellegardes [Mme de Cintré's family], at my rich and easy American" (*Art* 35). What had once been construed as true to life is now retrofitted not as realistic but rather as unfortunately romantic and, hence, more fanciful than accurate.[14]

With respect to ostensibly western modes of storytelling, James's change of opinion about his work has its analogy in the novel itself, insofar as James further identifies Newman as a westerner by making him an accomplished purveyor of the notoriously nonrealistic tall tale: "Newman had sat with Western humorists in knots, round cast-iron stoves, and seen 'tall' stories grow taller without toppling over, and his own imagination had learned the trick of piling up consistent wonders" (97). As a western humorist, Harte had in 1869 defended himself as "a humble writer of romance" (*Selected Stories* 3), a designation that presumably sets him at odds with that which James comes to represent. However, as demonstrated in chapter 1, Harte endeavored not to deflect accurate representation through an accumulation of "consistent wonders" but rather to offer a corrective to earlier misrepresentations, to dispel (in theory, if not in practice) the very "wonders" piled up by earlier writers. In the decades between James's defense of his novel's realism and his dismissal of it as a romance, though, the term "romance" becomes the dominant generic marker for western literature, one frequently used to challenge the premises of realism (recall Thompson and the Western Association of Writers).

Then again, "romance" became the very mode for representing something understood as the real West. In one of the more significant genre productions of western romance from the turn of the century, Owen Wister's *The Virginian,* the author offers in his preface "To the Reader" a rationale that very much amounts to a claim to realism:

> Sometimes readers inquire . . . [w]as such and such a thing true? Now to this I have the best answer in the world. Once a cowpuncher listened patiently while I read him a manuscript. It concerned an event upon an Indian reservation. "Was that the Crow reservation?" he inquired at the finish. I told him that it was no real reservation and no real event; and his face expressed displeasure. "Why," he demanded, "do you waste your time writing what never happened, when you know so many things that did happen?" And I could no more help telling him that this was the highest compliment ever paid me than I have been able to help telling you about it here! (*The Virginian* x)

Of course, this is not to say that Wister's cowboy novel *is* realistic, even if it earns the stamp of an insider's approval of authenticity (the cowpuncher's). But by asserting that it is so, Wister blurs the lines between realism as the depiction of the real and romance as the depiction of the imagined. His defense of the novel as historically accurate is in this regard even more telling. He writes: "We know quite well the common understanding of the term 'historical novel.' *Hugh Wynne* exactly fits it. But *Silas Lapham* is a novel as perfectly historical as is *Hugh Wynne,* for it pictures an era and personifies a type. . . . Any narrative which presents faithfully a day and a generation is of necessity historical; and this one presents Wyoming between 1874 and 1890" (*The Virginian* vii–viii).

Often deployed in the romance-realism debate as a euphemism for romance, the "historical novel" is here configured as an accurate representation of a period that simply no longer exists. Wister's preface thus comes fairly close to revealing that beyond regional distinctions, the romance-realism question was more fundamentally a matter of content than it was of form or style.[15]

These positions on romance and realism enumerated by Wister, James, and Norris begin to demonstrate for the idea of fiction in the late nineteenth century what Michael Davitt Bell contends was equally true for novelists in the antebellum period: to wit, American romance, despite claims to the contrary, developed in large part as a writerly theory of mimetic fidelity, as a claim to realism. The point is a tricky one, no doubt, particularly since many late-nineteenth-century American writers so frequently saw "romance," with its idealist typology and historical focus, as the enemy. However, Bell persuasively argues that romance is realism insofar as it attempts to match its representations with its audience's understanding of the world. The rhetorical emphasis may have been on the fanciful products of imagination, but the literature was supposed to have been referentially grounded in the often nationalist materials of what Hawthorne called the "Actual" (Bell, *Development of American Romance* 15–19). At the risk of leveling important theoretical and historical distinctions, then, it should be stated that as the century advanced, practitioners of both realism and romance concerned themselves primarily with finding the best way to represent the world, with giving textual access to something real. The lawyer and novelist Albion W. Tourgée, for one, offered in 1889 that "on every novelist rests alike the same obligation of truth-telling. 'Realist,' 'Naturalist,' 'idealist,' 'romanticist,' only that and nothing more, can be demanded of them—that they paint life as they see it, feel it, believe it to be" (qtd. in Thomas 7).[16]

To the extent to which it concerns writing from and about the West, the relationship between realism and romance has often been perceived in large part by the oppositional terms suggested by Henry James: realistic and romantic novels maintain representational goals that pull in two entirely different directions. However, James's attempt years later to apply the tag "romance" onto a text he had himself once defended as being in full accord with his own expectations of how the world really is suggests otherwise. But what may have changed for James, more than anything else, are the definitions. The relationship between the terms "romance" and "realism," then, is not so much oppositional as it is dialectical or even complementary,[17] and the American West, the locus of much interest in representationally accurate (i.e., realistic) modes of romance, serves as a linchpin in the debate. Howells, whom Thompson accuses of being something of an unwitting western romanticist, demonstrates by the example of his own work the specific function of that linchpin, of how the West as both an idea and a region plays the role of a mediating concept in genre development.

The Western Howells

Taken as a whole, Norris's critical writings express praise for Howells as a critic and novelist more often than they complain about his aesthetic sensibility. For one, Norris shared Howells's fond appreciation of Tolstoy's novels. And in an essay published one month after his "Plea for Romantic Fiction," Norris argues that among the ranks of American novelists, only Howells could be said to qualify for inclusion in "an American School of Fiction."[18] To Norris's regret, however, this singular quality of Howells's fiction is at once a cause for celebration and for lamentation: "But one swallow does not make a summer, nor does one writer constitute a 'school.' Mr. Howells has had no successors" ("An American School" 109). Given Norris's preference for romance as the best means to write about and represent the real, the lack of successors might not in Norris's estimation really be all that significant. Nevertheless, this latter essay of Norris's contains a telling moment well worth noting, one that casts its author, if only for a moment, as obliquely Howellsian. Having distanced himself from Howells on generic and stylistic considerations, Norris then turns abruptly and realigns himself with the Dean of American Letters along regional lines. Continuing his praise for Howells's accomplishments as a novelist, Norris asserts, "Of all the producers of American fiction he has had the broadest vision, at once a New Englander and a New Yorker, an Easterner and—in the Eastern sense—a Westerner" ("An American School" 109). Is Norris referring here to Howells's upbringing in Ohio (which, for one from California, would certainly be western "in the Eastern sense")? Or, if taken as a parallel construction, does Norris's sentence imply that Howells is western by virtue of his current residence to the west of Boston (New Englander is to Easterner as New Yorker is to Westerner)? Norris's equation is certainly ambiguous, yet as he nominates Howells as the sole producer of a fiction properly understood as exclusively American, he clearly endows his subject, however briefly, with a title more often and more accurately reserved for Norris himself, namely, that of western writer.

Norris may very well have been taking his cue from Howells himself, who by the turn of the century had taken to casting himself as a westerner in a number of autobiographical memoirs and essays.[19] Considered in tandem with the idea of a mimetic dimension to romances of the West developed above, Howells's tendency for reminding readers of *Harper's* and *Atlantic* of his frontier origins helps to illuminate quite clearly Howells's use of the West. In short, the West as both idea and place very much mattered to Howells's sense of realistic virtue and value. Consider, for instance, the novels that Howells wrote immediately before, during, and after the time when, as Norris might put it, he went "west" from Boston to New York: *A Modern Instance* (1882), *The Rise of Silas Lapham* (1885), *Indian Summer* (1886), and *A Hazard of New Fortunes* (1890). In these books, which arguably constitute Howells's finest and most compelling string of realist novels, something loosely known as the American West provides an occasional but very persistent and distinctive flavor. In *A Modern Instance,* for example, Howells stages the final dénouement, the divorce of Marcia Gaylord and Bartley Hubbard, in an Indiana courtroom, a sequence conceived of and presented as taking place in "the West."[20] Also, a resolution toward liberty via the West is further hinted at when the narrator reports in the closing pages that Bartley's unscrupulous journalism has put him six feet under in an Arizona town called Whited Sepulchre, a name that, taken from Matthew 23:27, humorously suggests an appropriate place of death for a well-deserving dissembler.[21] In *Indian Summer,* Howells portrays Theodore Colville very much as a "westerner" (he too is from Indiana) whose sensibilities serve him well in the expatriate high society of Florence, Italy. On several occasions the narrator reminds us that Colville's long career as a newspaperman in the small town of Des Vaches, Indiana, has given him a pragmatic outlook that both alienates him and, to a degree, protects him from the salon society to which he returns relatively late in life.

In *The Rise of Silas Lapham,* published in 1885, the very year of Howells's "go west" relocation to New York, the title character makes his fortune with the discovery of what he figuratively calls "a gold-mine" (9).[22] In speaking of his special paint and his ambitions for how it could be used to enhance American scenery, Lapham tells a resurrected Bartley Hubbard:

> I never saw anything so very sacred as a big rock, along a river or in a pasture that it wouldn't do to put mineral paint on it in three colors. I wish some of the people that talk about the landscape, and *write* about it, had to bu'st one of them rocks *out* of the landscape with powder, or dig a hole to bury it in, as we used to have to do up on the farm; I guess they'd sing a little different tune about the profanation of scenery. There aint any man enjoys a sightly bit of nature—a smooth piece of interval, with half a dozen good-sized wine-glass elms in it—more that *I* do. But I aint a-going to stand up for every big ugly rock I come across, as if we were all a set of dumn Druids. I say the landscape was made for man, and not man for the landscape. (13–14; emphasis in original)

The emphasis in this passage may not be on anything explicitly western, but the issues it raises regarding the value of scenery borrow quite directly from contemporary debates regarding the visual West, in particular the implications for scenery found in Muir's writings. Indeed, depicting in part a theme quite familiar to New England, namely, the value of nature and how best to represent it, Howells does so not in the transcendental mode familiar to the region, but rather in terms familiar to both the literary and the industrial West of the 1880s.[23] Notably, Lapham at one point notes that a key motivation for going into the paint business was that "it was just after two or three boats had burned up out West, and a lot of lives lost, and there was a great cry about non-inflammable paint" (9). Lapham's paint industry begins, however indirectly or figuratively, as a western enterprise. More precisely, as Martin Bucco has shown quite extensively, *Silas Lapham* as a whole contains a "compelling western dimension" in which the "foreground" of Boston constantly bears an "implied West in the background" (309).

A trio of "westerners" populates Howells's 1890 novel *A Hazard of New Fortunes* as well: the charmingly entrepreneurial magazine founder Fulkerson, his pragmatically level-headed editor Basil March, and Dreyfoos, the Indiana farmer turned natural gas millionaire who puts up the capital for the literary magazine at the heart of the story. As this last example of Dreyfoos should indicate, Howells's oft-discussed anxieties about and explorations of upper-class privilege, middle-class taste, social access, representational (i.e., realistic) ethics and imperatives, and so forth play out in the shadow of a natural resource bonanza. Howells repeats this point about raw material use on the figurative level. For one, Fulkerson's start-up literary enterprise, in attempting to work out an entirely new scheme for profit sharing and artist remuneration, requires the recruitment and development of new talent, a process that occupies Howells for a good part of the middle of the story. Similarly, at the very beginning of the novel Fulkerson tells March, "I like you because you're a western man; and I'm another. I do cotton to a western man when I find him off east here, holding his own with the best of 'em, and showing 'em that he's just as civilized as they are." March responds somewhat skeptically: "I think we western men who've come east are apt to take ourselves a little too objectively, and to feel ourselves more representative than we need" (9). In March's use of "need" rather than "are," Howells implies that westernness, while not a fully "representative" set of characteristics, nevertheless works in March and Fulkerson's favor as they become "civilized" in the eastern sense. In and of itself westernness does not make for a superior eastern man, but March and Fulkerson are better people, Howells suggests, because they are westerners who have refined their manner in the East.[24] One significant aspect of *Hazard,* then, is the manner in which the novel positions both characters and events in figurative relationships to raw materials.

In all, a good number of Howells's most significant novels touch on issues, questions, and characterizations popularly associated in his day with the American West. In particular, Howells repeatedly sketches characters in whom a touch of westernness makes all the difference. Granted, "the West" is a highly and notoriously mutable term (much as "realism" is as well), and as places on a map, Indiana and Ohio easily fail to sustain the imaginative associations more common to, say, Whited Sepulchre, of which there is only one in the entire Howells canon.[25] However, these states were at one time very much understood as the nation's western frontier. As traits, "the simple, the natural, and the honest" suggest the associations of both place and character that Howells would like readers to see in the direct, pragmatic, level-headed, and above all western Basil March and Theodore Colville. Moreover, the idea of the West operates simply and honestly when it doles out justice to the deserving Bartley Hubbard.[26] Howells thus depends very much on the mutability of the term. "The West" is useful to Howells as a concept that in turn helps him to think of realistic fiction as dealing in "the truthful treatment of material" (*Criticism and Fiction* 319). The West, simply put, provides Howells with a key source for such material.

Nowhere is Howells's reliance on a particular idea of the West as conceptual raw material more pronounced than in the sketches and autobiographical essays collected in *Literary Friends and Acquaintance* (1900). It is in these essays, written and published in the late 1880s and 1890s, that Howells argues that his own westernness proved to be a crucial ingredient in his development as both an artist and a representative man of realism. In the chapter "My First Visit to New England," for instance, he begins by simultaneously elevating and downplaying the importance of literate culture in the Ohio town he calls his native "inland city":

> We looked to England and the East largely for our literary opinions. . . . [T]he Atlantic Monthly counted many readers among us; and a visiting young lady from New England, who screamed at the sight of the periodical in one of our houses, "Why, have you got the Atlantic Monthly *out here*?" could be answered, with cold superiority, "There are several *contributors* to the Atlantic in Columbus." There were in fact two: my roommate, who wrote Browning for it, while I wrote Heine and Longfellow. But I suppose two are as rightfully several as twenty are. (8; emphasis in original)

Right from the first, Howells sets up a condition in which the West functions both to strip away stereotypes held in the East, thereby emphasizing the vitality of the West, and to provide an image of a certain provincialism that still requires a touch of eastern sophistication and refinement. The overall effect is to render the West, dare one say it, more realistically, using it as the foil to establish that which really matters in the East—not pretense and supposition but straightforward, pragmatic representation.

This pattern of both elevating and debunking the idea of the West repeats itself at virtually every stop on Howells's retrospective progress through the countryside of his literary ancestors, a journey collectively described as having a profound effect on "my young western consciousness" (20–21). At his first stop, James Russell Lowell "asked me about the West, and when he found that I was as proud of the West as I was of Wales, he seemed even better pleased, and said he had always fancied that human nature was laid out on rather a larger scale there than in the East, but he had seen very little of the West. In my heart I did not think this then, and I do not think it now; human nature has had more ground to spread over in the West; that is all" (28). To the family of James Fields, publisher of the *Atlantic Monthly,* Howells "patriotically bragged of the West a little" (40), and to Oliver Wendell Holmes he strove "to give the Autocrat [a] clear image of our social frame in the West" (43). Nathaniel Hawthorne "was curious about the West, which he seemed to fancy much more purely American, and said he would like to see some part of the country on which the shadow, or, if I must be precise, the damned shadow, of Europe had not fallen. I told him I thought the West must finally be characterized by the Germans, whom we had in great numbers" (49). Finally, regarding his meeting with Ralph Waldo Emerson, Howells recalls:

> He began to ask me about the West. . . . I did not find what Emerson had to say of my section very accurate or important, though it was kindly enough, and just enough as to what the West ought to do in literature. He thought it a pity that a literary periodical which had lately been started in Cincinnati should be appealing to the East for contributions, instead of relying upon writers nearer home; and he listened with what patience he could to my modest opinion that we had not the writers nearer home. I never was one of those Westerners who believed that the West was kept out of literature by the jealousy of the East, and I tried to explain why we had not the men to write that magazine full in Ohio. (57)

Ironically enough, Howells finds himself confronting the clichés and romantic misconceptions about the West held by his literary forebears. Indeed, they do get the *Atlantic* out here, and probably *Harper's* as well, a fact that renders the West a much more complex and interesting (and realistic) place than the stereotypes held by Emerson and his cohort would have it be.

Of course, as Howells tells it, the men he visits think of him as more of a westerner than he himself might have done. However, the designation is useful to Howells, as in a later essay in the book where he notes that Lowell had tried in vain to cure him of the diction and syntax of realism that he had learned in the West (198). According to Howells, the West is ultimately not refined enough to produce adequate, quality literature. For an idea of how that will eventually come about, though, the reminiscences in *Literary Friends and Acquaintance* imply that Howells himself will in his own person provide the catalyst if not the primary exemplar. The ostensible transition from romance to realism and from westerner to Boston Brahmin is of course far from complete in Howells's figurative representation in the memoir, but it is obviously very important to Howells that he limn the passing of the torch in these terms. In a passage reminiscent of the Fulkerson-March exchange in *A Hazard of New Fortunes* about "representative" western men, Howells provisionally agrees with Lowell's contention that "I should have an advantage with readers, if not with editors, in hailing from the West; I should be more of a novelty. I knew very well that even in my own West I should not have this advantage unless I appeared there with an Eastern imprint" (90–91). The new and representative literary man of the age, replacing the Brahmin of Boston, will be not an easterner but a westerner who has been tempered by the East. Finally, it is worth noting that when Howells issued a revised edition of *Literary Friends* in 1910, he symbolically completed the transfer of literary authority from East to West by adding at the end of the book, after his essays on the likes of Lowell and Emerson, reminiscences of two of his favorite contemporaries, Harte and Twain, both identified as westerners.

The West mattered to Howells, in a way that far exceeded his editorial advocacy of western writers. As often as not, it is the idea of the West, and also of westernness, that made the crucial difference in both Howells's criticism and his fiction. It is an idea that buttressed the principles of representation that he construed as simple, natural, and honest. What Emerson had in an earlier time depicted as a need to look not to "retrospective" forms but rather to an unalloyed "Nature" for the foundations of a national philosophy, Howells reconfigured as "the West," thereby exemplifying the extent to which western nature had by Howells's age become the chief source of American raw materials.[27] Wister's *The Virginian* ends by noting, in the very last paragraph, that the eponymous hero will not suffer because of the closing of the open range: "But the railroad came, and built a branch to that land of the Virginian's where the coal was. By that time he was an important man, with a strong grip on many various enterprises, and able to give his wife all and more than she asked or desired" (503). Once a noble cowpuncher, the Virginian has become a successful resource baron. On a similar note, Charles Dudley Warner's "Studies of the Great West" for *Harper's* also concludes by first praising "the most exquisitely beautiful natural objects" to be seen around Helena, Montana, and then adding that a recent jubilee day celebrated "a new competing [railroad] line to the East, [that] opened up the coal, iron, and wheat fields of north Montana" (569).

To this trend of representing the West belongs Silas Lapham's paint, that is, Howells and his idea of realism as an enlightening record of the products of nature. By virtue of his fighting for a specific definition of realism (and by extension of society) while simultaneously extolling and exploiting the utility of the West as a literary asset, Howells stands very much at the intersection of those cultural crosscurrents that offered the West as a font of the real and realism as the goal of textual representation. Contrary to Thompson's reading of *The Rise of Silas Lapham,* when Howells wrote of the West he did not fall into romance. Rather, he used the West as raw material for the real, the natural. Thus, when Norris proclaimed for himself the inheritance of accurately representing the West, while he may have called it a non-Howellsian romance, he nevertheless relied on the same assumptions about the West's realness that had motivated Howells's own writing. To be sure, Norris endeavored to change the terms by which that realness was recognized; his efforts to do so are the subject of the chapter to follow.

4

1902

The Generic Imagination in Transition

In 1902 the West changed. For one, Bret Harte died in May of this year, and with his passing so too passed a particular way of looking at and representing California and the American West. Eulogizing Harte in *Harper's Monthly,* W. D. Howells offered that the "wild America" which Harte had with literary brilliance "half discovered, half created" was "no longer to be found on our map" ("A Belated Guest" 251). As Howells notes, Harte closed his prolific career in England, "where his last twenty-five years were passed in cultivating the wild plant of his Pacific slope discovery. It was always the same plant, leaf and flower and fruit, but it perennially pleased the constant English world. . . . [H]e did not keep on doing the wild mining-camp thing because it was the easiest, but because it was for him the only possible thing" (253). Beneath Howells's praise lies the implication that at some point in his career Harte ceased to be of much importance or relevance to American audiences and writers. This is not to say that by this time Harte's popularity was a greatly diminished thing, for at his death Harte was on the verge of a canonization in the popular imagination that would take him well beyond the orbit of a strictly literary history. However, by 1902 the figurative and representational landscape of the American West was changing, as turn-of-the-century westerners began to reconsider the usefulness of gold mining as a foundational narrative for literary realism. By this time, those who would make a claim of realism regarding their representations of the West have on their minds something other than the once-ubiquitous mining narrative. Frank Norris, for instance, who coincidentally died only five months after Harte, not infrequently theorized about the future of western literature by making very plain his opposition to the past as signified by Harte. His novel *The Octopus* works to limn in historical terms a western economy in transition from mining to agribusiness but does so without once making explicit reference to Harte's tales. By 1902 Harte's mining stories had begun to lose their place as foundational pillars of the generic imagination, and as a consequence the focus of western American literary realism changed as well.

The lenses through which western writers and readers, as well as the rest of the nation, saw the West underwent a fundamental change in 1902 as a result of several overlapping cultural and material phenomena. For one, 1902 heralded the publication of Owen Wister's *The Virginian*. The best-selling popularity of this novel would skyrocket the genre Western from dime-novel status to that of a dominant and highly influential force in American cultural production.[1] And on a materially different but nevertheless related front, in 1902 the photographic technician Edwin Porter began directing silent film shorts for Thomas Edison's motion picture production company. As 1902 turned into 1903, Porter directed what would prove to be one of the most popular and significant films of the silent era, *The Great Train Robbery*, widely hailed as a major achievement in early narrative film production and, significantly, the first cowboy movie. Richard Slotkin best sums up the facts of Porter's achievement:

> Edwin S. Porter's *The Great Train Robbery*, produced for the Edison Company in 1903, has long figured in the folklore of American mass culture as the progenitor of narrative cinema: "the first story film," the first to use a close-up, "the first Western." In fact, many of its technical and narrative innovations had been anticipated in earlier productions. The legend is closer to truth in identifying *The Great Train Robbery* as the foundation of the Western as a movie genre. The film was a commercial success on a scale that no single movie had previously achieved. (231)

Slotkin thus concludes: "The history of the Western as a film genre begins with the decision to imitate Porter's work and repeat its success" (231). In tandem with *The Virginian*, Porter's short but hugely successful film would irreducibly (and irreversibly it seems) associate the western landscape with the exploits of the lone, hypermasculinized gunfighter. As Jane Tompkins, Lee Mitchell, and others have recently argued, both the figurative space of the twentieth-century West and the gender dynamics played out in that space fundamentally shifted after 1902.

The mainstreaming of the formula Western, however, constitutes but one aspect of the shifting generic imagination, for Harte's death had the effect of confirming what many had already come to see as the end of a particular version of the West: after 1902, the cultural West is no longer predominantly a mining space. In terms of genre fiction, it becomes the demesne of the cowboy. And with respect to resources, the West of literary realism becomes a space framed by yet another landmark 1902 event, the passage of the Newlands Reclamation Act, which established the Bureau of Reclamation and initiated the era of federal dam building and irrigation. To put it more succinctly, the Newlands Act re-creates the West as a region defined and delimited by the availability of water.[2] This further change in the cultural frame of reference signifies a key alteration in the sense of what makes the West seem "real," the sense of what takes place in its ostensibly natural spaces and how that realness is best represented. Western writers such as Norris and also Mary Austin will after this year in large part no longer represent mining as the primary means of establishing the "realness" of the Far West in their prose. And in making their respective claims to representational verity, they will no longer invoke Harte as their unavoidable predecessor, as John Muir had earlier felt the need to do in order to describe the Sierra Nevadas for his scenically oriented audience.

As the twentieth century begins, Harte becomes instead materially associated with the historical and geographic zones of his tales. In 1899, for instance, an article in *Land of Sunshine* magazine makes minor celebrities of "two cheery old Argonauts" named Chaffee and Chamberlain, grizzled veterans of the Gold Rush who, reportedly, were the "originals" on which Harte based the characters of "Tennessee" and his "Partner" (Bicknell 325).[3] On similar grounds, in 1901 the *Bookman* publishes what is ostensibly the first piece in what would become over the next thirty years a cottage industry in tourist writing, namely, an article describing a tour through "Bret Harte's Country" (see W. M. Clemens). The name "Bret Harte" thus takes on, in the years right before his death, a material referent in the landscape he presumably described. In the process, "Bret Harte" becomes less a signifier for a distinctly literary history as it becomes one for a place and time. In the transformation, it becomes easier for western writers to think of Harte less and less as their antecedent in western prose.

Ironically enough, Harte's ultimate erasure from the western writer's lexicon finds its motivation in part in a move figuratively suggested by

Harte himself. As argued in chapter 1, Harte's tales had been instrumental in initiating a narrative form, and by extension a lens through which to understand the West, in which the incidents, traumas, and successes of the California Gold Rush are shunted off into the foggy, distant past. As early as 1894, a reviewer for the *Atlantic* does just that, consigning both Harte and that for which he stands into the recesses of a bygone era. Anticipating Howells's eulogy somewhat, a "Comment on New Books" entry on Harte's *A Protégée of Jack Hamlin's, and Other Stories* argues that while Harte may still be an accomplished yarn-spinner, "his stories are not so well worth telling. In the California of nowadays Bret Harte would not find so much that really suits his literary aptitudes" (705). Hinting at the question of Harte's local color realism, this review plainly avers that those things to which Harte's narratives ostensibly refer no longer exist—the tales no longer point to anything real and, hence, one is hard pressed to think of them as realistic.

In the decade leading up to 1902, in fact, a number of self-identified western writers began to express widespread dissatisfaction not only with Harte as a writer about California but with the way in which his treatment of the Gold Rush had become synonymous with the West as a whole. Writing as a traveling reporter for *Harper's Weekly* in 1892, Richard Harding Davis observed that reading Harte had ill-prepared him to encounter the mines and miners in the mountains above Colorado (*West from a Car-Window* 59–60). Kate Chopin, while praising "Luck of Roaring Camp" in 1900 as a foundational moment in western American literary history, nevertheless endeavored to distance Harte as a predecessor of representational accuracy: "But the West of today is . . . no longer the West of . . . Bret Harte. . . . Mining camps are not so very far from the police station, and the bucking broncho is colliding with the automobile. . . . [Harte] has naturally had his followers, but it is pleasing to note that the great majority of western writers have observed with their own eyes and have chronicled their individual impressions" ("Development" 71). As Chopin rightly points out, by the turn of the century the West is a more complex space, and the hallmarks of reality such as the mine are no longer those which most warrant writing about. And in 1902, Mary Austin levels the Harte genre with a satire in the *Atlantic* called "Jimville —A Bret Harte Town." It is in this very manner that the literary West ultimately changes in the years leading up to 1902: the writerly process for determining and verifying both representability and representation ceases to concern itself predominantly with mining.

To be sure, this is not simply a case of the realism of a later generation supplanting the popular imaginings of an earlier, self-proclaimed "humble writer of romance" (Harte, *Selected Stories* 3). As the previous three chapters have demonstrated, while late-nineteenth-century writers fought hard for distinctions between the two, they nevertheless borrowed heavily from notions of both "romance" and "realism" to get at in writing what Henry James in a short story called "The Real Thing."[4] In the West, the claim to realism shows up with equal force in genre productions considered both romantic (i.e., Harte's Gold Rush tales) and realistic (i.e., novels, nature writing). Thus, the cultural and representational process by which Harte and mining are phased out of the generic imagination needs to be attended to, for it is immensely instructive of the role played by genre fiction in establishing the boundaries of realism. Turn-of-the-century genre productions such as cowboy Westerns, imitative satires, and romances provided the (unreal) foil against which the realist's crises of representation were perpetually measured. Norris's fiction, which engages the many styles listed above by often proclaiming itself a true and accurate representation of the West, provides a telling example of a generic imagination in transition: Norris was perfectly positioned in the literary spaces between two different versions of the West, and the name "Bret Harte" figures prominently in this process of moving from one version to the other. Even as the mining tale gains as a form of romanticized history-telling, the perceived realness of the turn-of-the-century American West changes, as does its literary realism, when "Bret Harte" no longer meets an assumed standard for accurate literary referentiality.

"The Fake"

In January 1894, a mere three months after the closing of Chicago's Columbian Exposition, San Francisco opened its own World's Fair, the California Midwinter International Exposition. Moreover, hoping to capitalize on the success of its predecessor, this West Coast version offered many of the same exhibitions and rides that visitors to Chicago would have seen. For this reason, one critic calls it San Francisco's "Midwinter Fake" (see Clary). And when a few years later Norris would satirize it in *The Octopus* as the "Million Dollar Fair," he too describes it as a notorious "Fake." According to the narrator of Norris's novel, "The people of the city were awakening to a Realisation of the Beautiful, to a sense of the higher needs of life. This was Art, this was Literature, this was Culture and Refinement. The Renaissance had appeared in the West" (315).[5] However, this "Renaissance" came at the hands of "decayed professors, virtuosi, litterateurs, and artists" who, according to Norris, provided very little cultural uplift. Instead, these "fakirs," as Norris calls them, did nothing more than pick the pockets of San Francisco's earnest but deluded bohemian ladies' clubs. Scholars, poets, Eastern mystics, Cherokee orators, and landscape painters well trained in the style of the Barbizon school—all constituted "the Fake," all were guilty of perpetrating "the eternal, irrepressible Sham; glib, nimble, ubiquitous, tricked out in all the paraphernalia of imposture, an endless defile of charlatans that passed interminably before the gaze of the city, marshalled by 'lady presidents,' exploited by clubs of women, by literary societies, reading circles, and culture organisations" (314). And, as Norris tells it, this cultural maelstrom of misrepresentation, artifice, and deceit predominantly centered on society's attachment to only one such poet/prophet/aesthete at any given time. However, this same society did occasionally organize itself into huge gala events such as the "Million Dollar Fair," which stands for Norris as monument to and apotheosis of the "Fake."

Notably, organizers and publicists for the Midwinter Fair exhibit a great deal of self-awareness: they appear to have known perfectly well that they were putting on a fake. *The Official Guide to the California Midwinter Exposition,* the standard souvenir booklet that any visitor might have picked up for ten cents and used as the primary reference to the fairgrounds, promises in its opening paragraphs: "We are aware that, following so closely upon the Columbian Exposition at Chicago, . . . the public mind will involuntarily connect them in some sort of way. . . . [We] hasten to assure our guests that the Midwinter Exposition is in no wise an imitation hurried into being by the contagious force of example, but the natural product of the last hundred years of California's existence" (13). But in a sense they protest too much. The presentation of this "natural product" in both print and on the fairgrounds proper strongly suggests that imitation and replication were key formal considerations in the design of the fair's major attractions. More to the point, the charge of "fake" leveled by critics is borne out by the fair's very raison d'être. According to Michael H. de Young, publisher of the *San Francisco Chronicle* and commissioner of California's delegation to the Columbian Exposition in Chicago, the explicit idea of the Midwinter Fair was to replicate for the city by the bay the effect that the Columbian Exposition had had on Chicago. Simply put, de Young hoped that his version of the fair would give San Francisco the economic boost that thousands of tourists would bring.

To this end, de Young borrowed outright many exhibits from the Columbian Exposition to provide the skeleton for his own extravaganza, contracting with the various Chicago commissions to disassemble their venues the moment they closed in October, haul them by rail to the West Coast, and then reinstall them in San Francisco in time for the Midwinter Fair's opening on 27 January 1894. The success of Chicago's exposition provided de Young with a time-tested, proven set of attractions. The former city's Ferris wheel, for instance, the first such apparatus ever built, was reproduced on a slightly smaller scale in Golden Gate Park and renamed the Firth wheel.[6] Similarly, a 300-foot-tall replica of Paris's Eiffel Tower (which stands 300 meters tall) was erected under the supervision of the man who served as commissioner of the French exhibits in both Chicago and San Francisco. Miles Orvell has shown that the Chicago Exposition was built upon "an aesthetic of replication." He writes:

> In the official exposition there were not only the imitation palaces made out of ephemeral stuff, but also replicas of home-grown structures: a reproduction of St. Augustine's Fort Marion offered by the state of Florida, for example, and a replica of the clock tower on Independence Hall—together with the actual Liberty Bell—displayed by Pennsylvania. Meanwhile, moored at the Lake Front were replicas of the *Niña,* the *Pinta,* and the *Santa María,* built in Spanish naval yards. As for the Midway, it featured replicas of German and Turkish villages, a street in Cairo (with dancers), a Moorish palace, a Viennese café, villages from Algeria, Tunisia, Austria, and Dahomey, a Japanese bazaar, etc., with people from these places as "actors." (35)

Most of the exotic locales Orvell mentions were reconstructed on San Francisco's own Midway, right down to the use of "natives" as "actors." In this respect, de Young's transplanted fair very much captures the logic of fakery that underlies such enterprises as world's fairs (see Rydell; Orvell).

The replicas of Columbus's ships, however, did not make the journey to the West. In place of their signification as the *modus transportus* of an origin story, the Midwinter Fair provided a stagecoach that was "no other than the famous one in which the late Mr. Horace Greeley was driven by Hank Monk" (*Official Guide* 106). Moreover, whereas Frederick Jackson Turner had used the occasion of the Chicago Exposition to proclaim the closing of the frontier, the Midwinter Fair offered a rich display of the "natural products" of that frontier. And in place of Columbus's so-called discovery, California offered the Gold Rush as the origin tale around which much of the fair's cultural displays were organized. Indeed, upon reaching the "extreme western end" of the exhibition grounds, visitors could enter a replica of a forty-niner gold camp that contained, significantly, the apparently real cabin in which Bret Harte had apparently stayed during a brief sojourn in the gold country.

In its blending of artifice and artifact, the Mining Camp of '49 not only provides the keynote example of the construction of the World's Fair, but also offers the key to the seemingly unrelated phenomenon of literary reputation. According to the appreciably biased *Official History of the California Midwinter International Exposition* (pub. 1894), this particular exhibit had been "perhaps more interesting than any, on account of its characteristic representation of life in the early days of California" (152). That this was so, the fair's boosters insisted, was largely due to "the realism of the representation" (153) offered by the scene. What matters here is not so much what visitors might have thought of the installation but rather the very specific grounds upon which the claim to realism is made. On the one hand, pieces such as Monk's stagecoach and Harte's cabin signify a certain level of museum-style historical authenticity, in that these objects are presumed to be the "real" ones connected with famous names. The "actual" cabins of several sitting U.S. senators and of Mark Twain and John Marshall (the discoverer of gold) stand, on the other hand, alongside "a complete model of Sutter's Fort" (*Official History* 153)—recall the real Liberty Bell in a fake Independence Hall. And Marshall's boots, knife, and "housekeeping utensils" keep company with a replica "placer mine showing the method of washing gold from gravel" (*Official Guide* 107). Finally, an immense dioramic (outdoor!) painting of Mount Shasta was praised for being "so well constructed and so artistically painted that it blended perfectly with the surrounding landscape." The pack mules responsible for drawing Hank Monk's stage apparently were fooled enough by this trompe l'oeil that they tried to eat the painted foliage, as were "visitors from abroad" led to believe "that they were really looking upon Mount Shasta. . . . [P]hotographs of the scene afforded an excellent idea of how easily the deception could be accomplished" (*Official History* 152). Realism is hereby achieved through deliberate and self-aware artifice, all of which amounts, in the words of the *Official Guide,* to "a most instructive object lesson" in history (107).[7] The Mining Camp of '49 stands unique among the fair's accomplishments, for in the *Official Guide* it is the only exhibit that succeeds not only as an "imitation," but as being "realistic" (107). While the distinction is perhaps negligible, it should be noted that of all the exhibits, realism appears to matter most with this one.

The self-professed rationale for the fair's existence lends credence to Orvell's observation that American culture in the 1890s resolved its tensions between imitation and authenticity largely by favoring those productions that were discernibly imitative in form (xv–xix). However, the persistent self-awareness with which de Young and company establish their claims to realism on the foundation of mimicry suggests that the logic of imitation is potentially more complex, that it signifies more than mere preference for a referential order of things that makes clear its own artifice. In a reading much more nuanced than Orvell's, and one which includes Norris within its purview, Walter Benn Michaels has characterized this period in history as being ideologically determined by "the logic of the gold standard," which in his formulation is essentially a logic which demands that inherent value, whether material, economic, artistic, or even in the establishment of the self, be equal to face value (22). If it looks like a duck and walks like a duck, it had better be a duck. However, a direct correlation between materiality and identity inevitably proves elusive, and so cultural productions such as Norris's fiction provide Michaels with an instance of a cultural logic divided against itself. In a culture that worries whether gold and silver are valuable because of some inherent quality or because, paradoxically, as metals they resemble money, the possibilities for accurate representation are tenuous at best. And the literary text, according to Michaels, can do no more than "exemplify" the culture of which it is a participant—not illuminate, or respond to, or even dialectically help shape its discursive framework (27, 174). What the example of the Midwinter Fair and its engagement with the literary dimension of material history suggests, and what Michaels's zero-sum game does not account for in its focus on the constitution and re-presentation of identity, is that the claim to making something *seem* real can provide a tangible bulwark against the unreliability of representation. This strategy for establishing the grounds on which both the real and its realistic representation are founded should be attended to more closely, for if you can safely imitate something presumably real, then it might very well be taken for granted that the referent in question in fact exists.[8]

Thus the question around which the fair organizes its approach to the Gold Rush past, a question evident in the mixing of replicated gold mills with the actual cabins of the rich and famous, is an inquiry into which form of representation is most trustworthy, the artifact or the artifice. According to the *Official Guide,* this problem is also of a distinctly textual nature:

> Many writers, not a few of the famous in their profession, who have visited California have been seized with the desire to write of it . . . but while their clever combination of nouns, verbs, and adjectives make very pretty reading—the will-o'-the-wisp spirit of California has ever eluded them. If the matter ended there it would be of comparatively little consequence, but it does not. Visitors come from the East with these descriptions in their memories if not with the books actually in their hands. (18)

Once in California, these misinformed visitors are inevitably disappointed to find that what they see does not match at points what they have read (Mary Hallock Foote anticipates this position as early as 1878, when she describes in an article for *Scribner's* the coastline around Santa Cruz and concludes that "the tourist sees the sensational side of California—its scenery and society; but it is not all included in the Yo Semite guidebooks and the literature of Bret Harte" ["Sea-port" 460]). The fair thus argues that, on a very basic level, textual representation has failed. Nonetheless, the *Guide* assures that with respect to California, "everything that has ever been written about it is true, at some time and at some place, but not all at once" (18). Given that the fair claims to provide a full and complete representation of "the natural product of the last hundred years of California's existence" (13), is one to infer that at the fair all those written impressions will, for a change, be found "all at once" in one place and time? Or will the fair offer a corrective to textual misinformation, replacing it with another, more "real" representation? The *Guide* does not address these questions.

However, the Mining Camp of '49, which, as indicated above, was central to both the mission and the structure of the fair, does provide answers. This exhibit promises, in very broad terms, to appeal to everybody. As the *Guide* states,

> For the old pioneer who spent a good portion of his life in just such a scene as this depicts, the camp will arouse stirring memories, while for the visitor from the East, the gentle "tenderfoot," as well as for the rising generations of the West, who have in imagination lost themselves in the Sierras with Bret Harte, crossed the Plains with Joaquin Miller or roughed it on the Comstock with Mark Twain, this exhibition will also be full of interest. (106)

Whereas the introduction to the *Guide* suggests that textual impressions may be unreliable, this passage offers that *both* forms of representation, the textual and the more materially grounded, will receive proper reinforcement and reification at the fair. And neither is offered as a corrective for the other. In fact, the construction of the camp as just that, a construction, largely serves to reify its hold on reality, allows reality to enter into the representation quite easily. For instance, the *Official History* boasts that one day the stagecoach to the camp provided "an accident which was really the only serious one occurring during the entire Exposition." Carrying to work a load of "employees of the camp, including the dancing girls and their partners," the stage spilled, "sending seven people to the hospital, three for stitches and two with internal injuries." Luckily, when all was eventually restored, "the fact that two of the male dancers did their parts on crutches did not detract from the show and was accepted as a pardonable further advertisement" (154–55). Even when bodily injury intrudes into the artifice of the camp, the exhibit is flexible enough to absorb the event.[9] As a presentation of historical narrative, the mining camp exhibit deftly balances the artifice of obvious representation with a deferral to the presumed realness of the artifact. Thus the "most instructive object lesson" offered by the camp inheres not so much in its presentation of mining life but rather in a textuality that is both mimetic and denotative—in short, it is both real and realistic.

In this context, Harte (as well as Twain) functions less as a literary antecedent than as a historical signifier whose presence confirms the reality of both his fictions and the locale in which they were set. The fair's presentation and use of Harte fairly indicates a shift in westerners' attitude toward him near the turn of the century. In the title of a recent and significant essay, Gary Scharnhorst asks "Whatever Happened to Bret Harte?," a question he answers by explicating the means by which Harte's name has been unfairly excised by recent revisions in literary historiography. But the question is also relevant to Harte's place in the representational schema of the Midwinter Fair. To recall, the fair offers a rationale for its existence based in part on the textual problem of California's representation, and indeed Harte's name is invoked as someone whose texts may have given "the rising generations of the West" an imaginative boost into the Sierras. However, no single portion of the mining camp exhibit itself makes specific reference to any of Harte's stories. The only Harte presence in the exhibit comes via the myriad of physical objects that correlate to the era signified by his tales. But the textual dimension itself is not engaged here—only the historical is, and this is done as a curative to textual misrepresentation.

Perverting Harte

A written text differs somewhat from a material representation erected on a piece of fairground, in that few observers, if any, would ever confuse the contents of a book with a miner's cabin. And so when Norris creates his parody of "the Fake" and its representational strategies, he does not pick up on the Mining Camp of '49 as a point of focus.[10] Instead, he aims his invective at the landscape painters of the period who offered hack imitations of the Barbizon aesthetic.[11] In doing so, however, Norris nevertheless engages the very same question that informs the creation of such an exhibit: does the discourse of mining, Bret Harte and all, adequately serve to represent the "natural product" of the West? In 1894 the Midwinter Fair answered this question by focusing a great deal of attention on the "extreme western limit" (*Official History* 152) of the fairgrounds, where a realistic mix of artifice and artifact was to be found. The representation of history is, simply put, both created and inherent in material objects. When Norris takes up the issue of California's cultural and economic history, most notably in *McTeague* (1899) and *The Octopus* (1901), he offers the assessment that the history signified by Harte and company does *not* adequately meet the representational needs of the region. However, Norris offers this opinion through a very specific form of imitation—parody. This strategy ties Norris into the tradition of western American realism insofar as both he and Harte rely on the forms of hoaxes and parody to shift the terms of referential truth. Consequently, Norris never fully shakes the specter of Harte. In this respect, Norris stands as a transitional figure in western realism; his engagement with and responses to Harte represent a discernible movement from one framework of representational verity (mining) to another (water).[12]

Three years after the Midwinter Fair, in 1897, Norris spent several weeks in residence at the Big Dipper gold mine near Colfax, California, during which time the not-yet-famous novelist completed the manuscript for *McTeague,* the book that would make him a nationally read author.[13] Both William J. Hug and Gary Scharnhorst have shown that the concluding chapters of this novel, with their abrupt departure from San Francisco, whirlwind tour through the Sierra gold country, and frantic climax in Death Valley, offer a subtle but effective parody of California Gold Rush literature and its most familiar spokeswriter, Bret Harte. Not surprisingly, then, in December of this same year, Norris took a further shot at his literary forerunner with the publication of a series of short, direct parodies of popular literary tastes called "Perverted Tales." As Scharnhorst points out, these sketches are remarkably reminiscent in both form and content of Harte's *Condensed Novels* (1867), a parodic collection Harte published exactly thirty years earlier when he himself was not yet famous ("Harte, Norris" 10). Where Harte saw fit to satirize James Fenimore Cooper, Charlotte Brontë, Victor Hugo, Wilkie Collins, and his favorite, Charles Dickens, Norris offers parodies of Stephen Crane, Ambrose Bierce, Richard Harding Davis, Anthony Hope, his favorite, Rudyard Kipling, and, of course, Bret Harte, parodying the latter's "The Outcasts of Poker Flat" with a perverted tale called "The Hero of Tomato Can."

While generally respectful of the other five writers on his list, Norris is quite ambivalent about Harte. On one occasion he writes that Harte alone rose above the "nameless hacks of the 'yellow back' libraries" who "defaced and defamed" the "tale of the West." According to Norris, Harte was "[the] one poet, [the] one chronicler . . . who understood that wild, brave life" ("A Neglected Epic" 121). Alas, Harte's promise proved to be greater than his accomplishment, for as Norris notes in another critical essay, "Harte was a writer of short stories and—oh, the pity of it, the folly of it!—abandoned the field with hardly more than a mere surface-scratching" ("An American School" 109). And, as already noted in the introduction, a third essay has Norris reflecting that

> we are quite ready to relegate the red shirt fellow with his stock lingo, his make-up, his swagger and his gallery plays, to the lumber room and the county jail. We are done with him. He was a characteristic once. . . . We distinctly do not want him to speak of his local habitation as "These 'ere diggin's," or to address us as "pard," or to speak of death as the passing in of checks, of the kicking of the

> bucket. He would not be true to Western life. ("Literature of the West" 105)

But such critical assessments would come later in Norris's career, in 1902 as a matter of fact. Five years earlier, as he was shaping his Big Dipper Mine material into the conclusion of a novel, Norris establishes *through parody* something of a pre-Norris canon, crafting a revealing portrait of his literary patrimony.[14] Thus does Norris initially enter into the dialogue on how best to be "true to Western life," by imitating to the point of parody. Even though Harte is, in the company of Kipling, Davis, Bierce, and Hope, clearly the odd man out, by writing in the same year both the conclusion to *McTeague* and "The Hero of Tomato Can" Norris unmistakably suggests that a comprehensive reevaluation of the history of Harte's literary terrain, figurative and otherwise, should be undertaken. Indeed, a year later Norris wrote to his friend Isaac Marcosson, "I have great faith in the possibilities of San Francisco and the Pacific Coast as offering a field for fiction. Not the fiction of Bret Harte, however, for the country has long since outgrown the 'red shirt' period."[15]

Norris's parody in "Tomato Can" operates as more than just a send-up of the "red shirt" period, for as with *McTeague,* so too in this piece does Norris offer a parody of his other literary bête noire, the dime-novel Western. For instance, Norris writes that his "Hero," John Oak-hearse, "betook himself leisurely down the one street of Tomato Can, languidly dodging an occasional revolver bullet, and stepping daintily over the few unburied corpses that bore mute testimony to the disputations and controversial nature of the citizens of Tomato Can" (175). The suaveness of the "Hero" and the sonorous rhythms of the language are unmistakably Harte, but the whizzing bullets and the piled-up bodies also suggest the demesne of a dime-novel shoot-out.[16] In 1902 Norris would rail more explicitly against the popular but "wretched" yellow backs that were an abomination to critical reading tastes; however, this critique also exists implicitly in the satire directed at Harte in 1897.

Norris's most sustained parody of the dime-novel Western, however, occurs in *The Octopus,* a novel that deploys genre parody as a crucial tactic by which the claim to realism is established. At the very outset of the story, the wheat rancher Harran Derrick exhibits a terrible misunderstanding of economic conflict, wishing for a resolution that very much sounds like the program of the Western. In complaining about how the Pacific and Southwestern Railroad sets its fees for shipping grain, he fumes, "Why not hold us up with a gun in our faces, and say, 'hands up,' and be done with it?" (11). As Walter Benn Michaels might say of this character, Harran is troubled by the fact that the railroad's actions do not match the reality of the situation as he perceives it—face value does not equal actual value. In other words, since Harran believes that the railroad's fee schedules are tantamount to robbery, he would prefer that the railroad's engagement with him actually look like a robbery. Significantly, Norris associates this literalist reading of economic reality with a literary form, with an event common to the popular Western. A similar misapprehension affects the principal character Presley, who is at the outset of the story intent on "giving true, absolutely true, poetical expression" to life in the West but who finds that "realism" (12) in the form of class conflict and the railroad intrudes upon his wish "to see as Homer saw, as Beowulf saw, as the Nibelungen poets saw" (41). The problem, as Norris poses it, is one in which the presence of a textual/literary history clouds the ability to render proper representation.

However, this recognition hardly leads to a Norris version of the dictum to "make it new," for Norris situates a significant parody of the dime-novel Western in an equation of representation more complex than the portrait of a misinformed wheat rancher would imply. Much as he (and Harte) had sought to establish initial legitimacy to his early writing career by publishing parodies of his literary predecessors, Norris in *The Octopus* deploys parodic imitation to make the claim to realism. In a tone decidedly more humorous than his depiction of Harran Derrick had been, Norris crafts one of the railroad's hired guns as a stereotypically villainous dime-novel cowboy. As Presley tells Annixter, another rancher, "[Delaney's] got the buckskin, and he's full of bad whiskey. . . . [He's] wearing all his cow-punching outfit, hair trousers, sombrero, spurs and all the rest of it, and he has strapped himself to a big revolver. He says he wasn't invited to your barn dance but that he's coming over to shoot up the place" (245). Needless to say, when Delaney does show up, the effect of his shoot-out with Annixter, as Norris describes it, is largely comedic. In a battle marked by "spurts of pale blue smoke jetting like the darts of short spears between men, expanding to a haze and drifting overhead," neither combatant really wants to shoot straight: "Both fired without aiming very deliberately. To empty their revolvers and avoid being hit was the desire common to both" (260). The party guests, however, believe they have just witnessed an expertly fought gunfight, and "All the legends of '49, the violent, wild life of the early days, were recalled to view, defiling before them there in an endless procession under the glare of paper lanterns and kerosene lamps" (263). That this event occurs halfway through the novel makes it a clear set-up for the contrasting irrigation ditch shoot-out of book 2. This latter episode, positioned as the climax of the novel and based on the historical events of Mussel Slough, Norris describes in much more matter-of-fact terms:

> Instantly the revolvers and rifles seemed to go off of themselves. . . . At first, it was nothing but a confused roar of explosions; then the roar lapsed to an irregular, quick succession of reports, shot leaping after shot; then a moment's silence, and, last of all, regular as clock ticks, three shots at exact intervals. Then stillness.
>
> Delaney, shot through the stomach, slid down from his horse. . . . Hooven, in attempting to rise from his kneeling position, received a rifle ball squarely in the throat. . . . Harran Derrick dropped where he stood, turning over on his face, and lay motionless, groaning terribly. . . . Annixter, instantly killed, fell his length to the ground, and lay without movement, just as he had fallen, one arm across his face. (521–22)

The ostensible realism of this moment, as moving as it may be, depends crucially on the antecedent parody of a shoot-out Norris positions near the end of book 1. In a very palpable sense, a form of representational legitimacy is thus conferred on the irrigation ditch slaughter by the parodic imitation presented in the barn dance.[17]

The most notable instance of parody in *The Octopus*, however, is Norris's send-up of the Midwinter Fair, or as he calls it, the "Fake." As Don Graham has shown, Norris uses the first chapter of book 2 to provide a detailed dismantling of the pretense and affectation he saw as rampant in turn-of-the-century bohemian society in San Francisco (Graham 74–94). Specifically, Norris describes an auction at which funds are to be raised for the "Million Dollar Fair," and the centerpiece of the auction is a painting reminiscent of the Barbizon school of landscape painting. The handiwork of a character named Hartrath, the painting known as "A Study of the Contra Costa Foothills" depicts "a couple of cows, knee deep in a patch of yellow poppies" and "a girl in a pink dress and white sunbonnet," all languidly posed "under the shade of a live-oak" (310–11). Dubbing this pictorial style "live-oak regionalism," Graham notes that paintings of this very genre had in fact taken most of the top prizes at the 1894 Midwinter Fair (85).[18] At Norris's auction, the narrative clearly derides those who appreciate art such as Hartrath's as being know-nothing aesthetes. Speaking of "atmospheric effects, of middle distance, of '*chiaro-oscuro*,'" Norris's viewers quibble over apparently trivial details: "It was decided formally that the reddish brown cows in the picture were reminiscent of Daubigny, and that the handling of the masses [presumably the girl in pink] was altogether Millet, but that the general effect was *not quite* Corot" (*Octopus* 311). Once again, Norris offers the opinion that an awareness of textuality, this time learned from "Art Books and painting classes" (311), creates a hindrance to both proper representation and its appreciation.

For Norris this was obviously a problem. As the venture capitalist Cedarquist complains to Presley, the entire city appears to be under the spell of putting on a "Million Dollar Fair" rather than investing its money in new industrial infrastructure: "We don't want fairs. We want active furnaces. We don't want public statues, and fountains, and park extensions and gingerbread *fêtes*. We want business enterprise. . . . San Francisco! It is not a city—it is a Midway Plaisance." Cedarquist concludes his diatribe by exclaiming, "California likes to be fooled. . . . Our state is the very paradise of fakirs" (303). Invoking the name of the polyglot, decidedly lowbrow strip of attractions found at both Chicago's Columbian Exposition and the Midwinter Fair, Norris suggests that the entire city is given over to a preference for cheap artifice over the real thing. Graham agrees, noting that "nothing in the decade [of the 1890s] so reflected the glaring disparity between nature and artifice, possibility and failure, as the Midwinter Fair" (91). However, as the above discussion of the fair has shown, and as Miles Orvell, Alan Trachtenberg, and Robert Rydell have argued as well, the Midway Plaisance in both Chicago and San Francisco is but one ingredient in a complex of representation that ultimately puts artifice in the service of realism. That is, the claim to realism of an event such as the Midwinter Fair depends very much on the artifice of the Midway setting off the other exhibitions.[19]

And so it is that yet again, as with the parody of a Western gunfight being placed in such a way as to give credibility to the shoot-out at the climax of the novel, Norris relies on the very strategy he disparages, a strategy that extends to the material construction of his own book. The particular aspect of Hartrath's painting that most directly aligns it with the complex of artifice and realism in which the fair functioned emerges in its presentation at auction. As Norris writes, it "was set in a frame of natural redwood, the bark still adhering" (310). Even this production, created in anticipation of the "Million Dollar Fair" and designed to help pay for the extravaganza, seeks to balance the construction of the painted artifact with "real" material.

On a metatextual level, the material object of Norris's novel—the book itself—shares this dimension of referentiality, for such a strategy perfectly explains the frontispiece map of the fictional San Joaquin locale in which the action of *The Octopus* unfolds, a map Norris and his publishers included in the first edition. As real bark serves as frame to Hartrath's painting, so does the ostensibly real map frame the fiction of the plot. Paul Civello writes that in *The Octopus* "traditional ordering principles . . . have already been destroyed before the action in the novel begins" (48). The presence of the map, however, suggests that some traditional form of ordering is still at stake in framing the narrative, even if philosophically and thematically Norris might offer otherwise. But whatever the intended design of the map, its function was perceived by reviewers very much as a document supporting the book's credibility and realism. The magazine *Town Talk* averred that "the book is furnished with an excellent map of the country around Bonneville, by which the story can be accurately followed" (133);[20] *Academy and Literature* noted that the map adds a "very business-like air to this novel," which is given as a bonus to an otherwise "complete" novel (162); and even Henry Boynton's negative review in the *Atlantic* complained that "photographs of a California wheat-field and a patent reaper and a tintype or two of the leading persons would have left still less for the imagination to do. But the author is a confessed realist" (172). The effect of the map, regardless of the fact that it maps a wholly fictional space with wholly fictional place-names and features, is to suggest that the tour Presley takes in chapter 1 of book 1 can be followed, timed, and matched precisely to the narrative. Once again, the presence of a presumably "real" artifact is put in the service of lending credibility to the artifice, to the fiction.

Norris appears quite aware of the function parody and imitation can have in the legitimation of a narrative's representational and canonical value. Consider the following description of the development, late in the novel, of Presley's literary reputation. It concerns the poem Presley has written in an impassioned fury over the mistreatment of the former railroad employee Dyke:

> Presley's Socialistic poem, "The Toilers," had an enormous success. The editor of the Sunday supplement of the San Francisco paper to which it was sent, printed it in Gothic type, with a scare-head

> title so decorative as to be almost illegible, and furthermore caused the poem to be illustrated by one of the paper's staff artists in a most impressive fashion. The whole affair occupied an entire page. Thus advertised, the poem attracted attention. It was promptly copied in New York, Boston, and Chicago papers. It was discussed, attacked, defended, eulogised, ridiculed. It was praised with the most fulsome adulation; assailed with the most violent condemnation. Editorials were written upon it. Special articles, in literary pamphlets, dissected its rhetoric and prosody. The phrases were quoted,—were used as texts for revolutionary sermons, reactionary speeches. It was parodied; it was distorted so as to read as an advertisement for patented cereals and infants' foods. Finally, the editor of an enterprising monthly magazine reprinted the poem, supplementing it by a photograph and biography of Presley himself. (394)

This passage is of course also meant as a parody, for the response to Presley's poem by San Francisco's bohemian set is hardly the revolutionary call to class consciousness that Presley had hoped it would be.[21] Nevertheless, recalling Norris's and Harte's self-positioning with respect to their published antecedents, the canonization and anthologizing of "The Toilers" only after it has been "parodied" and co-opted by advertising strongly suggests that parodic imitation is a key component in any text's move toward significant marketplace value, toward legitimization. *The Octopus* thus invokes a great deal of satire and parody for the very specific purpose of defining its own legitimacy as a literary production. It does so, parodically, in the above description of a reputation built in part on the fact that it can be parodied; it does so in its use of the dime-novel Western to set off the historically "real" events of the Mussel Slough shoot-out; and it does so in the satirizing of bohemian aesthetic taste in order to suggest that artifice does not beget truth in realism. The process by which Presley's poem achieves its canonization is precisely the same process by which *The Octopus* achieves its force as literary history. It is a process remarkably similar to that by which Norris sought to craft his own literary patrimony through parody, and it is a process further invoked in 1902 when Mary Austin attempts to make her reputation by satirizing Harte with her "Jimville" piece in the *Atlantic*. Finally, it is a process evident yet again in the fact that one year after *The Octopus* provided readers with a scathing parody of the Western formula, *The Vir-*

ginian and *The Great Train Robbery* indelibly etch that formula into the representational lexicon of the West.

"Dying Fires"

This chapter has argued thus far that the representational logic behind the change in Harte's reputation—how, when, and why—develops along correlative paths in the realm of material, cultural history and in the transitional fictions of Frank Norris. In both cases we see the delegitimization of one narrative framework for realism in favor of another. But with respect to the actual representation of mining, the question still remains to be asked: whatever happened to Bret Harte? As noted earlier, in *The Octopus,* a large historical novel bearing the subtitle "A Story of California" and built around a "real" historical event, Norris refrains from invoking his predecessor Harte, whose writings and persona at the turn of the century clearly stood for a great deal of California history. Nor does Norris offer a sustained stab at the "red shirt" period similar to the satire of the concluding chapters of *McTeague*. Rather, his historical representations in *The Octopus* are of a mining industry in transition, and in this manner does Norris at least gesture toward the discursive and material industry that gave shape to the history of the region. Among the novel's insertions of the mining past stands most prominently the figure of Magnus Derrick, the tycoon wheat rancher and father to Harran who, "when all was said and done, . . . remained a Forty-niner. . . . It was the true California spirit that found expression through him, the spirit of the West . . . the miner's instinct of wealth acquired in a single night" (298). Derrick's fellow rancher Annixter at one point supposes that "Derrick thinks he's still running his mine, and that the same principles will apply to getting grain out of the earth as to getting gold. . . . Get the guts out of your land; work it to death . . . and then when your soil is exhausted, sit down and roar about hard times" (28–29). This assessment, in fact, quite accurately describes the manner by which wheat farming supplanted mining in the mid- to late 1870s as California's primary source of revenue. Kevin Starr observes: "Drawing upon the existing infrastructure of the mining era—its financial resources, its foundries and iron works, its labor pool, its inclination toward an innovative, labor-saving technology—wheat brought these structures and operational patterns into the next era of agricultural growth, establishing a direct link between mining and agriculture" (*Inventing the Dream* 132).

At one point during the fund-raising auction for the fair, Derrick fantasizes about wide-open Asian markets for his wheat in the following terms: "He saw his wheat, like the crest of an advancing billow, crossing the Pacific, bursting upon Asia, flooding the Orient in a golden torrent. It was the new era. He had lived to see the death of the old and the birth of the new; first the mine, now the ranch; first gold, now wheat" (321). Not only is the character of Magnus Derrick a forty-niner, but the very assumptions, capital, and labor practices that structure his massive wheat operation are emblematic of his mining roots.

On a more subtle basis, Norris briefly hints, again through Derrick, at the key, transitional legal battles fought in the 1870s and 1880s between the wheat and mineral industries. In 1882, concerned that the persistent filling and raising of riverbeds with silt and tailings from the mines would force farmers in the Central Valley to depend less on river transport and more on the railroads, the farmers took the upriver mines to court. In the landmark *Woodruff v. North Bloomfield* decision of 1884, the mining companies in and around the town of Marysville were permanently barred from all hydraulic mining activity on the Yuba River (Kelley 212–42). At the end of the narrative, when Magnus has lost both his fortune and his senses, Norris has the Derricks move to a town identified as Marysville, where Mrs. Derrick will "teach—literature" at the local seminary, as she had been doing before her marriage (621). Having personally failed to replace gold with wheat, Magnus must now sit by as his wife uses her literary training to earn an income. By thus drawing textual production into the economic framework, Norris suggests that the sort of representations that make money—that is, the popular stuff to which both Norris and Presley are opposed—is also a fall from grace. It might thus be inferred that a failure to see the world as it "really" is, as a place in which the goldfield ethos no longer works, is also a failure of textual representation. This point is signified by Mrs. Derrick's return to teaching the sentimental, artificial "literature" and the approach to reading about which she and Presley had quarreled in the early chapters. And in what is perhaps an unwitting irony on Norris's behalf, his rancher returns to a place that is identified, if by nothing more than its name, with the mining region that was shut down precisely so that farmers would not become too dependent on the railroad. Whereas *The Octopus* does not dramatize in its plot the replacement of mining with wheat, Norris does situate the tale within a historical context in which the transition from a mineral economy to an agricultural one is represented in a number of the salient details. Significantly, neither Harte nor his texts are among those details.

What has happened to Harte, then? From the above reading of *The Octopus,* one might suspect that Norris has successfully removed Harte from his lexicon of the West, that the "Story of California" could finally manage without the once inevitable reference to an earlier version of the tale. But not all readers were of a mind with Norris, and it probably rankled him more than a little to read in 1901 the following *Washington Times* review: Norris's latest book, writes the reviewer, will "go further to make Mr. Norris, dealing with modern California wheat, what Bret Harte was to the early gold country" (McElrath and Knight 112). A year earlier, this same newspaper had offered in a review of Norris's *Blix* that its author was "not in the least like Bret Harte" (McElrath and Knight 62). However, Norris's ambitious "A Story of California" now draws a favorable comparison to Harte, insomuch as it frames Harte as the inevitable forerunner to all that Norris could hope to achieve in the representation of California. As if in direct response, Norris published soon afterward a short story that explores the effect of such a comparison on a novelist from the West: "Dying Fires," which first appeared in the *Smart Set* in July 1902. Significantly, with this tale Norris also returns to the Colfax/Big Dipper mining region that had provided material for *McTeague.*

"Dying Fires" tells of Overbeck, a young writer from Colfax who writes a "good" and presumably realistic first novel and, as a result, is brought to New York by a prominent publisher, much as Norris himself had been. Of Overbeck's novel Norris writes:

> He completed it in five months, and, though he did not know the fact then, the novel was good. It was not great—far from it, but it was not merely clever. Somehow, by a miracle of good fortune, young Overbeck had got started right at the very beginning. He had not been influenced by a fetich [*sic*] of his choice till his work was a mere replica of some other writer's. He was not literary. He had not much time for books. He lived in the midst of a strenuous, eager life, a little primal even yet. (215)

Drawing attention here to the representational dynamic of imitation versus an authenticity born of ostensibly unmediated, empirical observation, Norris offers the idea that the presence of a literary past would only have been a hindrance. In one sense, this is what the story argues, in that Overbeck, who falls in with a group of New York bohemian aesthetes, cannot repeat his initial success at writing. As Norris tells it, under the influence of the aesthetes Overbeck begins to think of himself and his work as "literary." Michael Davitt Bell has suggested that to call oneself a "realist" or, in the case of Norris, a "naturalist" was to a great extent the result of a wish to disassociate oneself from the "literary" (*Problem* 47–48). In *The Octopus* Norris had depicted a tension between Magnus Derrick's wife on one side and Presley's beliefs as an artist on the other, a tension that hinged on the notion that "the literary," favored by Mrs. Derrick, represents a dangerous territory fraught with misrepresentations and feminizing forces. For young Overbeck, the consequences of falling in with a group of "literary" folk is no less than the total and irreversible quashing of his creative talents.

Somewhat strangely, Norris introduces Harte, among others, as a possible antecedent to Overbeck's somehow uninfluenced achievement. The bohemians tell Overbeck that "he had succeeded where Kipling had ignominiously failed. They said there was more harmony of prose effects in one chapter of 'Bunt McBride' than in everything that Bret Harte ever wrote. They told him he was a second Stevenson—only with more refinement" (226). The narrator has already observed that Overbeck had taken no influence from books, that his achievement was a text free from imitation. And by signifiers such as "prose effects" and "refinement," we are meant to understand that the comparison to Harte is a specious one offered by a group of know-nothing "third raters" (232). And yet, these "literary people" tell Overbeck that he far exceeds Harte, that in fact his text succeeds where Harte's had failed. Does this comparison align their praise with that of the narrator? Or should it be ironically understood that the bohemians find similar comparisons to Norris's favorites Kipling and Stevenson and yet do not fully understand what it is they are praising by also lumping Harte in the equation? In all likelihood, the praise of the Bohemians is designed to signal that they did not understand the achievement of Overbeck's *The Vision of Bunt McBride,* that all they could see was the antecedents—Harte, Kipling, Stevenson—but that they missed the essential truth which the narrator tells us is really there. It is not imitative of Harte, they only think it is.

If Norris's references to Harte in "Dying Fires" are ambiguous, then a series of further Colfax/Big Dipper stories also published in 1902 are even more so. Though none of these mining tales involve the young writer Overbeck, two of the them employ Bunt McBride, the title figure of Overbeck's marvelous first novel, as narrating storyteller.[22] In "A Bargain with Peg-Leg" McBride recounts how at a Nevada rest home for consumptives he stole the artificial leg of a bumptious gambler and then used it as a club to negotiate his own continued safety; and in "The Passing of Cock-Eye Blacklock" McBride tells how another unlikable character had conveniently dispatched himself by making the fatal mistake of going fishing with dynamite in the company of a dog who loved to play fetch. The result was "a big enough hole in the ground to bury a horse an' wagon, let alone Cock-Eye. . . . So we planted him there, an' put up a board, an' wrote on it" (97). Both of these tales offer parodies of the dialect stories made famous by Harte and others, and they are also notable for including the mining tale's emphasis on physical injury within the range of their satire.[23] In January 1902 Norris complains of characters who "address us as 'pard'" and say "these 'ere diggin's," yet at the same time he composes for (presumably remunerative) publication a number of dialect tales which, although they are primarily satires, nevertheless employ as narrator the subject (and perhaps also narrator?) of an ostensibly "good" and realistic western novel. To say the least, Norris is at this point in his career notably ambivalent about his and his fiction's relation to Harte.

Because of Norris's death in 1902, whatever resolution Norris may eventually have worked out is never more than forthcoming. And so he leaves texts that, with respect to the genre forms first initiated by Harte, offer a view of a transitional generic imagination. Norris cannot quite get rid of Harte—the former writer's tactics of realism by dialectic tie him to the Gold Rush in more ways than simply through content or region. He cannot accept Harte's tales as indicative of the "real" West, yet he cannot keep him out of his own representations of that same West. It would thus remain for other western writers, both during and after 1902, to complete the transition.

Coda: Water

John R. Milton hails *The Octopus* as the first western novel, largely by virtue of its epic ambitions to universalize the "outdoor" experience of western life (101–2). Milton may actually be right, although Helen Hunt Jackson's *Ramona* and the Colorado and Idaho mining novels of Mary Hallock Foote strongly suggest otherwise, particularly if one is disinclined to get caught up in the romance versus novel debate of formalist criticism.[24] Nevertheless, Milton's claim does help to point out that Norris's novel indeed operates on a dimension hitherto unfamiliar to most western readers. Kevin Starr also praises *The Octopus* along such lines, noting the manner in which the novel dramatizes the shift in 1880s California from a monocultural mining economy to an agricultural and, as suggested by the railroad, eventually an industrial one (*Americans* 196–200). But Norris's "A Story of California" signifies yet more than that. With respect to Norris's desire to render, through Presley, the true West, one more observation needs to be made. *The Octopus,* or at the very least its first chapter, offers something not yet seen in any widely circulated literary prose from California, for in his first chapter Norris offers a vision of an emerging world in which economic, political, and social relations are determined not by mining but rather by water.

As many careful readers of *The Octopus* have observed, the oft-cited bicycle tour in chapter 1 of book 1 moves through a rich mix of land, people, stories, literary modes, and technology (see Ellis; Hochman 77–78). Yet no single critic has thus far observed that this opening chapter marks its progress with water, that at each stopping point Presley, the bicyclist, finds water. To wit: he begins by a saloon (3); he has his first encounter, with the ranch hand Hooven, by a watering trough and tower where Hooven has come to fill the tank of a water wagon (4–7); his next meeting is with Harran Derrick, who at the moment is occupied with setting up a sprinkler on his father's front lawn (7); next Presley crosses the irrigation ditch by Hooven's house, the site of the novel's final shootout (14). After crossing the railroad tracks and stopping for lunch at another saloon (another watering hole, so to speak), he heads for the foothills source of Broderson Creek (23); along the way he stops at Annixter's ranch house, which is conspicuously marked by the creek running nearby and the artesian well in the front court (24); Presley then listens briefly to "the trickle of the unseen fountain" at the Mission (30). Once past the Broderson Creek spring Presley heads into the dry ranges of the area, and it is here that he encounters Vanamee the desert ascetic ("leaning upon an empty water trough" [31]) and has his brief epiphany about the Homeric, epic quality of the West—a reverie rudely interrupted by a train that rams through a group of sheep at a spot between the irrigation ditch and the creek (49–51). Given that the rest of Norris's novel does not sustain this attention to water offered in the first chapter, it seems entirely likely that Norris was unaware of this particular figurative dimension of Presley's ride. Whatever the case, the opening of *The*

Octopus is unmistakably marked at each of its dramatic beats with water. As such it provides a vision of the "arid West," as it will come to be known in the twentieth century.[25]

Foote's novel *The Chosen Valley,* about a failed irrigation venture at an Idaho mine site that was first serialized in the *Century* in 1892, cogently anticipates the turn toward water that would, in the century to come, dominate both western material culture and the generic imagination that frames readers' perception of the West. As such, it and a number of other writings by Foote gave people prior to 1902 plenty of opportunity to contemplate an arid West in literature.[26] However, Foote's novel is in some measure still a mining story, whereas a more profound move away from mining narratives can be traced to the confluence of both literary and political matters in the period directly adjacent to the publication of *The Octopus*. Writing about *The Grapes of Wrath* (1939), another story of California, David Cassuto has identified water as "the privileged signifier" of Steinbeck's novel (Steinbeck was born in 1902). After 1902, the same could be said of the West as a region: water becomes the privileged signifier. This is not to say that Norris establishes twentieth-century western literature any better that Foote does, only that his example provides evidence of a significant shift in the generic imagination. In questioning and ostensibly rejecting the representational efficacy of Harte's fictions, Norris suggestively led the way for western literature to slough off mining altogether and open the floodgates to water as the key generic component of the literary West. Norris still relied on expressions of parody, imitation, and so on, tactics that tie him to using the Gold Rush as his primary historical, cultural, and textual antecedent. However, subsequent writers will find that by representing an almost exclusively hydraulic West—that is, by representing not mines and miners but westerners and their water resources—the frames of reference around which claims to realism could be built bring with them a whole new range of representational crises, primary among them being an inquiry into the very reliability of the realistic representation of nature. The first such encounter will come from the author of a California book called *The Land of Little Rain*.

5

"I Know What Is Best for You"

Post-Howellsian Realism in Mary Austin's Desert Narratives

Nature writers, it seems, are particularly apt at knowing a valuable story when they tell one. John Muir, for one, relished the success he had in bartering a Bret Harte story for information. Likewise, Mary Austin, who has in many ways been recognized as the next-generation inheritor of Muir's California legacy, recounts a similar instance of tale swapping in "The Land," the introductory essay to *Lost Borders,* her 1909 collection of desert stories. Austin's narrative about narrative value, however, differs significantly from Muir's in that Austin does not borrow her tale from Harte; rather, she makes a point of coming up with her own.[1] Beginning with the observation that "You can get anyone to believe a tale that has gold in it" (157), Austin recalls spending "a whole afternoon" inventing a fictitious provenance for a gold-flecked potsherd that her Owens Valley friend Dr. Woodin had brought to her. "Afterward," she continues, "my friend went to hold down some claims in the Coso country, and I north to the lake region where the red firs are, and we told the pot-of-gold story as often as we were permitted" (158). Austin then relates how, months later, a traveler had told her of hearing the tale in his passage through the Coso area and, even later, how "a prospector from Panamint-way wanted to know if I had ever heard of the Indian-pot Mine which was lost out toward Pharump" (158). Within about a year, Austin tells us, her tale had achieved a referential credibility very close to that of "desert myths" (159).

Austin's pot-of-gold invention presents a number of notable assertions about the value of storytelling. In addition to the obvious drawing power of a mining-region story that purportedly documents "a lost river bedded with precious sand" (158), Austin's narrative also indicates the extent to which landscapes become known by their names. In just under two pages, Austin mentions such places as Coso, Lone Pine, the "lake region," Panamint, Gunsight, and Bryfogle, with an additional comment about the many instances of local knowledge that may never "get into the reports of the Geological Survey" (159). This "tell the boys" story, however, is ultimately a cautionary one about the uncertainty of knowledge: "First and last, accept no man's statement that he knows this Country of Lost Borders well," Austin writes, adding that "a boast of knowledge is likely to prove as hollow as the little yellow gourds called apples of Death Valley" (159). Ironically, Austin's initial motivation for creating the potsherd fiction, she confesses, came about because "I was sore then about not getting myself believed in some elementary matters" (158). Austin spins a cautionary tale about the untrustworthiness of desert narratives precisely because some listeners had not trusted her assertions about desert knowledge. Coupled with the fact that "The Land" as an essay serves to introduce a series of stories that ask to be taken as realistic representations of desert life, Austin's position on knowledge and believability comes across as strangely ambiguous, or at the very least contradictory: she knows the stories and can be trusted to tell the truth, but no more so than others might be trusted to do the same. Austin's claim to realism thus bears a high degree of contingent uncertainty, and her alternating self-depiction as storyteller and skeptic provides a conceptual gloss on her approach to and thinking about realism as a literary and representational enterprise.

Austin is in many ways the most explicitly Howellsian of western realists. In her own criticism and theoretical essays about the practice of writing, she espouses an approach to realism that is very much like that proffered by W. D. Howells, whose tenure at the *Atlantic Monthly* (and later *Harper's*) set the terms for many of the representational issues Austin takes up at the start of her career. In a reflective essay from 1921 entitled "How I Learned to Read and Write," she explains that "when about 1900 I began seriously to devote myself to a writing career, I made a list of the magazines for which I meant to write in the order of their literary importance, with *The Atlantic Monthly* at the top" (14). As Nancy Glazener has shown in extensive detail, the *Atlantic* was at the turn of the century one of the nation's key arbiters of class, distinction, and taste while serving, not coincidentally, as the major venue for genre debates over realistic literature, including realism in nature writing.[2] Thus, when Austin fully inaugurates her career with the advance publication in the

Atlantic of several chapters from *The Land of Little Rain,* she very much announces herself as a realist in the *Atlantic* camp.[3]

In one of these *Atlantic* pieces, a sketch called "Jimville—A Bret Harte Town" published in November 1902 and which later appears as a chapter in *Little Rain,* Austin strikes a notably Howellsian pose. In December 1903 and more than a year after Harte's death, Howells would lament that by the time his friend had left California, "the age of observation was past for him. . . . He saw nothing aright, either in Newport, where he went to live, or in New York, where he sojourned . . . or if he saw it aright, he could not report it aright" (*Literary Friends* 250). Austin offers a notably similar assessment of Harte's failed ability for accurate representation a year earlier, writing in "Jimville" that Harte had "carried his young impression away to be worked out untroubled by any newer fact. He should have gone to Jimville" (*Land of Little Rain* 65). Beyond such parallel assessments, Austin comes still closer to expressing a Howellsian ethos a few paragraphs later when she asserts: "If it had been in mediaeval times you would have had a legend or a ballad. Bret Harte would have given you a tale. You see in me a mere recorder, for I know what is best for you" (68). Here Austin clearly and succinctly nominates herself as a writer whose ethical discernment presumes to validate the recording and presentation of "mere" facts and observation, in that she provides her own version of Howells's admonition not to run "the risk of overmoralizing" by merely heaping fact upon fact (Howells, *Criticism and Fiction* 302).

Harte and Norris may have been acquaintances of Howells's (not to mention two of his favorite authors), and Muir and Mary Hallock Foote may have been published in the *Atlantic, Harper's,* and the *Century* more frequently than most other writers from the Far West, but it is Austin who most deliberately and thoroughly pursues the Howellsian model of morally inflected critical discernment, an approach to writing more or less evident throughout all of her extensive oeuvre. With respect to "Jimville," considered in the context of its initial publication in 1902 in the *Atlantic,* the sketch engages both a textual history and a particular approach to accurate written representation, asking: How do we know a place if not through that which is written about it? When it appears just one year later as chapter 6 of *The Land of Little Rain,* Austin's "Bret Harte Town" functions vitally in the middle of the book by also endowing a text committed to describing the desert in ways that might have escaped the knowledge of others with the lens of a moral Howellsian realist. And by acknowledging the distinction between being a "mere recorder" of facts and a writer who "know[s] what is best," Austin will use her book to inquire into the limitations inherent in writing about one's environment.

As an instance of western American literary realism, *The Land of Little Rain,* precursor to *Lost Borders* and largely Austin's most important book, represents a major contribution to American realism in general and to western realism in particular. For one, it provides a more precise and advanced instance of the shift in the generic imagination detectable in Norris, in that it limns a progressive move away from the representation of mining and individualism and toward that of water and community.[4] Along the way, Austin's treatise on a land known for having "little rain" rethinks the representation of water and, more broadly, the representation of nature in a manner not strictly consistent with the ethos of a nature writer. Austin is even more of a writer in the tradition of American realism than is acknowledged in Lawrence Buell's contention that "the Austin persona beats Harte's in realism, in toughness, *and* in bonding to the environment" (*Imagination* 49).[5] Indeed, to think of her as writing not about nature but about the realism of nature writing and, more broadly, about how the real (natural, social, material, personal) intersects with a received tradition of western prose is to see Austin reworking the very definition of Howellsian realism as she sees it. Initially in *The Land of Little Rain* and subsequently in a long and varied career dedicated to cultural criticism, Austin adjusts the realist's position from one of moral discretion to one of epistemological inquiry. Coming from the West, Austin reinvigorates the idea of realistic representation, and as a post-Howellsian she endeavors to represent "the simple, the natural, and the honest" so that she may interrogate its representability. Notwithstanding the confidence of her "Jimville" assertion about knowing best, in her writing Austin investigates realism's capacity to know anything for certain.

"Mistaken for Poetizing"

Recalling in her autobiography the only substantive meeting she had ever had with Howells, Austin writes that when she queried him about the "shallow and slight" characterizations of women in his novels, he snidely responded, "That's the way it strikes you? One has to write what one knows" (*Earth Horizon* 330).[6] If her own writing is any gauge, Austin presumed to know something about almost everything, a tendency recognized by more than a few contemporaries. Carey McWilliams asked in a letter to his friend and fellow Californian, "Is there any limit to the catholicism of your interests? Naturalist, novelist, short story writer, historian, publicist, etc.,—You are awe-inspiring."[7] And Henry Nash Smith, who along with Austin served as a member of the editorial board for the *Southwest Review,* observed in 1931: "She interests herself in the Boulder Dam controversy, in the reform of the Indian Service, in the censorship rider on the last tariff bill, in the recovery and preservation of Spanish colonial folk-songs and folk drama. . . . She is connected with almost every enterprise which shows any tendency to enrich and deepen the life of the West" (33).[8] As a novelist she wrote essays on how a novel should be constructed; as a poet she wrote an extensive and much-debated theoretical treatise on American poetic form; as an essayist and critic she reflected on the formal characteristics of "the essay of opinion"; and as a playwright she wrote articles exploring the theory, function, and execution of theatrical presentation.[9] Her essays on topics ranging from women's education to natural science to foreign policy with regard to Mexico appeared in magazines such as the *Atlantic, Harper's, Scribner's,* the *Nation,* the *New Republic,* the *Saturday Review of Literature,* and *Bookman.*

And yet, despite the obvious breadth and complexity of her interest and knowledge, Austin's enduring reputation rests almost exclusively within the canon of nature writing. More to the point, of the more than 250 articles, essays, and op-ed pieces Austin published in her lifetime, not a single one concerns the theory, criticism, or practice of nature writing. In short, nature writing was not a subject about which she had much to say. The reason for this is quite simple: Austin never thought of herself as a nature writer. Considering that her 1903 masterpiece *The Land of Little Rain* has become a vital component of ecocriticism and the canon of American environmental literature, such an assertion may very well be moot. However, the definition of nature writing as Austin herself historically understood it is well worth attending to. Her work did not fit the generic definition as it was known in her lifetime, nor did she seek in any concerted way to align herself with the genre. A central purpose of this chapter will thus be to destabilize Austin's canonization as a nature writer and, subsequently, to suggest a revised framework for seeing and reading her work as that of a realist. The test case for this examination will be Austin's ostensibly realistic treatment of that most fundamental natural element of the western region from which she came, the one named in the very title of her first book, water. When we look at her treatment of this element in what has since become a hallmark of American nature writing—doing so, however, in the context of what she felt to be her cultural obligations as a writer—a very different author comes to light. Specifically, what in Austin's writings has thus far been viewed chiefly as the textual representation of an unalloyed nature will, upon closer examination, appear as but one element in her career-long commitment to a morally inflected cultural criticism.[10]

To gain, first, a sense of the means by which the non–nature writer Mary Austin has been effectively forgotten by the canonizers of American literary history who came after her, we need only begin with the ostensibly appreciative commentary of one of her closest friends and colleagues, Columbia University's Carl Van Doren. In his introduction to a 1950 commemorative reprint of *The Land of Little Rain,* which includes a great many Ansel Adams photographs of the Owens Valley,[11] Van Doren effectively sets Austin in the margins of the American literary canon:

> When, years ago, I wrote a study of her work which stressed the prophetic aspect of it, she smilingly complained that I had done her an injustice by calling her a seer without telling how good a cook she was. She did not lose the woman she was in the prophet she became—and might not become if she had found wifehood more abundant and motherhood less cruel. Much as she was admired and valued by men, she was distinctly a woman's woman. The men in her audiences listened to every word she said, but the women hung on her words, acknowledging her power while trying, I suppose, to guess her secret. (xi–xii)

Van Doren turns what had probably been a wry, ironic comment about culinary skill into a detrimental indicator of literary merit.[12] And his point is clear: his friend may have been the author of some fine books—"wells driven into America to bring up water for her countrymen" (xiv), he calls them—but it is as a woman and not as a writer that she is best remembered.

Not surprisingly, Austin was always keenly interested in the dynamics of gender and authorship. The concluding paragraph of "The Land," for instance, speculates, "If the desert were a woman, I know well what she would be like" (*Lost Borders* 160). In this respect, Austin's warning to "accept no *man's* statement" (emphasis added) may very well be an instance of her gender politics. Striking a similar note when she responds to a negative review of *The American Rhythm* by Lewis Mumford, Austin avers that

> I have unreservedly committed myself to the feminine approach. I express myself as freely and as definitely in my literary medium, as I do in my social life, as a woman. I have always believed that there is a distinctly feminine approach to intellectual problems and its recognitions is indispensible to intellectual wholeness. All that I have ever, as a feminist, protected against, is the prevailing notion that the feminine is necessarily an inferior approach.[13]

Thus, for much of her career Austin actively sought (and succeeded more often than not) to publish her work alongside that of such cultural critics as John Dewey, Carl Van Doren, and Van Wyck Brooks, to have her "feminine approach" be taken as seriously and be as widely considered as the points of view of her male colleagues. As Melody Graulich affirms, "Austin did not reject man's way of seeing but wanted society to have the benefit of both eyes" ("Afterword" 391). Austin playfully expresses this commitment to equal voice in a 1931 letter to her longtime friend Sinclair Lewis. In proposing that the two of them collaborate on a trilogy of novels about western water, Austin assures: "Dear friend, don't turn this aside because of a traditional objection to collaborating with a woman. I know I'm feminine, damnably feminine, and not ashamed of it, but I'm not ladyish. You can count on my behaving like a gentleman" (Pearce 142). Such a rich mix of gender tags strikes hard against the notion that any one person, male or female, is necessarily confined to any one specific role. At the very least, such passages indicate just how complex were Austin's understanding and awareness of the means by which gender (and the perception of it) could inflect authorship.

As numerous commentators have pointed out, writing about nature in America has frequently been one of the more severely gendered of literary productions.[14] Such was especially the case at the turn of the twentieth century, when Austin began her own writing career. It was at this point in history that a group of young women established the first Thoreau Society, another woman wrote the first doctoral dissertation on Thoreau (Buell, *Imagination* 45), and, on the other reverse side of the issue, President Theodore Roosevelt brought his advocacy of all things strenuous to bear on the "nature fakers" controversy.[15] However, while there is no doubt that a significant portion of Austin's work engages in what criticism now calls nature writing, Austin resisted this designation. In the only explicit mention of nature writing she ever published, a brief moment in her 1932 autobiography *Earth Horizon*, Austin complains that "when the Naturist reports upon himself, it is mistaken for poetizing" (188). The not-so-gender-neutral pronoun "himself" hints at Austin's understanding of just how bifurcated the field was in her time. As a woman writer and as a writer from the West, Austin continually fought against being doubly marginalized.[16] It should thus be reasonable to assume that Austin would wish to avoid being marginalized by the publishing industry on yet a third count. Indeed, as the following brief genealogy makes clear, Austin had very specific reasons for wanting to avoid being known as any specific sort of (mere) genre writer.

The category known as "nature writing" developed in almost perfect simultaneity with Austin's professional writing career. This is not to say that nature writing as an identifiable practice did not occur before this time—in addition to Thoreau, the names John Muir and Susan Fenimore Cooper no doubt also come to mind. Rather, "nature writing" developed as a genre both critically and culturally recognized *by name* in the very same years encompassed by Austin's national publication record, which roughly spans 1900 (her first *Atlantic Monthly* publication) to 1934 (her death). A 1902 *American Monthly Review of Reviews* essay by Francis W. Halsey on "The Rise of the Nature Writers" first sets the terms by which authors such as Muir, John Burroughs, John James Audubon, and Ernest Thompson Seton come to be recognized as comprising a specific and discrete genre. According to Halsey, the increased market proliferation of books on flowers, birds, and animals (Halsey's three categories of "Nature-books") owes itself to a shared ambition to provide "an authentic record of things known and seen,—things no one else had known so intimately, seen so accurately, and described so delightfully" (570). In Halsey's taxonomy, "Nature-books" stand unequivocally in direct opposition to fiction, and they do so by having responded to "the impulse which each year drives more and more city people to spend longer seasons in the country" (571). With the advent of middle-class ecotourism so too is a distinctive literary category born.

Four months after the publication of Halsey's survey, the definition of nature writing received an important gloss in Burroughs's "Real and Sham Natural History," published in the *Atlantic* in March 1903. As Halsey had observed, Burroughs was by this time both nature writing's most important progenitor (Thoreau notwithstanding) and its best current practitioner. In what proved to be the opening salvo of a heated, decade-long public debate about "nature fakers," Burroughs complains that a great deal of currently popular natural history writing contains "too much sentiment, too much literature" (299). Such writing is not "true to the facts" of nature, which one may gain only through a "deep and abiding love of Nature, and of power to paint her as she is" (303, 299). Irritated by an apparent lack of such love and power in the inventive and engaging (not to mention terrifically popular) animal stories by writers such as E. T. Seton, William J. Long, and Jack London, Burroughs laments that "fact and fiction are so deftly blended . . . that only a real woodsman can separate them" (301). He then offers himself as just such a qualified reader: "I can believe many things I have never seen or known. I discredit them [the 'sham' nature writers] because they are so widely at variance with all we know of wild creatures and their ways" (308). That is, Burroughs claims to know for certain that the "glaring counterfeit" animal stories that are his target do not accord with what he already knows to be true about nature. He confidently concludes: "There are many, very many, things in our own natural history that I do not know; I add a little to my knowledge of it every year" (308). By this formula, nature writing does provide an inquiry into the nonhuman world, but more importantly, it offers a means of testing and confirming what one already knows.

With the appearance in 1923 of Norman Foerster's *Nature in American Literature,* this budding genre assumed yet a further dimension of respectability, namely, that conferred by the academy of American literature taking shape at the same time.[17] At the very least, in becoming the subject of academic inquiry, nature writing gained another degree of cultural legitimacy. A professor of English at the University of North Carolina, Foerster frames his project as charting the "development of this naturalistic movement in American literature from Bryant to Whitman and the typical essayists of the present century." Echoing the generic claims made by Burroughs twenty years earlier, Foerster adds: "With only two or three exceptions, all of our major writers have displayed both a striking curiosity as to the facts of the external world—an intellectual conscience in seeking to know them with exactness—and an ardent emotional devotion to nature because of her beauty or divinity" (xiii). Seven years later, Henry Chester Tracy similarly claims that the nature writer is "an ardent lover and observer of the life out-of-doors, wholly and naïvely responsive to its lures, unhappy if long deprived of its contacts" (5). However, unlike Foerster, who attempts to connect the representation of nature in already canonical American texts to their "classical and Christian" antecedents, Tracy hopes to delineate an altogether "new literature" and demands, much as Halsey had done before him, the recognition of nature writing as a discrete and unique genre. Published in the highly significant year of 1930, which Kermit Vanderbilt has labeled "an annus mirabilis of American critical debate" (358), Tracy's *American Naturists* belongs squarely in the critical literature of a new academic category.[18] And while Tracy himself was not affiliated with a research institution (he taught at a private high school in Los Angeles), his book, with its inclusion of Austin in the roster, nevertheless helped establish an academic canon of nature writing that has carried largely untouched to the present.[19] Austin is by this time canonically isolated as a writer of nature appreciation texts, leaving the door wide open, as it were, for Van Doren to discount her largely for being a woman writer of only marginally valuable literature.[20]

Over the course of her career, Austin expressed many of the thematic and ethical concerns raised separately by Foerster, Tracy, and the "nature fakers" controversy, particularly with regard to the question of how one comes to know nature and how one might communicate and represent that knowledge. However, and this is the significant point, Austin never aligned herself with this ethos by claiming "nature writing" as the primary descriptor of her work. She never fully considered herself a part of this literary movement. Her specific reasons for doing so may be gleaned from two brief moments of reflection offered at the end of her career, the only times Austin ever wrote about her craft as nature writing (notably, only one of these ever made it into print). In the full passage from *Earth Horizon* cited earlier, Austin discusses the response of one attuned to nature. Describing the pleasures of peeking out over a garden fence at an uncultivated, "not utterly ruined" landscape, Austin writes:

> I am torn in my vitals. This is the way a Naturist is taken with the land, with the spirit trying to be evoked out of it. This is the authentic note of confession for which autobiographies are supposed to be written, for which they are quite certainly read. It is time somebody gave a true account. All the public expects of the experience of practicing Naturists is the appearance, the habits, the incidents

> of the wild; when the Naturist reports upon himself, it is mistaken for poetizing. (188)

Austin offers here what may be taken as a brief definition of nature writing that speaks directly to the criteria set forth by Halsey thirty years earlier: although her contemporaries understood nature writing as the mere reportage of "the appearances, the habits, the incidents of the wild," Austin would rather see it as an expression of the personal, visceral exchange possible between writer and subject. This may very well be a definition consistent with more recent assessments of Austin's inclusion in the canon.[21] But in 1932, and most certainly at the beginning of her career three decades earlier, Austin came across as uncomfortable with the generic category as it had been handed to her. She clearly preferred not to be dismissed for "poetizing" her material.

Austin's other commentary on nature writing comes in the form of letters she exchanged with Henry Tracy, who consulted with Austin while preparing the manuscript for *American Naturists*. In response to his initial query for guidance, she wrote back: "First of all, 'American Naturist' doesn't seem to me to be an appealing title, though I confess I cannot suggest anything better."[22] And in response to his question concerning her own impressions about her contribution to the field, she responded that her works on the Southwest

> have fairly cracked the shell of unfamiliarity of desert nature. I would be appalled at the number of young poets who have got themselves known by pharaphrasing [*sic*] one or another of my outdoor books in verse, if I did not know that it is frequently the business of writers to furnish the public with vocabularies in which new categories of nature and society may be discussed.
>
> Another thing that you can charge to me, and that is revealing and fixing, through my translations and expositions of Indian poetry, the primitive approach to nature, so that it can never again be misapprehended as it has been in the past.[23]

This letter shows Austin thinking of herself not as a cataloger of "the appearances, the habits, the incidents" of nature, as noted in the *Earth Horizon* definition, but rather as having contributed an enabling intelligence to the culture at large. She has (in her own opinion, to be sure) accurately explicated "the primitive approach," and she has produced a lexicon for the "nature and society" of the desert by which future writers and readers may know the region. Austin is not interested in "representing" nature. She is after something altogether different, something involving the communication of an acquired knowledge of which nature is only one small part: a specialized perspective applicable to a whole range of subjects.

In a series of notes on essay writing and form that Austin composed sometime after 1927, in preparation for an article or possibly a lecture, Austin argues that above all else the prospective essay writer must have what she calls "a privileged point of view."[24] Situating her comments specifically in relation to what she calls "the essay of opinion," a form that requires "the creative thinker to place his conclusions at the service of the public," Austin declares that in fact she finds it "impossible to think of the essay as a distinct literary form, irrespective of the subject treated. . . . I can not imagine such a thing as making special excursions after 'material,' nor do I believe that any one of the notable essayists of our time does so." Identifying Lytton Strachey and Bertrand Russell as being among the form's best practitioners, Austin posits that "such men concern themselves with special study in fields for which they are especially equipped, and they write as they think." Form, in other words, arises directly out of content, and content in turn derives from the authority of a qualified essayist who "know[s] more than is generally known by readers on that subject." Thus, according to Austin, the potential essayist should "choose then, that point from which his own intellectual [*sic*] is the widest, and remain there consistently throughout his exposition. Leave it to other essayists from other points of privilege to complete the survey."

Austin identifies her own point of privilege as "the origins of culture," the understanding of which requires "that I must play a creative part in modern culture, not only at home but in as many contemporary societies as possible." This far-reaching goal of Austin's would certainly explain her proclivity for producing opinion pieces on the many subjects she engages over her thirty-two years as professional writer and commentator, as it would explain her concept of the naturist as being a contributor to the *cultural* understanding of a region (e.g., her letter to Tracy). Considering Austin finally as a writer of this ilk, it is safe to conclude that she did not, in the main, think of herself as a practicing nature writer. Rather, as only a very small number of scholars outside of Austin studies have come to realize, she may very well be labeled an early-twentieth-century cultural critic. But one might ask, does such a recognition necessarily diminish the force of Austin's writing about nature? Certainly not. It does, however, open up the possibility of seeing in her work elements of a cultural critique heretofore not fully recognized.

Criticism and Water

About no subject was Mary Austin more knowledgeable than western water resource issues. A resident of California's Owens Valley at a time when the city of Los Angeles managed to appropriate the lion's share of the valley's water resources, Austin learned firsthand of the social and cultural dimensions of this particular aspect of nature. But to write about water in a land of little rain was not necessarily to write about nature. Notably, in revising the first draft of her autobiography, Austin removed a significant number of passages in which she further discussed her ideas on the role of the naturist. As Rae Ballard has shown in her comparative study of the various manuscript drafts of *Earth Horizon,* every passage on nature writing that Austin deleted before publication had initially been placed in sections of the book in which she also discussed her experience in the Owens Valley (135–36). In doing so, Austin avoids drawing a connection between water issues and nature writing, preferring to explicate the former at the expense of the latter. Writing about water, for Austin, is not entirely a matter of writing about nature, and her reasons for thinking so, beyond the literary marketplace issues raised in the section above, may be adduced from her responses to what has been called the Owens Valley water grab, which presented Austin with an epistemological problem.

With the passage of the Newlands Reclamation Act in 1902, the Department of the Interior began the search for semi-arid western lands to "reclaim," to render fit for homesteading and agricultural enterprise. And one of the very first designated projects was to be established in the Owens Valley. With the federally funded construction of a reservoir and canal system, an irrigation system could be put in place that would transform the already productive valley into one of the West's most lucrative agricultural centers.[25] The U.S. Forest Service's chief engineer in California, J. B. Lippincott, began surveying in the valley as early as the spring of 1903, before the Reclamation Service had even become a fully operational government agency (Kahrl 40; Reisner 62). One year later, in the fall of 1904 and less than a year after the publication of Austin's first book, two Los Angeles associates of Lippincott's also paid a visit to the valley (Lippincott was at the time on the payroll of both the federal government and the city of Los Angeles). Fred Eaton, a former mayor of Los Angeles, and William Mulholland, chief engineer of the City Water Company, took a leisurely buckboard ride from the city through the desert to the valley. Rumor has it that the Los Angeles Aqueduct they would soon build was surveyed and laid out along the trail of discarded whiskey bottles that marked their initial foray into the valley. By the spring of 1906, after a series of mostly legal but certainly unethical arrangements between Los Angeles and the Reclamation Service, the greater portion of the Owens River was not being used on irrigable land in the valley but rather was being held in reserve while Los Angeles built its 250-mile aqueduct. By 1906 the water of the Owens River was well on its way to fulfilling its "proper destiny" in an irrigation ditch connected to Los Angeles, and in April of 1906 so too did a disappointed and frustrated Mary Austin leave.[26] In her autobiography Austin refers to this period as one beset by endless "lies and misrepresentations" (*Earth Horizon* 308); she never came back to the valley.

However, Austin did make at least one concerted effort to address the situation, with an essay that may very well be considered her first foray into essay-oriented cultural criticism. On 3 September 1905 she published in the *San Francisco Chronicle* an admonitory op-ed article simply titled "The Owens River Water Project," a document familiar to historians of western water but largely unknown to scholars of Austin's literature. She begins this piece by suggesting that Los Angeles's attempt to siphon away the Owens River raises the more fundamental question of "how far it is well to destroy the agricultural interests of the commonwealth to the advantage of the vast aggregations of cities" (19). After presenting her version of the Owens Valley story, a version in which the Bureau of Reclamation duplicitously helps Los Angeles officials exaggerate their water needs and thus justify appropriating as much water as the Owens River could provide, Austin broadens the scope of the issue to suggest that "every considerable city in the State is or is about to be confronted by a water problem. . . . [T]heir own water problems are likely to be shaped by it [the Owens Valley situation] more or less" (19). Cautioning the voters of Los Angeles, who on 30 August (the date given in Austin's byline) are little more than a week away from voting on an unprecedented $23 million bond measure to pay for the aqueduct, Austin posits that a city capable of deceiving the farmers and ranchers of Inyo County out of their water access might be equally capable of putting one over on its own residents. And referring at the end of the piece to Mulholland's back-room collusion with Lippincott and the Bureau of Reclamation, Austin concludes, "In a republic[,] government is not supposed to have a private ear" (19). At stake for Austin, then, is nothing less than fair and democratic state governance.

With respect to the regional cultures and industries that make up Austin's California, the Owens Valley situation also threatens to rid the land of little rain of a vital and productive community. Alluding in her conclusion to her initial question about the virtues of destroying agriculture in favor of a faraway city's need, Austin asks again, "But what is to be gained by the commonwealth if it robs Peter to pay Paul?"[27] For every one of the city's material gains there will be, according to Austin, a corresponding and irrevocable loss to the society and culture of the rural region from which the water is taken. This is finally the thesis point Austin develops for her San Francisco readers:

> The entire success of the Los Angeles plan means the entire destruction of the improvements of Inyo, the return of great acreage of orchard and alfalfa to desertness, the wiping out of the best of the few remaining chances for people of limited means to obtain Government land, the retarding of the development of the rich mineral districts of Tonopah and Bullfrog by destroying their only available base of agricultural supplies; in short, it means that whatever Los Angeles gains is lost to the State otherwise.

Austin sees in the Owens situation a harbinger of the water battles that every California city would eventually have to fight, and so her warning is finally not so much for the people in Los Angeles but rather for the metropolis to the north. The battle of Owens Valley/Los Angeles is perhaps lost, but San Francisco, at work during this time on plans to dam Hetch Hetchy Valley just north of Yosemite National Park, may yet be stopped from making the same mistake of depleting a cultural resource in favor of a material one.[28]

Austin does however briefly express the hope that events may yet turn in favor of the valley. Suggesting that if Los Angeles had come "openly, with fair-mindedness" to negotiate for water, there would be plenty to suit the needs of both the city and the valley, Austin offers the confidence of personal knowledge: "On my own acquaintance with the sources of

Cottonwood creek, I venture to assert that enough good water could be developed." Similarly, she argues for maintaining the spirit of the federal government's intentions in the valley when she comments that "everybody who has ever read the [Newlands] reclamation act *knows* that it was instituted not to make rich cities, but to provide homes for the people on otherwise unreclaimed land" (emphasis added). And Austin's sense of moral propriety emerges when she explains her motive for publishing the essay in San Francisco instead of in Los Angeles: "Perhaps it is not worth while, in their present uninformed condition, raising the question of civic morals with the people of Los Angeles, but it is worth while for other cities to consider" the case. The "mere recorder who knows best" from "Jimville" has now, in an early venture into cultural criticism, invoked the Howellsian realist's dual tenets of knowledge and moral propriety.

When Austin decides to write *The Ford* a decade later, she not only draws on what she knows of this aspect of California's resource history but also works the issue of knowledge into the very texture of the novel's narration. Published in 1917, *The Ford* presents a thinly veiled fictional account of the Owens Valley water situation. It tells the story of a foothills farming and ranching community that successfully fights off an attempt by the city of San Francisco to appropriate its water rights and dam the "Arroyo Verde" river on which much of the local economy and culture depends. Austin also depicts a fictionalized rendition of the Bakersfield, California, oil boom, as an early dramatic set piece that foreshadows the more pressing water battles that occupy the greater part of the plot. As such, *The Ford* quite plainly aligns itself with the tradition of resource-based claims to realism. But more importantly, it shows Austin's continuing conviction that western water resources signify not questions of nature but rather questions of knowledge and representation.

At the very end of *The Ford*, the character of Rickart, a rancher turned venture capitalist who spearheads the attempt to dam the "Tierra Longa" valley and divert its water, informs Kenneth Brent, Austin's inexperienced, naive main character and Rickart's chief opposition in the water deal, that there is oil under Brent's land. Stunned that his opponent in the water struggle had all along known more about his land than he himself could have known, Brent arrives at an epiphany of sorts about how the resource business is conducted. As Austin's narrator explains, "The key to the Old Man's success was, after all, knowledge, knowledge of land and minerals, knowledge of law, and, more than everything else, knowledge of men" (437). Similarly, Austin paints Brent's journey in the novel as one of self-discovery, as a journey toward self-knowledge. About Brent's future she at one point notes, "He could never reason the thing out, but all at once he would Know" (204); about his ability to participate in San Francisco Bohemian coffeehouse debates she writes, "There was a great deal, Kenneth felt, that could have been said to this [capitalism's evils], but he did not know enough to say it" (234); and about his adolescent responses to women she explains, "Beyond being pleasantly aware of the proximity of the fair and unmated, young Brent knew very little of women" (182). Later in the story, key events hinge on the actions of Brent's sister Anne, who becomes a shrewd and successful real estate speculator and who trumps San Francisco's water ambitions through an almost prescient understanding of Rickart's plans. After reading about "some unconsidered source" for future water in a San Francisco newspaper, Anne "could never really say whether or not her conscious intelligence took hold of the possibility that this slightly indicated source might be the waters of the Arroyo Verde, but, obeying some obscure impulse, Anne had blue-penciled the paragraph" (359). Anne's intuitive guess about the eventual waterway proves to be correct, and when she thwarts Rickart by proactively securing on behalf of the valley's residents crucial water rights, her brother can only exclaim, "Oh Anne! If I had only known . . . " (424; ellipse in original).

Long on polemics but short on the subtle, rhythmic language that marks *The Land of Little Rain,* Austin's earlier treatment of Owens Valley water, *The Ford* is largely a political novel, as Melody Graulich has aptly described it.[29] Indeed, with respect to subtlety of theme, *The Ford* is almost unnecessarily direct and repetitious. In almost every chapter (of which there are twenty-five) the reader is explicitly told that "knowledge" is somehow at issue. For reasons such as these, Henry Nash Smith did not much care for the novel's execution as fiction, despite his admiration for the ideas with which it wrestles. *The Ford,* Smith writes, offers an "analysis . . . of the openly Scythian big business of the beginning to the century [in California], but the characters suffer because of the author's interests in social forces. . . . She is too much interested in ideas to be able to give herself up to the almost a-moral mirror-passion of the great dramatist or novelist" ("Feel" 20). But as demonstrated earlier, Austin's concept of the opinionated writer is very much tied to a moral approach to representation. Indeed, it is precisely her moral vision that enables her to posit the figurative relationship between water and knowledge. At one point early in the novel, a young Kenneth overhears his parents fighting over the family's lack of money and his father's inability to get his foot in the door of any sort of lucrative land deal: "Sentences like these [his mother used] ran on and mingled in the boy's mind with the tinkle of water dropping from the flume and the riffle of the wind across the chaparral by which the Torr' seemed to breathe. In that impressionable hour between day and dark, the two streams sunk and watered the roots of being" (54). Indebted to William James's notion of a "stream of consciousness" perhaps more literally than her contemporary modernist writers were, Austin concisely and figuratively offers a vision of the means by which land and consciousness become one.[30] As a result of heeding his particular stream of consciousness, young Kenneth Brent will eventually find the moral strength to resist both a law career in San Francisco and, with his sister's knowledge, that city's attempts to co-opt the water. In writing *The Ford* Austin was keenly concerned with wrapping the problem of knowledge within the representation of a struggle for natural resources in general and for water in particular.

But why so insistent? Why should a novel about the Owens Valley water grab focus so assiduously on the necessity of acquiring proper knowledge? At one point Austin addresses the problem of how certain pervasive representations of the West have given over to a false knowledge about the region. Specifically, she holds up to ridicule a consumptive New York playwright and his sister who both insist on seeing the West solely "in the key of Owen Wister and the Sunday Supplements" (242). Similarly, in another instance Austin describes a rabble-rousing local newspaper editorial as containing "the usual veiled allusion to the local octopus" (110). Coupled with the novel's across-the-range transposition of Owens events, this reference suggests that Austin hopes with her novel to augment Frank Norris's *The Octopus* (1901), a similar tale in which far-off big city interests run roughshod over the lives, property, and resource claims of agricultural workers at the southern end of the San Joaquin Valley. Whereas Norris had portrayed the struggle between wheat ranchers and the railroad taking place in the shadow, as it were, of an irrigation ditch, Austin renders the context of water her most explicit motivator of the plot. By invoking the "Sunday Supplements" and their dime-novel rendition of regional characteristics, by transposing the salient details of the Owens Valley conflict into the southern reaches of the San Joaquin, and by including Hetch Hetchy and the Bakersfield oil boom as parts of the plot, Austin appears once again keenly interested in revising, as she had sought to do with "Jimville," the received literary history of the region.[31]

Then again, Austin may simply have been giving voice to a frustrated wish to recover a landscape already lost, a nostalgia born of her encounter with historical forces that are anything but literary. Such is the tenor of David Wyatt's dismissive appraisal of *The Ford:* "Austin was unable to relinquish in imagination what she had already lost in fact. In this undoing of history, the people win. . . . *The Ford* becomes a fantasy of redemption through real estate" (*Fall into Eden* 92). That is, since the Owens Valley could not be saved from the rapacious city of Los Angeles, Austin could at least save a fictionalized version of it from the city of San Francisco. Ironically enough, Wyatt has in a more recent book offered a means by which to reconsider this assessment, although he does so not by reevaluating his position on Austin's novel (he never even mentions it) but rather by trying to account for the many-storied, contradictory, and often confusing historical accounts of the Owens Valley events. In *Five Fires* (1997), he concludes that "the refusal of that history to yield up a master narrative or even verifiable evidence about human acts and intentions raises questions about how much we can come to know about the past" (140–41). Perhaps unaware of the ramifications for his own earlier dismissal of *The Ford,* Wyatt in his assessment of the frustration inherent in the Owens story confirms the very problem with which Austin wrestled. That Austin eventually expresses this problem by combining so overtly the representation of water with a thematics exploring the ramifications of adequate knowledge suggests that she saw the two issues as being very much related.[32]

Before leaving the Owens Valley for good in 1906, Austin attempted at least twice to combat the "lies and misrepresentations" that were giving shape to the growing crisis of appropriation. The first effort was her aforementioned article for the *San Francisco Chronicle*. The evidence for Austin's other attempt, however, is largely anecdotal, reported by Helen MacKnight Doyle, Austin's friend and physician in the Owens Valley town of Lone Pine and one of her first biographers. In her book *Mary Austin, Woman of Genius* (1939), Doyle tells how at the height of the struggle, Austin made a special journey to Los Angeles: "She interviewed the most powerful of the agents of Los Angeles. After that interview he said, 'By God, that woman is the only one who has brains enough to see where this thing is going!' " (218). Presumably an interview with William Mulholland, who by most accounts of the Owens water deal certainly qualifies as "the most powerful of the agents," this tempting tale unfortunately lacks outside confirmation. The want of corroborating evidence is particularly noteworthy since Doyle purports to know that Mulholland (if it was really he) had made this assessment *after* Austin left the office—who was there to record the comment?[33] Whether true or not, however, Doyle's tale shows that even in apocryphal anecdote, the connection between water and knowledge adheres to Austin, a connection that was central to her concept of and approach to the work of a writer.

In the 1920s Austin became deeply involved once again in a controversial western water issue, namely, the building of Boulder (now Hoover) Dam on the Colorado River near Las Vegas and, subsequently, the over-apportioning of the Colorado's water to meet the agricultural needs of seven different states. Reflecting on her own involvement in the issue, Austin writes in her autobiography:

> My Governor appointed me a delegate to the Seven States Conference. I said what I had to say, being profoundly convinced against it [the dam]; but I discovered there is little one can say against an enterprise that will not come to the proof for perhaps fifty years. The other New Mexican delegates were for it, and the Conference was so heavily weighted by Los Angeles that there seemed nothing to say, in any case. None of us will live to see that *débâcle*. I withdrew from the Conference, although not from foresight and opposition. If I am mistaken in what is to eventuate, it will be the first time my prophetic gift has failed me. I never went back to Inyo. The city of Los Angeles bought the towns there, the house I built. The place is given over to desolation. (*Earth Horizon* 362–63)

Note the apparent non sequitur at the end of this passage. In the midst of an explanation of her involvement in the negotiations over the allocation of the Colorado, Austin connects once again with the Owens Valley. In claiming that the other delegates to the Seven States Conference gave little or no credence to her "privileged point of view" regarding the long-term *structural* ramifications of building a dam without consideration of local *culture,* Austin is prompted to recall similarly that the culture of Inyo was never to be the same after Los Angeles had taken the water. To the very end of her career Austin cared about the Owens Valley as the signal event in her perceived relationship between knowledge—

knowing "what is best for you," "a privileged point of view," and so forth —and western water.

This point of view finally holds throughout Austin's desert narratives, and it represents a key point on which she had perhaps hoped to cap her long and wide-ranging career.[34] As she worked on her autobiography in the early part of 1931, she also took a moment to pitch to her friend Sinclair Lewis what she called her "River idea," in the letter in which she promised to behave "like a gentleman" (Pearce 141). Hoping to convey to Lewis the scale of her experience with western water issues, Austin explains:

> I know everything that needs to be known: How the Indians learned irrigation and taught it to the Whites; how the cities "framed" the farmers and stole the river for the use of the realtors, all the bitterness and greed; how three lives and fortunes are sacrificed to every title to irrigated lands. I was appointed to the Seven States Conference on the Colorado. I know all about the corruption both commercial and political that goes to that business. I lived through the Owens River theft and know why the Watterson brothers still languish in jail. I know why the San Francisquite Dam went down— I think I know what threatens in Boulder Dam. (Pearce 142)

Austin thus suggests that the two novelists combine the points of view for which each has the privilege of special knowledge: "We might pool our separate knowledges in a work of fiction around the destiny of one of those rivers which have meant so much to the development of the west" (Pearce 142). Austin would contribute her knowledge of the water, of course, including what she terms her "intensive" knowledge of American life and culture in the Southwest. Lewis, for his part, would provide his "extensive . . . knowledge of the country" and assist Austin in avoiding a pitfall she had encountered in writing her Owens Valley novel, *The Ford,* fifteen years earlier: she tells him, "Every little while my material disappeared into the intricacies of male life beyond my capacity to follow it." Austin concludes her offer by saying: "I want to see these things told in imperishable form as you can do it, and as I can't alone. If you feel we can't do it together, then buy my knowledge and do the books for yourself. Nobody knows this as I do. In twenty more years it will be impossible for anybody to know it as directly and completely, and in two or three hundred years more such a book as you could write will be pertinent and readable" (Pearce 142). Knowledge is the key to this issue, so much so that Austin proffers it as a material resource in and of itself, as something Lewis could in fact "buy" from her. Moreover, that Austin would seek to tie her fortunes to a writer whom the Nobel Commission praised in 1930 for the brutal realism of his satire clearly suggests that Austin saw realistic fiction as a means well suited to the expression of one's "privileged point of view" concerning western water.

Simply put, Austin's understanding of realistic representation as a problem of knowledge arises directly out of her consideration of issues connected to water resources. Water sets the terms for Austin's thinking about realism. Viewed in this context, then, a context in which the author resists the genre label of "nature writer" and sees the representation of water issues as a cultural problem, a title such as *The Land of Little Rain* suggests an enterprise in realism that bears only provisionally on the representation of nature as nature. That Austin's first book predates the "Owens Valley theft" by several years matters very little. As the following analysis of a rarely interpreted but—in the light of Austin's commitment to epistemological questions—crucial segment of *The Land of Little Rain* will demonstrate, Austin's apperception of a relationship between water issues and questions of knowing is present from the start. By thus using the rest of Austin's career to challenge the prevailing critical opinion of her first, and in many regards most complex, book, we finally see that her "privileged point of view" regarding desert spaces and those who inhabit them prompted her not to represent "the appearances, the habits, the incidents of the wild" but rather to interrogate their human and social dimension.

"Other Water Borders"

As noted above, Austin's choice of title for her first book clearly underscores the importance of water to the region. As the reader slowly discovers, the near-litotes of "little rain" does more than just signal an awareness of aridity as the defining environmental condition; it indicates the resource by which Austin examines the epistemological and ontological bases of the desert's social fabric. Water, it can be said, figures virtually everywhere in this book. For example, in one particularly relevant instance, the three consecutive essays of chapters 10 through 12, Austin figuratively follows the Sierra snow from high up in the range to its eventual dispersal as irrigation water. Chapter 10, "The Streets of the Mountains," begins its narration among the snowy peaks of the high Sierra and explores the narrow and precipitous canyons that high alpine, seasonal streams have carved into the hills. Notably, while the chapter's topic is ostensibly free-running and natural, Austin establishes through her "street" metaphor the eventual observation that the snows will ultimately meet their destiny in a human context. Chapter 11, entitled "Water Borders," next follows the snowmelt as it courses through meadows and lakes on its way into and through the foothills. Drawing on Thoreau and hinting at the question of knowledge, she notes: "The lake is the eye of the mountain, jade green, placid, unwinking, also unfathomable. Whatever goes on under the high and stony brows is guessed at" (114). Finally, in chapter 12, an essay entitled "Other Water Borders," what began in "the Sierras of the Snows" (103) finishes its journey in the irrigation ditches of the Owens Valley. And it is here that Austin's interest in explicating the problem of knowing becomes most explicit.

Austin begins "Other Water Borders" by expressing what would become one of the twentieth century's keynote assertions about life in the American West: "It is the proper destiny of every considerable stream in the west to become an irrigating ditch. It would seem the streams are willing" (123). As Austin formulates the issue, the fate of water is ultimately and irrevocably linked to the will and thirst of human communal activity.[35] Austin adds a note of ironic doubt by suggesting that any apparent accord between the water's will and the irrigator's desire merely "seem[s]" to be the case, that water's complicity in human endeavors may very well be less than voluntary. In the Owens Valley, what little rain does fall is irreversibly destined for the "irrigating ditch," the will of water notwithstanding. This recognition prompts Austin to begin the second paragraph of this same chapter with a portrait of the determined but murderous Amos Judson, who jealously hoards water from the communal irrigation ditch by perpetually sitting "asquat on the headgate with his gun" (123). According to Austin, Judson, after more than a decade of driving away competitors such as the Montañas and the Clarks, is finally forced into a water-sharing compromise by Frau Diedrick, who appropriates Amos's seat early one morning and protects *her* claim to irrigation water with "a long-handled shovel across her lap" (124)

Austin's thumbnail sketch of neighborly aggression and eventual compromise is indicative of the fundamental cultural role played by water, of which Austin is keenly aware: turned into canals by and for humans, the resource reciprocally operates as the catalyst by which human social behavior is determined. In other words, while human choice ostensibly governs the fate of water, water's presence consigns humans to their own fated behavior. Austin thus refers equally to water and human when she observes that affairs at the Judson headgate are marked by "the repose of the completely accepted instinct" (124). Echoing an almost identical passage from her chapter on Jimville, a relic mining town, Austin subtly suggests that the thing known as "instinct," far from being a governing force of nature, is in fact the *result* of the dynamic played out between a community and its resource of choice. Indeed, one of Austin's stated ambitions in this chapter is to comment on what she alternately calls the "Homeric" and "squalid" history quality of the valley's "water-right difficulties." She writes: "Unless you have known them you cannot very well know what the water thinks as it slips past the gardens in the long slow sweeps of the canal" (124). To know about the Owens Valley's "water-right difficulties" is to know what the water thinks—an ambitious goal, to say the least, but also a goal indicative of the extent to which the sight of an irrigation canal inspires in Austin the desire to know something, anything, for certain.

However, such absolute confidence ultimately eludes her. After her opening discussion of the Judson feud history, Austin moves to an extensive account of the many flora to be found along the sides of irrigation ditches. Wondering how it is that certain herbs and plants come to be recognized for their medicinal value, she asks:

> It seems the secrets of plant powers and influences yield themselves most readily to primitive peoples, at least one never hears of the knowledge coming from any other source. The Indian never concerns himself, as the botanist and the poet, with the plant's appearances and relations, but with what it can do for him. It can do much, but how do you suppose he finds it out; what instincts or accidents guide him? How does a cat know when to eat catnip? Why do western bred cattle avoid loco weed, and strangers eat it and go mad? One might imagine that in a time of famine the Paiutes digged [*sic*] wild parsnip in meadow corners and died from eating it, and so learned to produce death swiftly and at will. But how did they learn, repenting in the last agony, that animal fat is the best antidote for its virulence; and who taught them that the essence of

joint pine (*Ephedra nevadensis*), which looks to have no juice in it of any sort, is efficacious in stomachic disorders? (126–27)

Clearly Austin wishes to differentiate between the more familiar Eurocentric forms of knowledge—those of the botanist and the poet, which are further suggested by the inclusion of the Latinate classification of the joint pine—and those gleaned from the establishment of a palpable communion with the natural environment (the troubling conceit by which Austin links Paiutes to cats and cows notwithstanding). Austin even admits to her own limitations when she describes the moment she "came first upon a wet meadow of *yerba mensa,* not knowing its name or use. . . . A little touch, a hint, a word, and I should have known what use to put them to. So I felt, unwilling to leave it until we had come to an understanding." Although she eventually learns of this plant's utility, such understanding never comes to Austin by way of direct communication with the plant. Rather, only after she sees "Señora Romero make a poultice of it for my burned hand" does she discover the secrets of the *yerba mensa* (127).

Considered as a whole, *The Land of Little Rain* stands in many respects as a meditation on knowledge. In her preface to the book, Austin announces: "For if I love a lake known by the name of the man who discovered it, which endears itself by reason of the close-locked pines it nourishes about its borders, you may look in my account to find it so described. But if the Indians have been there before me, you shall have their name, which is always beautifully fit and does not originate in the poor human desire for perpetuity" (3). And while she cautions the reader that genuine knowledge about "the heart and core" of a place is "not to be come at in a month's vacation," she nevertheless offers her home as a place where the passerby may stop to pick up valuable and interesting information: "But if ever you come beyond the borders as far as the town that lies in a hill dimple at the foot of Kearsarge, never leave it until you have knocked at the door of the brown house under the willow-tree at the end of the village street, and there you shall have such news of the land, of its trails and what is astir in them, as one lover of it can give to another" (4).[36] By emphasizing place-naming conventions, learning through immersion, and the value of word-of-mouth information, Austin sets the tone for a series of essays that will explore the various means—empirical, historical, mythological, mystical—by which one may arrive at familiarity with or knowledge about a particular environment. Returning thus to the example of "Other Water Borders," the possibility for such knowledge is directly tied to one's engagement with water not as nature but as a natural resource—the primary manner through which most westerners come by this particular aspect of the natural environment. Austin's final point in the chapter is to mention the many birds that nest in the shallows of the tulares, those marshy, reedy spots that serve as the "last and inevitable resort of overflow waters" (128). Circling back to the subject of water, Austin concludes the chapter by admitting that "one wishes for, but gets no nearer speech from those the reedy fens have swallowed up. What they do there, how fare, what find, is the secret of the tulares" (130). Some places and plants, it seems, may never yield to human understanding.

A contemplation of what presumably can and cannot be known in living and observing the life of the irrigation ditch, the slightly anomalous "Other Water Borders" chapter of *The Land of Little Rain* actually makes explicit what is otherwise implicit in the rest of the book: knowing about a natural environment is more a matter of knowing how humans situate themselves on the land than it is one of cataloging the biota. To be sure, this distinction accords well with the defining characteristics of "an environmentally oriented work" as outlined by Lawrence Buell: "The nonhuman environment is present not merely as a framing device but as a presence that begins to suggest that human history is implicated in natural history," and "Human accountability to the environment is part of the text's ethical orientation" (*Imagination* 7). These criteria describe Austin's project quite accurately. But the point here is that by juxtaposing Austin's work with a contemporaneously burgeoning popular and academic subgenre of literary nonfiction, and by understanding the manner in which Austin saw her writing as a contribution to the epistemological concerns of her day, we see that Buell's definition functions retroactively: it construes as nature writing that which Austin saw as a culturally engaged, realistically motivated criticism.

Historically and contextually speaking, Austin is at her most interesting as an essayist and cultural critic who wrote not of nature but rather of community. Adopting such a perspective has the potential to integrate her first and best book, *The Land of Little Rain,* more fully into the larger context of a career devoted to the social novel and the question of cultural production. As far as Austin is concerned, the genre of nature writing represents but one element in the interrogation and explication of the connection between people and environment. Thus does she differ significantly from the self-proclaimed nature writers of her time. Buoyed by academic recognition, the definition of nature writing advanced by Burroughs during the "nature fakers" debate, while motivated by the potential knowability of nature, amounts to little more than the (re)presentation of what one already knows of "the appearances, the habits, the incidents of the wild." In contrast, Austin's interest in the land of little rain is social and cultural. Henry Nash Smith, for one, recognized this difference. Commenting in 1931 that recent academic opinion had begun to lump Austin together with "Thoreau, Muir, Burroughs," Smith suggests instead that "between Mary Austin and any of these there is this important difference, that her interest in the environment . . . is, in the real sense, ethical, and thus political. She is seeking not a retreat from men, cities, and society, but a real avenue of approach to them" ("Feel" 23). That Smith appears never again to mention Austin in his long and distinguished career, with its turn to Twain studies and the analysis of (largely male-based) myths of landscape and nationhood found in *Virgin Land* (1950), is all the more evidence that the perduring canonical association of Austin with a marginalized nature writing had come to seem inevitable, however wrong it may be.

And what of realism as a genre form? In a 1932 essay entitled "Regionalism in American Fiction," Austin writes: "Art, considered as the expression of any people as a whole, is the response they make in various mediums to the impact that the totality of their experience makes upon them, and there is no sort of experience that works so constantly and subtly upon man as his regional environment" (97). Here she quite straightforwardly offers a definition of culture, literature, and society in interaction that derives from her education at the hands of the Southwest's water controversies. Howells, she writes in this essay, is not a regionalist—as a proponent of canonical realism, of course, he would be the first to concur. However, Austin continues: "But it has always seemed to me that Howells was the first, and the most eminent, of the American novelists responsible for the thinning out of American fiction by a deliberate choice of the most usual, the most widely distributed of American story incidents, rather than the most intensively experienced. Between Howells and Sinclair Lewis we have the whole history of that excursion of the American novelist away from the soil" (101–2). Later in the essay Austin confers the title of "realists" on those who favor the tendency to be regionally specific (103), thus turning the definitional table on the canon of American realism. According to Austin at the end of her career, realism may very well be ethically inflected, but it should first and foremost be literature that pays attention to the particulars of place. In striving for "the most widely distributed" stories, the writings of Howells and also of Lewis thus signify the beginnings of a move *away* from realism, a move Austin herself hopes to counter.

Admittedly, this closing example is more suggestive than comprehensive, yet the implication is finally this: beginning her career as something of a self-styled Howellsian critic, Austin very rapidly adapts the tenets of realism to the explication of the cultural dimension of water, which in turn provides for a theory of literary realism that is largely antithetical to that of Howells. Beginning with a critique of "romance" ideality and its preference for typology, Howells developed an argument about realism that relied on the moral imperative to tell properly all that is known about "the simple, the natural, and the honest." Austin, on the other hand, finds that determining what is simple and what is natural is not always so easy. Driven to epistemological considerations more by the experience of resource water than by any other interaction with the natural world around her, especially in the instance of the water ditch, Austin finds that the ability to know is greatly limited. Such a lack of full knowledge, it would seem, comes part and parcel with living on the land. A visitor to Austin's "brown house under the willow-tree at the end of the village street" would receive not only valuable information but also the proper, informed instruction on that which cannot be conveyed. Taken as a "realist's" approach to writing, this dual concern for properly useful knowledge and for the moral discernment required to process and represent that knowledge configures realism as epistemological inquiry.

6

Hard-Boiled Nature

California, Detective Fiction, and the Limits of Representation

In at least one respect, W. D. Howells became by the 1930s what "Bret Harte" had come to stand for in the last decades of the nineteenth century: a mark of what not to do as a writer, particularly if one feels somehow obligated to render accurate and real-seeming representations of the worlds that novel-reading Americans had come to know. Sinclair Lewis famously denounced an overly genteel Howells in his 1930 Nobel Prize acceptance speech. Mary Austin developed a western approach to realism that had been Howellsian in genesis but which ultimately became skeptical of the representability of nature that was implicit in the dictum to write about "the simple, the natural, the honest." And when Erle Stanley Gardner, the author of dozens of mystery stories and novels, complained to Raymond Chandler that "as literature my stuff still stinks," Chandler defended the integrity of his friend's fiction by sneering, "Who says so—William Dean Howells?" (Chandler, *Selected Letters* 70). That a genre writer remembered for his highly stylized, noir-ish explorations of the underbelly of Los Angeles crime should (in 1946) even be thinking of Howells might seem strange, especially considering that Chandler's point is that detective fiction should not be held to the outdated standard of excellence represented by the genteel and wordy realism of another era.[1]

Yet in Chandler's invocation of Howells as a negative example there is nevertheless the hint that the *idea* of realism still matters, in that Chandler favors Gardner's detective novels partly for the believable representation of the character Perry Mason. In this regard, both Gardner's insecurity and Chandler's assurance of quality rely on the extensive association that detective fiction has with the representation of the real, with literary realism. As Dennis Porter concisely sums up the generic roots of the detective story from Arthur Conan Doyle to Agatha Christie and from Mickey Spillane to Sue Grafton, maintaining representational fidelity to a known reality has always been a part of the detective genre project: "Although at its outer limits the genre overlaps with the gothic novel and science fiction, on the one hand, and the novel of manners, on the other, mainstream detective fiction respects the conventions of the realist tradition. . . . Further, detective stories present themselves to their readers as substitute worlds or mirrors that reflect directly the reality beyond" (115). Similarly, D. A. Miller's *The Novel and the Police,* a Foucauldian study of panoptic surveillance in the British Victorian novel, also finds formal and ideological correlations between the so-called realism of the nineteenth century and fictions involving the detection of crime. And most recently, R. Gordon Kelly's detailed analysis of current book reviews and internet-based electronic discussion lists has shown that the idea of realism continues to adhere among those who read detective stories: " 'Realistic' . . . is the readers' term of choice. . . . [T]here is no term of higher praise, and few come close to matching it for evaluative power" (169). Although not descriptive of the texts themselves (Kelly focuses instead on the analytical vocabulary of contemporary readers), Kelly's research nevertheless demonstrates that the idea of "realism" is a primary consideration in how readers approach and consume detective fiction. As will be shown below, both Chandler and his pioneering predecessor Dashiell Hammett were very much this sort of reader.

Noted with even less frequency, however, is the hard-boiled novel's specific provenance as an exercise in literary realism.[2] Indeed, whenever realism is discussed in relation to hard-boiled fiction, the former is invoked largely for the sake of contrast. Joan Copjec's Lacanian reading of film noir, for instance, which relies on and augments Miller's arguments, posits that the hard-boiled novel represents a very specific departure from turn-of-the-century realism. According to Copjec, whereas the realistic text is marked by "intersubjective network[s] of perceptions," detective fiction stresses the extent to which a person may be counted as such only after he or she has been quantified as a statistic of one sort or another: "In detective fiction, to be is not to be perceived, it is to be recorded" ("Private Space" 171). Also reading in a Lacanian mode (which is, curiously, the only mode of analysis in which the comparison to realism has yet been made to any substantial degree),[3] Slavoj Žižek first distinguishes the detective novel from the realistic one and then separates the hard-boiled novel by yet another degree (48–49, 60–61). He does so largely by explicating the manner in which fictional detectives in both the classical and hard-boiled forms can be seen evading or participating in, respectively, the production of cultural desire. In the main, such interpretations can be quite useful in that they elucidate "changes in the so-called *Zeitgeist*" (Žižek 48), particularly in how the semiotics of deductive analysis change between Conan Doyle in the 1890s and Chandler in the 1930s. Historically speaking, though, there exists a very specific correlation between realism and hard-boiled fiction, and as Chandler's reply to Gardner begins to suggest, California's hard-boiled writers felt they had a stake in the idea of realism. That is, much as their western predecessors had done, they lay claim to realism as their particular stake in authority and authenticity, thereby entering into a continuity of literary history that bears further inquiry.[4]

The cultural product known as hard-boiled detective fiction, which enters its most mature phase with Chandler's 1939 novel *The Big Sleep*, signifies an important confluence of the several patterns of western claims to realism that have been the subject of the preceding five chapters. As partially self-aware rewriters of literary history, the western claimants to realistic prose covered thus far—among them Dame Shirley, Bret Harte, Mark Twain, John Muir, Frank Norris, and Mary Austin—have repeatedly engaged questions of accuracy and truthful representation as they appear in popular genres such as the mining tale, the Western, nature writing, and, as this chapter will discuss, the hard-boiled detective novel. They have done so, moreover, by invoking (either as formal and ideological challenge or as reifying principle) the proper and accurate representation of the West's natural splendor, a choice in representation that has brought the West's natural resource industries into the domain of textuality. To this trend finally belongs the work of Hammett and Chandler, for the claim to realism known as hard-boiled fiction is unmistakably a product of the American West. Chandler, renowned for his Anglophilia, nevertheless at one time semi-jokingly referred to himself as a westerner, writing to a friend that although he had been born in Chicago, "I was conceived in Laramie, Wyo., . . . and if they had asked me, I should have preferred to be born there" (qtd. in MacShane 3).

This chapter, however, will not suggest, as many critics have done previously, that hard-boiled fictions are western by virtue of their being Wister-like cowboy narratives set in modern urban environments.[5] Rather, as a textual claim to realism from and about the West, the hard-boiled detective novel engages fully the historical contingency of such previous claims. It embraces the representation of nature's bounty and the problems inherent in such representation on a level only hinted at by the other texts in this study. The California hard-boiled novel stands as something of a final synthesis of western American literary realism. It achieves this status by rendering visible a number of patterns and assumptions that earlier texts in this tradition only hint at: the conflict over art and artifice, the function of genre both in and as a literary history of realism, and the material value of the body as it stands in relation to natural resource industries.[6] Hammett writes of miners in Montana and Chandler of oil barons and water reservoirs in southern California; collectively, through their engagement with the generic imagination surrounding gangsters and violence,[7] their novels reinscribe into the matrix of resource representation the human body that was first elided in Harte's reconfiguration of the mining tale. More to the point, if the more familiar representations of the American West postulate a natural world more or less inviolate, then the realistic project of Hammett and Chandler argues that a nature without cultural and material intervention by humans is little more than a useful but potentially misleading fiction.

Reading for the Real

The claim to realism in western detective fiction begins in many respects with the former detective Dashiell Hammett, who was very much the sort of reader R. Gordon Kelly describes. Hammett expected the detectives he encountered in books to behave very much like real ones, and in the 1920s he began to apply these readerly expectations of realism to his own development of an ostensibly realistic detective fiction. To this end, well before he ever published his first novel in 1929, Hammett successfully established himself as an expert on both the work of the detective and mystery writing, offering his interpretation of the mystery novel form as the most authoritative one. Drawing on his much-traveled years with the Pinkerton Detective Agency (1915–21), he wrote such articles as "From the Memoirs of a Private Detective," an epigrammatic essay published in the *Smart Set* in March 1923, only three months after his fictional short stories had begun appearing regularly in *Black Mask*, the flagship magazine for detective pulp stories.[8] During this period in the mid-1920s Hammett further honed his skills at persuasive writing by working as an advertising copywriter in San Francisco, which, as William Marling notes, helped Hammett "bring the experience of his travel into narrative focus" (106).[9] And regarding narrative focus more broadly, Hammett, the former detective and copywriter, developed a recurring concern for the relation between truth and realistic fiction, between the facts as they may really be and the authoritative and accurate presentation of those facts. Clearly, Hammett felt quite strongly that the detective and his work must be properly represented in writing: in a word, it must be real. In his *Smart Set* "Memoirs," for instance, he offers the following observation, labeled no. 27: "The chief difference between the exceptionally knotty problem confronting the detective of fiction and that facing the real detective is that in the former there is usually a paucity of clues, and in the latter altogether too many" (89). By the end of 1926 Hammett had been hired to write reviews of mystery novels for the *Saturday Review of Literature,* and in this forum he even more fully expressed his concern that mystery writers provide accurate representations of crime and detection. Relying on his status as a detective-turned-writer, Hammett used these reviews to make a case for realism in the mystery genre.[10]

In his very first review essay for *Saturday Review,* published in the 15 January 1927 issue and entitled "Poor Scotland Yard!," Hammett presents both his bona fides and his critical expectations with the following opening paragraph: "In some years of working for private detective agencies in various cities I came across only one fellow sleuth who would confess that he read detective stories. 'I eat 'em up,' this one said without shame. 'When I'm through my day's gum-shoeing I like to relax; I like to get my mind on something that's altogether different from the daily grind; so I read detective stories'" (510). Presented with five novels for review, including *The Benson Murder Case,* the first of twelve Philo Vance mysteries by S. S. Van Dine, Hammett concludes that his former fellow sleuth "would have liked" them very much.[11] To this erstwhile colleague, mystery books offer no representation or, rather, no re-presentation of what he sees in his daily work. That Hammett has seen the same things is of course clear from the opening line: "In some years of working for private detective agencies in various cities I . . . " By thus measuring his and his colleague's experience as detectives against the representations offered by fiction, Hammett effectively positions the traditional mystery novel as something of a fantasy, entirely unhinged from reality. Thereby he succinctly assesses the lack of authenticity in current mystery writing.

In his keen concern for realism in the reading experience, Hammett was hardly alone. Roughly six months after the appearance of "Poor Scotland Yard!," *Black Mask* published an editorial designed to instruct its readers on what to expect from the magazine. Entitled "The Aim of Black Mask," editor Joseph Shaw's column offered that "detective fiction, as we view it, has only commenced to be developed. . . . [A]ll other fields have been worked and overworked but [detective fiction] has been barely scratched." Thus setting apart his nascent form from "all other fields" of literature, Shaw then cautioned that "to be convincing . . . [such fiction] must be real in motive, character and action . . . must be plausible . . . clear and understandable. . . . Therefore, word has gone out to writers of our requirements of plausibility, of truthfulness in details, of realism in . . . the portrayal of action and emotion" (June 1927; qtd. in Nolan, *Black Mask Boys* 25). Significantly, one of Shaw's predecessors, George W. Sutton, published another such editorial in 1922 called "How to Read Black Mask Stories," which implored readers not to skip pages and not to read ahead to the ends of stories (Nolan, *Black Mask Boys* 22). Hard-boiled fiction was a developing genre very much concerned with the function/contribution of the reader.[12]

It is certainly safe to assume that Hammett approved of such programs for accuracy in the writing—and reading—of this sort of detective story, which may be inferred from the frequency with which he places emphasis, in both his reviews and his fiction, on readers and reading. In his review of *The Benson Murder Case,* for instance, Hammett maintains an oblique emphasis on reading well beyond the opening lines about his former colleague. Evaluating the gap between his knowledge of the world and that which is (in Dennis Porter's terms) presented to him through his sampling of new mystery novels, Hammett finds an egregious representational crime in S. S. Van Dine's description of a victim's untimely death. Hammett summarizes:

> Alvin Benson is found sitting in a wicker chair in his living room, a book still in his hand, his legs crossed, and his body comfortably relaxed in a lifelike position. He is dead. A bullet from an Army model Colt .45 automatic pistol, held some six feet away when the trigger was pulled, has passed completely through his head. That his position should have been so slightly disturbed by the impact of such a bullet at such a range is preposterous, but the phenome-

> non hasn't anything to do with the plot, so don't, as I did, waste time trying to figure it out. (510)

Since the corpse has maintained its readerly pose ("sitting in a wicker chair . . . a book still in his hand"), Hammett is able to suggest a corollary to the act of reading with both his futile attempt to "figure it out" plot-wise and the experiences of the fellow sleuth mentioned in the opening of the review. By implication, reading is very much like detective work.

The uninformed, unquestioning reader of genre tales comes under similar fire in a review Hammett published in December 1928. "Most of the people in this book [Carolyn Wells's *The Tannahill Tangle*]," he complains, "are detective-story readers and they spend a lot of time talking about detective stories, which is bad enough, but their dialogue reaches its real depths when they indulge in what is supposed to be sophisticated banter" (qtd. in D. Johnson 62).[13] Like *The Benson Murder Case,* this book elicits one of Hammett's favorite adjectives, the same one used in assessing the state of Alvin Benson's body: "preposterous." To Hammett, a reader who has signaled that he is accustomed to reading both books and crime scenes, the clues offered by the authors of these various mysteries clearly do not corroborate his expectations of realism; hence they are "preposterous" in their representations.

This readerly relationship between detectives and clues, frustrated as it had been in Hammett's attempts to glean a plot-based solution to the unrealistic positioning of Benson's corpse, provides one crucial angle by which Hammett addresses the inadequacies of contemporary mystery writing. As item no. 27 from his *Smart Set* essay affirms, Hammett sees a fundamental difference between the apperception of clues in fiction and the same in reality. Continuing his frank assessment in "Poor Scotland Yard!," he complains that in the Van Dine novel, "The authorities, no matter how stupid the author chose to make them, would have cleared up the mystery promptly if they had been allowed to follow the most rudimentary police procedure" (510). Similarly, "When information concerning a mysterious box of jewelry accidentally bobs up everybody resolutely ignores it, since it would have led to a solution before the three-hundredth page" (510). The detectives in this fiction bear a deeply flawed relationship to the clues at hand: they cannot see them for what they are, even when they appear in plain sight before them. This problem of ostensibly not seeing things for what they are is Hammett's crisis of representation, the one against which he will begin to define a more realistic genre of detection.

The problem of the plainly visible clue is, of course, the premise behind Edgar Allan Poe's "The Purloined Letter," as well as of the subsequent strong reading of that story offered by Jacques Lacan, to which Joan Copjec is indebted.[14] Concerning the noir detective, Copjec explains that the investigator

> is always able to extract a letter, a corpse, a clue that was literally undetectable before he arrived on the scene. It is the signifying description of the scene and not the "scene itself," the referent, that is submitted to the work of detection. . . .
>
> We might even argue that the detective distinguishes himself from the police by virtue of his passion for ignorance, not for eliminating it. For while the police search for the telling clue, the index, in the belief that at this point reality "impresses" itself on the symbolic, "brushes up against it" and thereby disambiguates it, the detective approaches the index as the point where the real makes itself felt in the symbolic, that is as the point at which the symbolic visibly *fails* to disambiguate itself. ("Private Space" 177–78; emphasis in original)[15]

The question of that which in California hard-boiled fiction "fails to disambiguate itself" will be considered in greater detail in the next section's discussion of natural resource representations. For the moment, though, Copjec's characterization of the detective, who detects that which was "literally undetectable before" and who is attentive not to a scene but to how a scene is descriptively understood, suggestively illuminates Hammett's concern for proper reading. Indeed, to illustrate her point Copjec turns briefly to one of Hammett's earliest *Black Mask* stories, "Bodies Piled Up" (December 1923), only the fourth story (out of an eventual thirty-three) to feature Hammett's serial detective, the Continental Op (Hammett would unveil Sam Spade in 1929). At one point in this story the Op, as narrator, explains his investigative philosophy: "From any crime to its author there is a trail. It may be . . . obscure; but since matter cannot move without disturbing other matter along its path, there always is—there must be—a trail of some sorts. And finding and following such trails is what a detective is paid to do" (84). In his reference to the criminal as "author," Hammett once again implies, if only obliquely, that the detective functions as a reader.

More telling in this regard, however, is the fact that the key to the case presented in "Bodies Piled Up" involves a particularly curious instance of misreading. Three murder victims have been found stacked up in a closet in room 906 of the Montgomery Hotel in San Francisco. After a prolonged investigation in which no connection between the victims and any sort of motive can be established, the Op determines that all three deaths, including that of a salesman named Develyn, are cases of mistaken identity, the innocent victims of a gangster assassin named Cudner. In his interview with another gangland hit man, Orrett, the Op gains confirmation of the fatal misreading, the key to which lies in the fact that at the time of the triple murder, Orrett, the intended target, had been registered in room 609. Looking for Orrett's room, Cudner takes a quick glance at the hotel register facing away from him at the front desk. Then, as Orrett tells the Op:

> "When you read numbers of three figures upside-down you have to transpose them in your head to get them straight. Like 1-2-3. You'd get 3-2-1, and then turn them around in your head. That's what Cudner did with mine. He was keyed up, of course, thinking of the job ahead of him, and he overlooked the fact that 609 upside-down still reads 609 just the same. So he turned it around and made it 906—Develyn's room."
>
> "That's the way I doped it," I said. (90)

In short, the murderer adjusted his reading where none was needed (apparently, the gangster Orrett is as good a reader as the Op, which indicates that such a skill is not particular to any single line of work). In Copjec's terms, the symbolic value of the upside-down number 609 in the register, a signifier hitched to the presumed reality of the room 609, failed to disambiguate itself, in that the real did not come through but rather was subsumed in the killer's readerly tendencies. As realism, this sort of mystery might not be any more convincing than is the book-holding corpse of Alvin Benson. However, as a measure of Hammett's concern for proper representation and as a constituent element of his particular claim to realism on behalf of the mystery novel, the problem and resolution of "Bodies Piled Up" offer a perfect indicator of hard-boiled fiction's self-encoding of its own reception as realism: to be a realist in hard-boiled fiction is to be a responsible reader.

A quick glance at some of Hammett's other fiction provides a significant number of similarly coded instances of reading and writing. Throughout *Red Harvest* (1929), Hammett's first novel, the Op worries repeatedly over how his reports from a case he is on in Butte, Montana, are being read by his supervisors at the Continental Detective Agency in San Francisco. In particular, the Op is concerned about writing truthfully the details of his investigation while keeping out his complicity in the bloodshed (one type of "red harvest" implied by the title; another allusion is to Butte's copper-mining industry). In the closing lines of the novel, the Op laments: "I might just as well have saved the labor and sweat I had put into trying to make my reports harmless. They didn't fool the Old Man. He gave me merry hell" (142). In *The Maltese Falcon* (1930), Sam Spade keeps a copy of "Duke's *Celebrated Criminal Cases of America*" on his night table (13), a book that the villain Gutman, the infamous "fat man," chuckles over in an idle moment (244–45).[16] Similarly, Spade's faithful secretary, Effie Perine, is frequently shown with reading material, whether the daily mail, a newspaper, or a magazine (29, 50, 266). Newspapers play a crucial role in this novel, in both revealing and obscuring truth. Early on Spade trusts them to conceal, through simple reportorial ineptitude, his client's identity. Yet, at the conclusion of the novel, after Effie reads in the papers that Brigid O'Shaughnessy, the killer of Spade's partner, has been arrested for murder, she implores, "Is that—what the papers have—right?" and Spade affirms that it is, that he has finally stage-managed it so (266). And a vital clue concerning the mysterious falcon's whereabouts comes to Spade by way of a newspaper (165–66). Finally, Hammett's *The Thin Man* (1934) opens with the former detective Nick Charles's encounter with the daughter of a former client, who asks him: "Listen: remember those stories [about his detective years] you told me? Were they true?" (4). Moments later this woman tells Nick's wife, "I was fascinated by him . . . a real live detective, and used to follow him around making him tell me about his experiences. He told me awful lies, but I believed every word" (5). Given that Nick Charles is the first-person narrator of *The Thin Man,* this opening exchange frames the entire novel, Charles's recollection of a case he and his wife solve, as possibly another of his believable lies, even as the first-person format of the genre conveys authority and authenticity. Of course, these works by Hammett contain many more complexities than are indicated by this brief survey. Nonetheless, their repeated emphasis on reading, storytelling, readers, and real-seeming believability strongly suggests that Hammett, and by implication the hard-boiled style he pioneered,[17] continued to value the act of reading as a means of detection.

Which probably helps to explain, at least in part, why Hammett's self-styled successor Raymond Chandler, writing over a decade later, makes an almost identical set of claims concerning realism and the hard-boiled novel—the method of the genre demanded it, since the continuity of readerly expectations and readership, in addition to that of form, was vital. Content-wise, Chandler's fiction echoes a number of Hammett's formulations regarding detection as reading. For one, Chandler's detective Philip Marlowe is an inveterate reader—among his scant personal possessions he counts "a few books, pictures, radio, chessmen, old letters, stuff like that" (*The Big Sleep* 96)—and the first Marlowe mystery, *The Big Sleep* (1939), involves a theft of books as a key event in one of the novel's two conjoined plotlines. Chandler also has Marlowe echo the argument of Hammett's dictum no. 27 when he comments on a suspect's story: "It had the austere simplicity of fiction rather than the tangled woof of fact" (103). And as in *The Maltese Falcon,* in this tale the newspapers also generally fail in their reports of criminal activity: "Their accounts of the affair came as close to the truth as newspaper stories usually come—as close as Mars is to Saturn" (72). Chandler's *The Long Goodbye* (1953), in addition to presenting a T. S. Eliot–quoting chauffeur, even contains an author as a key principal character, one who provides a challenging foil for Marlowe and, according to many critics, is Chandler's most autobiographical characterization.

But such connections are circumstantial and on the level of the thematic, whereas Chandler's indebtedness to Hammett's construction of the realist's position is more complex. Consider, for example, the various twistings and turnings of the mystery in *The Big Sleep*. In this novel Marlowe is hired by an old, wealthy southern California oil baron, General Sternwood, to investigate the reasons behind a petty blackmailer's attempt to squeeze the General for the relatively paltry sum of one thousand dollars. Several bodies pile up in conjunction with the blackmailer's stolen pornographic books, and in the process Marlowe also ends up searching for the General's missing son-in-law, Rusty Regan, who married the General's older daughter, Vivian. This search brings Marlowe into contact with a number of other criminal figures, including a Los

Angeles crime boss who has placed his own wife into hiding in order to give the impression that she too is missing. All of these characters, plus the murder and/or suicide of the Sternwood chauffeur (this death is never explained), make for a complex chain of events.

At the end of the novel, when a satisfactory solution seems far from attainable, Marlowe takes a moment to explain his methodology to his client:

> I'm not Sherlock Holmes or Philo Vance. I don't expect to go over ground the police have covered and pick up a broken pen point and build a case from it. If you think there is anybody in the detective business making a living doing that sort of thing, you don't know much about cops. It's not the things like that they overlook, if they overlook anything. I'm not saying they often overlook anything when they're really allowed to work. But if they do, it's apt to be something looser and vaguer. (129)

The "something looser and vaguer" that the police have missed and which Marlowe uncovers is the fact that the convolutions of the *plot*—the concatenation of narratives presented equally to Marlowe and to the reader of the book—bear virtually no relation to the meaning of both the blackmail and the disappearance. The majority of pages in *The Big Sleep*, which is narrated in the first person by Marlowe, recount events that in no way lead to the solution of the mystery. The solution lies not underneath the tangle of events but rather tangentially: the son-in-law is already dead at the beginning of the story, murdered by the General's other daughter, Carmen, and the blackmailer had guessed at this and was testing with a relatively small, unrelated touch for money to see whether the General knew it too. Marlowe solves this mystery not by decoding a sequential narrative but rather by examining that which the narrative has not accounted for—the motivation behind a blackmailer's seemingly insignificant try for cash.

Notably, Marlowe explains his approach to the whole problem by referring to the writing of detective fiction. His emphasis on "pick[ing] up a broken pen" echoes the textual side of detection invoked by the names Holmes and Vance, and both references have to do with writing and reading. Indeed, the problem that ultimately confronts Marlowe the narrator is a series of unreliable narrations. These come to him first from the General, then from Sternwood's daughter Vivian Regan, from Sternwood's other daughter, Carmen, from Eddie Mars the gang boss, and even from the police, in the person of Captain Gregory, head of the Missing Persons Bureau and a practiced dissembler (see 73–77). Through all of this, Marlowe's method of investigative deduction closely echoes the "detective function" formulated by Joan Copjec's analysis of Hammett's Op in "Bodies Piled Up," and it is presented once again as a methodology marked by a sort of reading. Marlowe, like the Op, looks not for the overlooked tidbit but rather tries to behold the scene in a manner altogether different from how the police do. He too is looking at the description of a scene rather than the scene itself, which is to say that Chandler's detective operates in much the same way as does Hammett's.

But this association alone does not yet make Chandler a western realist. For that connection, we can begin, as we did with Hammett, by taking him at his own word. And once again, a significant western writer's claim to realism appears in the pages of the *Atlantic,* a publication that, as the preceding discussions of Harte, Muir, and Austin have shown, has repeatedly proven instrumental in the codification of the West's many subgenres. In an *Atlantic* review essay called "The Simple Art of Murder" (1944), for which he suggestively adapted his title from Henry James's "The Art of Fiction" (1884), Chandler compares himself favorably to Hammett specifically on the grounds of realism.[18] According to Chandler, the genre of detective fiction as a whole has been sadly lacking in competent realists and, not surprisingly, Hammett's achievements rank him among the few who have succeeded in writing a realistic mystery. Dennis Porter has classified the attention to realistic prose among detective story writers as "a search for an appropriate idiom" (132). In Chandler's opinion, Hammett has done precisely this: "He had a literary style, but his audience didn't know it. . . . I believe this style, which does not belong to Hammett, or to anybody, . . . is the American language" (58). What for Hammett had been largely (although not exclusively) a problem of seeing clues for what they are, Chandler adapts into a problem of style, of language.

As befits a self-professed realist, though, Chandler needs his own crisis of representation by which to distinguish his realism, and in presenting his case he reiterates much of Hammett's program for realism as a necessary requirement of mystery writing. Just as Hammett had taken issue with the "preposterous" contrivances of books such as *The Benson Murder Case,* Chandler devotes much of "The Simple Art of Murder" to dismantling a highly popular novel, A. A. Milne's *The Red House Mystery* (1922).

Like Hammett before him, Chandler finds fault with mystery fiction in which the police are not allowed to behave like police (54–55). And he complains similarly about the useless dialogue: "The only reality the English detection writers knew was the conversational accent of Surbiton and Bognor Regis" (57). In contrast, Chandler praises the realism of his predecessor for having given "murder back to the kind of people that commit it for reasons. . . . [A]nd he made them talk and think in the language they customarily used for these purposes" (58). Here again Chandler's interest in the language of the text manifests itself in praise for fictional characters who speak as he would have real people speak—that is, he prefers realism in dialogue.

Even more self-consciously focused on issues of diction and style than Hammett appears to have been, though, Chandler concludes "The Simple Art of Murder" by qualifying his opinion of an increasingly ubiquitous Hammett style:

> The realistic style is easy to abuse; from haste, from lack of awareness, from inability to bridge the chasm that lies between what a writer would like to be able to say and what he actually knows how to say. It is easy to fake; brutality is not strength, flipness is not wit, edge-of-the-chair writing can be as boring as flat writing. . . . There has been so much of this sort of thing that if a character in a detective story says "Yeah," the author is automatically a Hammett imitator. (58)

And mere imitation does not a realistic writer make. Chandler's point is that the verbal imitation of toughness does not equal real toughness—artifice does not equal art. (In a notable twist to Hammett's persistent concern with what one picks up by reading too many genre stories, Chandler describes in *The Big Sleep* one particular crook who is more bluster than threat as having "the elaborately casual voice of the tough guy in pictures. Pictures have made them all like that" [48].) Chandler's reproach of those who would write "Yeah" as a shortcut to authenticity may thus be read as an elitist complaint against the proliferating popularity, in books as well as in movies, of an easily copied hard-boiled style first pioneered by Hammett.

Consequently, Chandler moves his definition of hard-boiled realism away from the predominantly mimetic definition proffered by Hammett (fictional cops should behave like real cops) and toward a realism of a slightly different yet still familiar stripe. As Stephen Knight has observed, "From Hammett he drew a writing style and a sense of urban corruption; the link is strongest in the early stories. Hammett had stopped writing before Chandler began and they met only once; he gave a starting-point Chandler moved away from" (137). Indeed, at the conclusion of "The Simple Art of Murder," after he has enumerated his objections to the traditional detective novel and has praised Hammett's realistic departure from that tradition, Chandler admits: "But all this (and Hammett too) is for me not quite enough" (59). To be sure, Hammett remains Chandler's model of the realistic mystery writer, in that Hammett's texts create what most mysteries do not: "an effect of movement, intrigue, cross-purposes and the gradual elucidation of character, which is all the detective story has any right to be about anyway" (59). However, sounding just a bit like Howells (who also emphasized character development over plot), Chandler explains that the realist writer of mysteries is ultimately accountable not to the timetable or the logic of the locked room but rather (to borrow from *The Big Sleep*) to "something looser and vaguer." Chandler argues, in one long sentence, that

> the realist in murder writes of a world in which gangsters can rule nations and almost rule cities, in which hotels and apartment houses and celebrated restaurants are owned by men who made their money out of brothels . . . a world where a judge with a cellar full of bootleg liquor can send a man to jail for having a pint in his pocket, where the mayor of your town may have condoned murder as an instrument of money-making . . . a world where you may witness a holdup in broad daylight and see who did it, but you will fade quickly back into the crowd rather than tell anyone. (59)

Considering himself such a realist, Chandler offers as a corrective his oft-quoted requirement for the moral detective, the epitome of the ethical self: "Down these mean streets a man must go who is not himself mean. . . . He must be, to use a rather weathered phrase, a man of honor. . . . He must be the best man in his world and a good enough man for any world" (59). And the mystery novelist's obligation is to create/represent such a man. This, in short, is a moralist's vision of realism, an ethical approach to representation.

Of course, critics have long recognized the moral as Chandler's particular demesne as a hard-boiled novelist—as explained above, Chandler claims as much himself, insofar as the ultimate project of "The Simple Art of Murder" was to present its author as an advocate of ethically motivated realism. The point of the present argument, however, is that this position arises directly out of Chandler's specific commitment to the idea of realism: he was not a writer of realism who also happens to embrace an ethical outlook, but rather a writer who assumed the mantle of "realist" in its fullest dimension. In addition to the terms elucidated thus far, Chandler also fits the mold of realist, as it were, in a number of other important ways. For one, he was an inveterate reader of Henry James, whom Chandler's biographer Frank MacShane has identified as a vital stylistic influence (31, 42). More significantly, Chandler's realism appropriated elements of the Howells legacy that range beyond a mere sense of moral propriety. Amy Kaplan has characterized traditional Howellsian realism as a genre marked by an insistence on social boundaries, which are policed by the realist who carefully demarcates the middle-class subject from both the destitute lower classes and the stagnant, corrupt upper classes (see Kaplan 44–64). Although he does not speak of Chandler as a realist, Fredric Jameson makes an almost identical point about the "socio-typological" system of class demarcations that operates in Chandler's novels (see "The Synoptic Chandler" 35–44). At the very least, Chandler shared Howells's propensity toward an elitism maintained in the name of democratic universality.[19]

Regardless, such scorekeeping of tendencies and characteristics seems unnecessary. Taken as a whole, the claims to realism made by Hammett and Chandler on behalf of the hard-boiled detective novel invoke formal and ethical requirements that serve as grounding assumptions in any representational program (Howellsian or otherwise) that purports to have a handle on reality, namely, proper and selective representation of presumably factual material. Whether any given text ever successfully satisfies these criteria is an altogether different question, one best left to a more aesthetically focused criticism. Meanwhile, the fact remains that hard-boiled writers from California thought of themselves as realists. More to the point, as readers both Hammett and Chandler professed a particular taste for representational accuracy, which with a certain degree of self-awareness they called realism. Consequently, their written works, which stood in part as attempts to provide like-minded readers with accurately represented material, may be understood as the products of realist writers.[20] And as the following section will show, what finally distinguishes hard-boiled fiction as *western* realism is the remarkable frequency with which the products of various resource industries were deemed significant enough to warrant ostensibly realistic representation.

Of Human Value *Redux:* Bodies as Resources

Quoting the opinion of Hamlin Garland, who was in turn speaking of Howells, Howard Horwitz affirms that American realism characteristically "is not 'reproduction'; [instead,] it represents 'the relations of things' and persons" and hence "is not a purely formal problem but an ethical problem, a question of allegiances" (195). Among the many relations and allegiances commonly associated with hard-boiled fiction—social, urban, technological, gendered—as yet rarely noticed and least commented on is its representation of nature. Horwitz's assessment indirectly raises the possibility of something approaching an ecological point of view (in re: nature and the broader "relations of things"). However, this is not to suggest that an explicitly ecological vision ever motivated the California hard-boiled novelist.[21] Such a reading would only reproduce on an ecocritical level the once popular but reductive reading of Chandler as a committed, disinterested diagnostician of social inequality.[22] Rather, what the representation of nature in Chandler, and to an extent in Hammett as well, shows is an explicit interrogation of the normative appeal to nature that historically characterizes a great deal of western American literature. Instead of depicting the natural world as something other than or beyond the corrupt and troubled social world of the detective, hard-boiled fiction argues that there is no nature without human intervention, that there is no such thing as a nature not already marked by a resource industry. It does so by limning the "relations of things" between Californians and their nature in such a way that situates the human figure as a bridge between the two; humans, in a sense, become natural resources.

As noted earlier, the title of Hammett's first novel, *Red Harvest,* alludes metaphorically to the color of both copper ore and human blood. More specifically, the "harvest" in Hammett's gangster-Western signifies equally the mineral wealth of a thinly fictionalized version of the Anaconda mines near Butte, Montana, and the scores of bodies that pile up in the wake of the Continental Op's attempt to clean up the town. That Hammett should want this connection between bodies and ore is clear from the opening lines of the novel. The Op narrates:

> I first heard Personville called Poisonville by a red-haired mucker named Hickey Dewey in the Big Ship in Butte. He also called his shirt a shoit. I didn't think anything of what he had done to the city's name. Later I heard men who could manage their r's give it the same pronunciation. I still didn't see anything in it but the meaningless sort of humor that used to make richardsnary the thieves' word for dictionary. A few years later I went to Personville and learned better. (3)

What the Op learns is that the bootlegger-controlled town has become corrupted in both name and civic spirit and that the one stands as a correlative for the other, that is, "person" into "poison." Commenting further on the effect of mining on both the town and its inhabitants, the Op notes that the mine's smelters had over time "yellow-smoked everything into uniform dinginess." He concludes:

> The result was an ugly city of forty thousand people, set in an ugly notch between two ugly mountains that had been all dirtied up by mining. Spread over this was a grimy sky that looked as if it had come out of the smelters' stacks.
>
> The first policeman I saw needed a shave. The second had a couple of buttons off his shabby uniform. The third stood in the center of the city's main intersection . . . directing traffic, with a cigar in one corner of his mouth. After that I stopped checking them up. (3)

In just these opening passages, Hammett already establishes a series of causal relations between mining, the vestigial evidence of nature ("ugly mountains" and "a grimy sky"), human beings, and a traditional symbol of urban authority (the police). In this respect he ever so faintly transmutes the familiar trope of the decrepit gold miner onto the level of "forty thousand people," moving it from the individual to the social.

Strictly speaking, though, in terms of genre Hammett has written not a mining tale but a detective-adventure thriller. Moreover, his fictionalization of mining activity does not borrow to any significant degree from the possible reality of conditions in 1929 Butte but rather comes out of the progressive, urban politics and demographics of 1920s San Francisco (see esp. Marling 108–9). Nevertheless, Hammett's figurative rendition of the allegiances between humans and their environment introduces a significant ingredient into the hard-boiled formula. Calling *Red Harvest* a "watershed moment in the history of the American noir novel" (106), William Marling affirms that key aspects of the traditional detective story, such as the detective's function in the recovery of social order, overlap in this novel with nascent elements of a hard-boiled form, such as the cinematically inspired fragmentation of narration and the general irrelevance of the mystery to the plot (recall the concatenation of narratives in *The Big Sleep*). On top of this, Hammett's first novel offers the crucial formulation of "person" becoming "poison," of people and scenery and city and ideology all begrimed by a natural resource industry. *Red Harvest* as both title and metaphoric representation of the "relations of things" in a western resource environment thus provides a suggestive clue to the manner in which human bodies in hard-boiled fiction become mere objects: they do so in relation to economies of resource extraction.

In the particular claim to realism by which hard-boiled fiction asserts its representational authenticity, the human figure plays a significant role. And this dynamic, suggestively introduced by Hammett's *Red Harvest,* reaches its zenith in the same place as do most formal and ideological aspects of hard-boiled writing, in the work of Chandler. As David Wyatt has said of Chandler's fourth book, *The Lady in the Lake* (1943), namely, that "people become 'somethings' in this novel" (*Fall into Eden* 170), so may be said of the rest of Chandler's canon. From the first book to the last, Chandler's Los Angeles is a town very much like Poisonville, a "deracinated urban hell" (M. Davis 37) in which the police are no less dishonest than the criminals, the weather and landscape serve as objective correlatives for corruption and urban grime (see Babener), and the human figure is more object than subject. And at its heart, much of this city is built over a resource industry matrix. In fact, Chandler's personal history strongly suggests that he should very well have had a very keen awareness of the extent to which a natural resource had given shape to the Los Angeles basin: from 1919 until 1932 he worked his way from accounting clerk to vice president of the South Basin Oil Company in Long Beach (MacShane 34–40; Marling 188–201). Moreover, as a company executive Chandler had social access to the houses of Los Angeles's many oil barons, including the West Hollywood home of oil pioneer E. L. Doheny, from whose $4 million mansion one could see Doheny's oil derricks in the not-too-distant La Brea/Baldwin Hills region (Ward and Silver 166–67).[23] Notably, this view from Doheny's terrace is precisely the view from the Sternwood mansion, also in West Hollywood, that Marlowe encounters in the opening sequences of *The Big Sleep*.

Approaching the front door of his client's baronial estate house, Chandler's narrator Marlowe first describes himself, in the opening paragraph, as "neat, clean, shaved and sober, and I didn't care who knew it. I was everything the well-dressed private detective ought to be. I was calling on four million dollars" (3). Marlowe's next paragraph describes the front portal of the mansion, after which he proceeds inside to his first meeting with a new client. And when he reemerges from the house, Marlowe describes the expansive view afforded by the fenced-in lawn:

> Beyond the fence the hill sloped for several miles. On this lower level faint and far off I could just barely see some of the old wooden derricks of the oilfield from which the Sternwoods had made their money. Most of the field was public park now, cleaned up and donated to the city by General Sternwood. But a little of it was still producing in groups of wells pumping five or six barrels a day. The Sternwoods, having moved up the hill, could no longer smell the stale sump water or the oil, but they could still look out of their front windows and see what had made them rich. (13–14)

Chandler returns to this landscape in the novel's climactic scene, to what he paradoxically calls "a daydream land." Here Carmen Sternwood attempts to do to Marlowe what she had done to her brother-in-law Rusty Regan: murder him for his sexual unresponsiveness and dispose of the body at the well site, in "the stagnant, oil-scummed water of an old sump iridescent in the sunlight" (132). Chandler's language draws attention to the unnaturalness of the scene, even as the phrase "iridescent in the sunlight" suggests a strange sort of attractiveness. Given the novel's attempt to critique overly conspicuous capitalism, this terrain functions as the location at which the hidden corruption of wealth literally bubbles to the surface, where everything is "oil-stained" and "motionless" (132).

Chandler communicates the idea of a reified human body through more than just the connection he establishes between corpses and the residual muck of an oil enterprise. At the start of *The Big Sleep*, sandwiched between Marlowe's arrival at the house and his contemplation of the far-off oil derricks, are scenes that narrate Marlowe's encounter with General Sternwood and his two daughters. These meetings allow Chandler to present the lead figures in the tale in metaphoric language that confuses and conflates the human with the nonhuman, the natural with the ostensibly not so natural.[24] In Sternwood's greenhouse–cum–sitting room, for instance, Marlowe discovers an "obviously dying old man" whose face resembled a "leaden mask" and on whose head "a few locks of dry white hair clung to his scalp, like wild flowers fighting for life on a bare rock." Reversing the man-plant metaphor, Chandler also has Marlowe notice in the greenhouse "a forest of [plants], with nasty meaty leaves and stalks like the newly washed fingers of dead men" (6). In the house proper Marlowe encounters a Carmen Sternwood who "walked as if she were floating" and who had "little sharp predatory teeth, as white as fresh orange pith and as shiny as porcelain" (4). Finally, at various points in the novel both Vivian and Carmen Sternwood are described as mechanical puppets controlled with "artificial" wires.

The most compelling juxtaposition Chandler draws between a human figure and a nonhuman artifact, however, is that which he establishes, again in the novel's opening sequence, between the façade of the Sternwood house and Marlowe himself. Fastidious and precise about his own appearance, Marlowe recalls: "I was wearing my powder-blue suit, with dark blue shirt, tie and display handkerchief, black brogues, black wool socks with dark blue clocks on them. I was clean, neat, shaved and sober" (3). The very next paragraph, the second one in the novel, has Marlowe noticing the mansion's immense entrance doors, over which he sees a "stained-glass panel showing a knight in dark armor rescuing a lady who was tied to a tree. . . . [H]e was fiddling with the knots on the ropes that tied the lady to the tree and not getting anywhere. I stood there and thought that if I lived in the house, I would sooner or later have to climb up there and help him. He didn't seem to be really trying" (3). Chandler of course hopes to strike an analogy between the stained-glass knight's fruitless efforts to save the damsel and Marlowe's eventual inability to do anything for the Sternwood sisters (he thinks "It wasn't a game for knights" when his gentlemanly attempts to rebuff Carmen's sexual aggressiveness prove ineffective [95]). However, the net result of the scopofilic correlation of human figure and house, even if only done ironically, further helps to establish the text's broadly conceived connection between humans and nonhuman material.

The figures by which *The Big Sleep* integrates human bodies both physically and metonymically into the material fabric of Los Angeles are not unique to this particular novel, though. In subsequent works, Chandler maintains this tendency as he continues to use the evidence of resource industries as foundation and backdrop. In *Farewell, My Lovely* (1940), for instance, Marlowe teams up with an intrepid, sleuthing woman named Ann Riordan, who lives off of the fortune her father had earned in selling oil-rich real estate. And *The High Window* (1942), in which a stolen gold coin provides part of the mystery, contains in the figure of the late Jasper Murdock a parody of Joseph Dabney, Chandler's former boss at South Basin Oil. What's more, when Marlowe's client Mrs. Murdock asks for a list of professional references, Marlowe gives, among others, the name "Oliver Fry of the Fry-Krantz Corporation, Oil Well Tools" (321).

Of course, there is much more at stake in Chandler's rendition of the natural world than mere reference to regional history. *The High Window,* which Chandler (among others) considered his worst effort, has prompted Fredric Jameson to ask why, despite its structural resemblance to other Chandler novels, "the novel fails to cohere, even in a formal situation in which the episodic is the law rather than the exception" ("The Synoptic Chandler" 38). The answer, according to Jameson, is that unlike the rest of Chandler's novels, *The High Window* offers no representation of nature. Jameson argues that nature, especially water, "the sign of the nonhuman axis of matter in these novels" (55), exists in Chandler's novels as somehow outside of the narrative world bounded by his sociology. What it does quite simply is "cancel" that narrative, in a manner that nevertheless renders the text as dialectically whole and complete. The "hard wet rain in the clearness of the foothills" described in the first sentence of *The Big Sleep* and which never lets up,[25] Rusty Regan's final resting place in the sump ponds of an oil field, the offshore floating casinos to which Marlowe experiences a nerve-shattering and discombobulating motorboat passage in *Farewell, My Lovely,* and the corpse-bearing mountain reservoir of Fawn Lake in *The Lady in the Lake* —these instances of "the liquid element" Jameson associates with "death itself" (52), a symbolic and dialectical force that cuts against the usual system of social and economic relations by which Chandler structures his detective's movement through the greater Los Angeles area. *The High Window* fails to satisfy largely because it does not contain the full "spatial outside or underside" (55) of Chandler's Los Angeles; despite its being a murder mystery, it contains no palpable hint of death, which comes by way of the intrusion of nature into the social schema. Jameson, to say the least, clearly enjoys Chandler for the way in which he (apparently) enables the reader to "[touch] on the outer edge of Being itself" (53).[26] But regardless of its validity as a description of the *effect* that comes from reading Chandler, Jameson's aesthetic/thematic interpretation of water, which falls on Chandler's just and unjust alike, does point out the semiotic importance of Chandler's nature: it organizes the narratives.

In Chandler's fourth novel, *The Lady in the Lake,* Jameson finds "an unusual semic combination of history, nature, and human production rare even in Chandler" (46). The reason, simply put, is the novel's ample yet very specific representation of nature. Set for almost half of its action high up in the San Gabriel and San Bernardino Mountains, which form the northern edge of the Los Angeles basin, *The Lady in the Lake* hinges its mystery on the identification of a body found submerged in Fawn Lake, a reservoir of decidedly artificial provenance. Built to look like an old mill, the dam responsible for Fawn Lake is in fact the product of Hollywood artifice: "Some movie outfit put it up three years ago. They made a picture up here" (495), Marlowe is told when he arrives. Puma Lake, the other resort-oriented body of water Marlowe encounters, is somewhat more real than Fawn, insomuch as it was really built as a water storage reservoir. Nevertheless, as with Fawn Lake, the narration emphasizes the human artifice by which Puma Lake is maintained, as evident in Marlowe's first impression: "The Puma Lake dam had an armed sentry at each end and one in the middle. The first one I came to had me close all the windows of the car before crossing the dam. About a hundred yards away from the dam a rope with cork floats barred the pleasure boats from coming any closer" (489). Published in 1943, this thinly fictionalized version of Big Bear Lake above San Bernardino eerily reflects its status as a wartime commodity (hence Jameson's "unusual semic combination of history [and] nature"). Half a century earlier, John Muir had observed that in these same mountains, "People mine here for water as for gold" (*Mountains of California* 374); in Chandler's handling, the water has very much achieved the status of gold, a resource worth protecting to the death. As Marlowe discovers in the course of his investigation, those armed government soldiers have orders to shoot anyone who threatens to compromise the integrity and security of the dam. Chandler thus paints a picture of a lake held prisoner, as it were, an ostensibly natural feature kept under strict guard by the people responsible for its existence.

But this is also the novel in which David Wyatt has observed the phenomenon of people turning into "somethings." As this chapter has argued, this key representational strategy of Chandler's is not unique to *The Lady in the Lake,* although in this novel it is certainly at its most explicit. On the final page, for instance, Chandler describes the death of the murderer whom Marlowe had been searching for. In trying to escape, the killer had run his car onto Puma Dam, had been shot at by the sentries, and had come to his ultimate end at the base of the dam, on the dry side. Watching the effort to recover the body, Marlowe notes that "they had moved the car enough to lift something out. Something that had been a man" (625). Likewise, the mysterious corpse for which the novel is titled, the one that Marlowe discovers in Fawn Lake and which consequently turns his missing person search into a murder investigation, receives a similar description. Looking into the lake, Marlowe observes:

> The depths cleared again. Something moved in them that was not a board. It rose slowly, with an infinitely careless languor, a long dark twisted something that rolled lazily in the water as it rose. It broke the surface casually, lightly, without haste. . . .
>
> The thing rolled over once more and an arm flapped up barely above the skin of the water and the arm ended in a bloated hand that was the hand of a freak. Then the face came. A swollen pulpy gray white mass without features, without eyes, without mouth. A blotch of gray dough, a nightmare with human hair on it. (499)

As the body that had been Crystal Kingsley becomes in this passage a "something," a "nightmare" of "gray dough," the lake gains a "skin." Along with such other objects as a "doe deer with a leather dog collar" (510), the "velvet shadow of a manzanita bush" (519), and a client with "the eyes of a sock animal" who "looked as big as a horse in a creamy shetland sports coat" (582), Chandler continues his figurative emphasis on a sort of cross-material hybridity. Finally, when Kingsley's body is recovered from the lake, Marlowe observes that "the thing that had been a woman lay face down on the boards with a rope under the arms" (503).

Regarding the autopsy of the lady in the lake, the local sheriff at Puma Lake tells Marlowe, "She drowned. . . . She wasn't knifed or shot or had her head cracked in or anything. There's marks on her body, but too many to mean anything" (614), which along with the complete lack of facial features makes her impossible to identify. And since the body cannot identify itself, it thus poses a problem of missing signification—in a word, it does not disambiguate. In the context of hard-boiled realism, this detail is important in that it once again compels Marlowe to solve a mystery not by reading the clues of the scene but rather by disentangling the narratives by which each of the principal characters expresses a relationship to the body (a task further complicated by an instance of mistaken identity). Marlowe has to figure out who people *think* the victim should be and then determine whose story/relationship best leads to an identification—and a murderer. As in *The Big Sleep,* Chandler's other resource-rich novel, Marlowe operates as Hammett's detectives did, by looking not at the referent for a solution, not at the thing itself, but rather at the description of the referent. In effect, he must read for the referent that fails to disambiguate itself materially.[27]

If, as Joan Copjec describes it, the hard-boiled detective seeks to "demonstrate that the surface of language never covers a depth" ("Private Space" 177), then what Marlowe ultimately discovers in his repeated encounters with human things and the like is the surfaces of so-called nature. A trip he takes into the country at the conclusion of *The Big Sleep* brings him to Realito, a former mining town that now holds "a cyanide plant where they make the stuff for fumigation" in California's many orange groves (110). Chandler's hard-boiled fiction argues that with respect to a presumably natural nature, resource industries *are* the surface, and the perceived depths are easily misread. That is to say, one cannot access a natural nature of any presumed value—scenic, biotic, ecotopic, and so forth—without passing through the material industries that have construed it as valuable.[28] And this applies equally to Chandler's reservoir under armed guard and the high Sierra tourist eco-wonderland promoted by Muir's picturesque renderings. As realism ("Real-ito") this formulation finally points to a significant problem in the appeal to nature as normative and nonhuman: nature, it seems, human or otherwise, cannot be counted on to provide the sole measure of reality. In his reading of late-nineteenth-century fiction's relation to the logic of the gold standard, Walter Benn Michaels offers the recovery of what he calls "not a meaning that has been obscured, but a meaning that has been, one might say, *read through,* as if it were transparent" (176; emphasis in original). This is precisely how hard-boiled fiction approaches the representation of nature: it makes visible once again that which has become materially transparent. In this respect, the connection between reading as detection and resources is finally most telling, in that what ultimately fails to disambiguate through representation is nature itself. The perduring fiction of the American West as a space of unalloyed nature is thus discovered as but one component of a natural resource economy, for in the West, nature is never very far away from a mine or a dam or an oil rig—there is no human-accessible "out there" that does not already contain an economic, technological, ideological human presence. The potential for representing a nature that is recognizable as such appears, to say the least, to be rather limited.

It would be worthwhile now to revisit, by way of some quite recent examples, the observation that the words in the phrase "western nature" function as a pair of mutually reinforcing simple abstractions. When the critic Richard Rodriguez published an essay called "True West" in the September 1996 issue of *Harper's,* both the essay and the responses to it were but the latest contributions to a long tradition of examining and explicating the realness of the American West in the pages of that particular magazine. Once again using California—specifically, his childhood in Sacramento—as the yardstick by which a "real" westernness could be gauged, Rodriguez observed that despite having "a Chicago-accented neighbor who spoke of California as the West" and a Mexican-born father who saw California as *el norte,* "any imagination I had of the West (a landscape suggested by studio backlots in Burbank, which was south) lay east of the Sierras." Rodriguez is not so interested in a geographic point on a map as he is in the extraordinary history of an iconographic aspect of the generic imagination. Thus, the multidirectional designations for a single place he had encountered in his boyhood lead Rodriguez to conclude that " 'West' is imaginary" (37), an American cultural and spatial concept designed to contain a loose arrangement of notions such as freedom through self-determinacy, the cowboy ethos, and the manifest "license to dominate Nature" (45). Indeed, paramount among Rodriguez's concerns are the ways in which popular discourses continue to "create" the West (and more recently Alaska) as "a pagan reserve—Nature sacrosanct" (46).

Three months later, *Harper's* published several letters to the editor in which self-identified western readers of the magazine expressed disappointment at having been told that they live not in a specific place but in an abstract metaphor. One writer from Culver City, California, admonished Rodriguez by referring to an ardent westerner who also happens to once have been the editor of *Harper's:* "The West is just a place, Mr. Rodriguez, neither better nor worse than other places. . . . Bernard DeVoto would not be amused." And a correspondent from Yakima, Washington, simply advised Rodriguez to "open your windows in the 'not East.' We're more than metaphor" (*Harper's* Dec. 1996, 5–6). This second response implies once again that most fundamental of associations Americans have with their western regions: the correlation of the place with the outdoors. If Rodriguez had really been interested in examining western reality, he needed only to have looked at the world beyond his window, or, by implication, at the natural environment. Of course, the majority of westerners today would in doing so find not an unalloyed nature but city streets and suburban yards, and so opening one's window on the West does not necessarily locate one in a Yosemite-like wilderness.[29] However, the empirical stance of the writer from Yakima is clearly in line with at least a century and a half of looking to an idea about the natural environment as a way of verifying the realness of the American West. That the assumption persists can be further deduced from a tale that William Least Heat-Moon tells of a man in a Strong City, Kansas, coffee shop who mutters the following complaint about a visiting historian from the East: "Couldn't tell a sycamore from a cottonwood, hadn't the least idea of what kind of tree to cut a wagon axle out of. He wasn't exactly sure what an ox is. He didn't know how to make hominy, hadn't ever skinned a squirrel or milked a cow—and he got paid fifty thousand a year to tell college kids about the West" (*PrairyErth;* qtd. in Kowalewski, *Reading the West* 15).

Taken as indicators of a perduring element of the generic imagination, the above examples demonstrate that, for some, being in the West still correlates quite clearly to being in a natural environment. Taken as literary events, as texts, they operate with equal familiarity as claims to realism that attempt to connect narratives of the "real" West with nature. And what is at stake in both instances amounts to the following question: Who, or what, has the requisite knowledge to determine what the West is really like? As this study has traced the textual and cultural history of a series of such claims, it has uncovered a body of writing within the movement of American realism that both exploits and lays bare the epistemological uncertainty of any claim to realism based on nature. The failure of nature to disambiguate itself at the end of a Chandler novel may thus be taken as the lasting achievement of western American literary realism. The writers who have used California's natural resources as a means of grappling with ideas about both the West and realism constitute a tradition that has long made evident, often through available and popular genre forms, the fact that somewhere just under the surface of "western nature" inevitably lies a natural resource industry. And in bringing this material and textual "reality" to light, western American literary realism suggests that when it comes to questions of knowledge about the West, whatever the answers, they are not to be found in nature. Genre literature, on the other hand, definitely has something to say about it.

Notes

Introduction

1. See Lynn, *Howells,* esp. 167–68.

2. Critical examinations of White are scarce. For basic information see Butte, Alter, and Seelye 317–19.

3. The phrase "west cure" appeared initially in Jennifer Tuttle's "To Rest or To West? Charlotte Perkins Gilman, Owen Wister, and the Sexual Politics of Nervous Exhaustion." See also Barbara Will's "The Nervous Origins of the American Western." Both Tuttle and Will examine the "rest cure" variation that Mitchell prescribed only for his male patients—head west and live vigorously—and which led to Wister's recovery from neurasthenia and subsequent success as the author of *The Virginian*.

4. The occasional discussion of western American literary realism has traditionally been restricted to assessments of historical accuracy or moral imperatives—over how many ridges a mountain man could reasonably be expected to ride in a day or what it means for a town to take the law into its own hands. See Westbrook, Milton, Tatum, and also Lyon's introduction to *The Literary West* (1–18). Little effort has been made, however, to connect late-nineteenth-century conversations about the West with those concurrently taking place over the idea of literary realism. Bredahl, in a study that at times pauses to consider the possibility of such connections, argues not for a reciprocity of discourse but largely for a distinction between twentieth-century eastern and western literary form in which the latter is separate from but occasionally an influence on the former.

5. Landmark examinations of California that have in some measure treated the state's cultural productions as a unique or special case include those by McWilliams, Starr, and Wyatt. By contrast, for an analysis that approaches the goals of the present study, see Fender on how the West as a whole was "plotted" in nineteenth-century narratives about California. Other notable cultural and

literary studies that have recently enlivened or expanded our understanding of the West include Allmendinger, Comer, Dorst, Robinson, and Rosowski.

6. This project shares Bill Brown's formulation of "the material unconscious," which "names literature's repository of disparate and fragmentary, unevenly developed, even contradictory images of the material everyday"—in *Traces of Gold,* natural resource industry materials—and which provides a means by which to assess "the pressure that such materiality . . . exerts on literary texts" and "the formalizing pressure those texts exert on the heterogeneity of lived life" (*Material Unconscious* 4). For Brown, this method allows for a challenge to the ideologies of inevitability posited by New Historicism that do little more than "recirculat[e] the dominant cultural memory" and reduce cultural history to mere text (5, 18). Similarly, the idea of a "material unconscious" focused on resources enables a view of the American West that directly confronts the problem of seeing the West as a space of unfettered, natural fulfillment. For a methodologically related study of the material culture of late-nineteenth-century American museums, see Conn. Also, for recent challenges to the "police academy" visions of literary realism offered by New Historicism, see Thomas, Dauber.

7. The phrase "conventional iconography" comes from Dorst (9), from his analysis of the "discourses of looking" by which the American West has become "the primary symbolic landscape through which the nation defines itself and the face by which it is most readily recognized throughout the rest of the world" (102). In a different context, Mary Louise Pratt has described this idea as "a basic repertoire of images" (125).

8. Notably, a rare dissenting opinion to this assumption at the time came from Bret Harte. In a letter for the *Springfield (Mass.) Republican* written roughly five months after his commentary on the Munchausen-like exaggerations of California descriptions, in September 1867, Harte sarcastically advised, "Go and see Bierstadt's wonderful 'Domes of the Yo Semite.' If what the critics say be true, he has given them an atmosphere so poetic, so delicious, that one does not care to see the original bleak, bare, coldly outlined and sharply incisive monoliths in their original, practical conditions. . . . Is it the haze which distance and a poetic memory lends to the past, or must we thank thee, O A.B., for granting us through that larger sense of consistency and harmony which belongs to art, the charm which nature has so churlishly denied us?" (*Bret Harte's California* 133).

9. See Mitchell's *Westerns* for a formalist analysis that draws parallels between the cultural work performed by Bierstadt's landscapes and Harte's tales (57–93).

10. Stephen Crane's "The Blue Hotel" offers a similar, albeit much more critical, view of the formative impact of reading genre fiction about the West. See also Richard Harding Davis's *The West from a Car-Window.*

11. See also Howard 3–35 for an illuminating discussion of genre forms and the construction of expectations; and Kaplan for an exploration of how realist authors such as Howells, Dreiser, and Wharton absorbed assumptions about

authorship into their own works and personae. On authorship and professionalism during the realist period, see Borus, Wilson.

12. My thanks to Nancy Armstrong for helping to clarify this point (e-mail to the author, 5 May 1998). See McKeon for an elucidation of the crises in representation and epistemology that led to the earliest "doctrines of realism" among English novelists such as Defoe, Fielding, Richardson, and Behn.

13. See Brown, *Reading the West,* and also Denning for discussions of the powerful cultural influence exerted by cheaply produced, widely distributed dime novels.

14. For a reading of western American literature's use of realism to provoke contemplation of the inadequacy of representation, in the context not of nature writing but of historical fiction, see Tatum.

15. Moreover, the majority of the essays in this anthology in one manner or another call for literary criticism to reanimate its representations of nature, as Christopher Manes argues in a piece entitled "Nature and Silence" (15–29), by letting nature speak for itself. Such a rhetorical move, with its faith in an "articulate" referent, may be read as a claim to realism. For analyses of the rhetorical strategies of environmentalists and their enemies alike, see the essays in Herndl and Brown.

16. Buell himself touches on ASLE's foundation and the related potential for constructing an environmental criticism out of western material in "Circling the Spheres" (483). Other instances of the use of the West in seminal ecocritical texts include studies by O'Grady, Slovic, and Teague, all founding officers of ASLE, and also by Erisman, Love. In the introduction to his recent anthology *The Literary West,* Thomas J. Lyon limns the development of western American literature as a narrative that begins with explorers' reports and native myths, enters the period of romantic fantasies, proceeds through the "realistic" coming-of-age period of the mid–twentieth century, and concludes with the "real" West now being written, in its most mature phase yet, through ecologically aware writing (1–18). He repeats this progressive narrative through realism to environmentalism in his survey of criticism (425–32). Finally, as to ASLE meetings, they have thus far been held in Fort Collins, Colorado; Missoula, Montana; Kalamazoo, Michigan (the non-western site); and Flagstaff, Arizona.

17. See Henderson for a discussion of how realist literary discourse helped both to narrate and to bring into effect the late-nineteenth-century capitalist transformation of California, i.e., "the turning of nature into money" (xi).

18. Michael Cohen ponders this very issue in his essay "A Brittle Thesis," in which he admits to being chagrined by the discovery that Muir's ecologically aware celebration of California's flowers, a celebration Cohen had shared in his book on Muir, *The Pathless Way,* was unbeknownst to both writers in fact a celebration of mostly non-native plant species from Europe. Remarking further that native peoples had also altered the local environment, Cohen admits that what he and Muir had taken to be completely and naturally nonhuman turned out

to have endured the effects of human enterprise well before Muir's moment of observation.

Chapter 1

1. Several print versions of this lecture exist, including an authoritative version published in the Standard Library Edition of *The Works of Bret Harte* (1894–1904). The text of this particular passage, however, comes from a *Springfield Daily Republican* review published the day after the lecture. In the authorized version Harte has removed the statement "I do not know that is strictly true," an emendation which suggests that Harte's 1872 challenge to the truth-value of the narrative had somewhat diminished a quarter-century later. This disparity between versions does not however significantly alter the observation that Harte was keenly interested in the representability of the Gold Rush. For an alternate but incomplete text of this lecture compiled from various newspaper reports, see Kozlay.

2. Harte's reference is to Charles C. Nahl's illustrations for *The Idle and Industrious Miner,* an 1854 booklet for which Alonzo Delano has long been the suspected author of the unsigned accompanying verses (see Walker, *Literary Frontier* 38). This attribution, however, is beginning to erode in favor of a California poetaster named William Bausman; see T. H. Watkins's introduction to the recent reprint of this booklet in *American West* magazine (39).

3. On Harte's use of ironic humor, see Kolb. Gary Scharnhorst has developed the interpretation of Harte's texts as satire in a number of instances: on "the Luck of Roaring Camp" as satire see *Bret Harte* 22–25, and on "Plain Language from Truthful James" see "Ways That Are Dark" 377–79. On the latter see also Duckett 242.

4. The figure of 67,000 westering immigrants comes from Holliday 83, 312.

5. On Davis as an early realist, see Harris. Notably, as was the case with many other texts and essays about American realism, "Life in the Iron Mills" first appeared in the *Atlantic Monthly*.

6. See Allmendinger 33–50 for an excellent recent discussion of Ridge's novel.

7. The extent to which Harte's ambiguous tone here succeeds in setting the terms for understanding the Gold Rush may be judged in part by Kevin Starr, who, despite his highly unfavorable view of Harte's representations, gives Harte exactly what he asks for: in *Americans and the California Dream,* Starr decries Harte for writing "sentimental melodrama" but three pages later proclaims that "the Gold Rush was both Iliad and Odyssey" (49, 52). See Scharnhorst's "Whatever Happened to Bret Harte?" for a discussion of the misinformed charge of sentimentalism leveled against Harte and the shaping of our current literary canon. For recent discussions of gender typing in both Harte's and Twain's Gold Rush tales, see Stevens, Stoneley.

8. The very next "Etc." item celebrates the announcement of Bancroft's soon-to-be-published *The Native Races*.

9. Assessing the decision to begin his *Works* with a five-volume account of California's pre-conquest inhabitants, Bancroft recalls: "I would gladly have avoided them. . . . My tastes in the matter, however, did not dispose of the subject. The savages were there, and there was no help for me; I must write them up to get rid of them" (qtd. in Walker, *Literary Frontier* 307).

10. While the technologically simple, individualistically driven placer phase of California's Gold Rush had been long gone by this time, mining as an industry had only just begun its dominance of the late-nineteenth-century economy in the American West (see Robbins 83–102). The discovery of the "Big Bonanza" on Nevada's Comstock Lode was at least half a year away, and booming rushes for coal in Wyoming and Colorado, for yet more gold in South Dakota, Alaska, and the Yukon, and for copper in Arizona and Montana were still to come before the turn into the twentieth century. By 1900, mining provided employment for 11 percent of the workers in Colorado, 12 percent in Idaho, 13 percent in Montana, and 15 percent in Arizona, while the national average stood at less than 1 percent (figures cited in Milner, O'Connor, and Sandweiss 433–43). For a discussion of the impact on literature of such economic growth, see Howard 30–32, 72–76.

11. Accounts of Clappe's career can be found in Marlene Smith-Baranzini's excellent introduction to Heyday Books's recent edition of *The Shirley Letters* (ix–xxxv) and in Lockhart. For a look into Clappe's later years (she died in a New Jersey nursing home that was managed by nieces of Bret Harte's), see Rodman Paul's "In Search of 'Dame Shirley.'"

12. The Clappes lived and worked for a while at Rich Bar on the Feather, in the same camp and at roughly the same time that a nineteen-year-old newcomer named Hubert H. Bancroft first mined and later clerked in his brother Curtis's dry goods store. Clappe mentions Curtis Bancroft several times, most frequently in "Letter Ninth" (60–67).

13. See Walker, *Literary Frontier* 30–35; Kowalewski, "Quoting the Wicked Wit of the West" 89–92. Clappe refers at one point to her epistolary representations as "the darker shades of our mountain life" (133); cf. Delano's call in *Pen-Knife Sketches* for telling the other side of mining life, namely, that left out of newspaper accounts.

14. As further evidence of this phenomenon, consider Frederick Law Olmsted, who came to the California goldfields in 1863 to serve as managing supervisor of the Mariposa Mine just west of Yosemite Valley (all biographical details from Roper 233–90). Disheartened and depressed by his Civil War work for the Sanitary Fund Commission in Washington, D.C., and frustrated in his attempts to retain full creative control over the ongoing design and construction of Central Park in New York City, the forty-one-year-old landscape architect essentially came West for his health. While traveling across the arid, sun-browned stretches

of the San Joaquin Valley, a deeply glum Olmsted wrote to his wife that he felt unsure of whether or not to use the word "beautiful" to describe the valley (Roper 240). Upon reaching the Sierra foothills, Olmsted wrote in another letter to his wife that "the desolation was somewhat relieved by multitudes of children's graves." These rounded-over piles of gravel, he would later learn, were in fact the tailings, or heaps of discarded rock, from the many mines in the area (F. L. Olmsted, *The California Frontier* 98). What is striking about Olmsted's initial response to the gold country is that he has picked up on one of the fundamental characteristics of western mining narratives, namely, the association of the material of the mines with the material of the human body. How Olmsted might have come by his observation is largely irrelevant to this discussion, whether it was by his having been an avid reader of books and periodicals from California, or by his having sensed a mood in his brief time in San Francisco, or even by the sheer coincidence of the particulars of his depressed aesthetic imagination. What matters is that Olmsted's metaphoric conflation of rock and body accords remarkably with what would over the course of a decade become a dominant thematic element in the popular discourse of mining.

15. See, respectively, "The Luck of Roaring Camp" (*Selected Stories* 7–17) and "Letter Fifth, September 22, 1851" (34–37).

16. In the 1860s, after giving up his publishing endeavors, Hutchings capitalized further on his earnings by taking up residence in Yosemite Valley and establishing both the valley's first tourist hotel and a sawmill where John Muir worked for a season.

17. All citations from this publication are taken from the photoreproduction available in the Yale Microfilm Series, *Western Americana: Frontier History of the Trans-Mississippi West, 1550–1990,* reel 277, item 2735. A facsimile reproduction, albeit one too small to read by, may be found in Walker, *Literary Frontier,* between pages 30 and 31. The text of Hutchings's lettersheet has recently been published in Kowalewski, *Gold Rush* 290–93.

18. Clappe, Harte, Twain, and even Muir all rely extensively on this familiar figure. Muir's debt to Gold Rush writing and, in particular, to this figure will be discussed in chapter 2.

19. Discussing Delano's important contribution to western humor writing, Henry Wonham points out that Delano's comic style "hinged on the contrast between exaggeratedly romantic images of western life and equally exaggerated accounts of abject poverty and hardship on the frontier" (91). Unlike Delano's "Old Block" sketches, which very much rely on this style for comic effect, Delano's cross-country account is framed in the much less humorous style of the travel narrative. Notably, the effigy sequence is one of only a handful of Delano's pieces to appear in both books (p. 36 in *Pen-Knife Sketches*). That this sequence works equally well in the context of both burlesque and overland journalism testifies to the textual significance of the author's encounter with the abject in the gold country.

20. In a similar satire, Harte writes in his 1868 poem "The Society upon the

Stanislaus" about a miner named Brown who, upon finding a pile of ossified bones, theorizes that they belonged to an ancient animal, until he is told by Jones that they were in fact the remains of one of Jones's mules.

21. And the controversy goes on: no longer considered a remnant of North America's earliest inhabitants, the skull nevertheless continues to generate debate over whether it belonged to a hapless forty-niner or to a 4,000-year-old native inhabitant. Carbon-based dating techniques, it seems, are not accurate enough. Thus, in archeological circles the question of identity is far from settled, and the Calaveras Skull still resides uneasily in the Peabody Museum at Harvard. See Taylor, "The Age of the Calaveras Skull"; Dexter.

22. See Duckett for a full and detailed exploration of the initially friendly but ultimately acrimonious relationship between Harte and Twain.

23. For background details concerning Clemens's interest and involvement in this matter, see Edgar Branch's commentary in Twain, *Clemens of the Call* 233–35.

24. See the publication history provided by editors Branch and Hirst in *Early Tales and Sketches* 1: 320–23. The *Evening Bulletin* ran its reprint three days later, on 31 October, and it appended at the end the first line of Twain's apology: "I take it all back." Whatever the case, Twain's stated goal of having a critique of the Spring Valley Water Company run in a San Francisco newspaper was ostensibly achieved. The other two papers, it appears, were completely taken in by the sensationalistic hoax. See also Highton 49–52; Fatout 99–112; Lillard.

25. The most comprehensive study of the hoax in the tradition of the Old Southwest humorists remains Kenneth Lynn's *Mark Twain and Southwestern Humor*. More recent studies of Twain's hoaxing include Jeffrey Steinbrink, *Getting to Be Mark Twain;* Don Florence, *Persona and Humor in Mark Twain's Early Writing;* and Bruce Michelson, *Mark Twain on the Loose: A Comic Writer and the American Self*. Both Florence and Michelson approach the hoax first as humor in the context established by Lynn and second as examples of ambiguous meaning and identity, while Steinbrink evaluates the persona of Twain.

26. "Dan De Quille" is the pen name of William Wright. It should not escape notice that in this arena of representation and reality, the writerly pseudonym was a very popular item. In addition to those of De Quille (Wright), Old Block (Delano), Dame Shirley (Clappe), and Twain (Clemens), San Franciscans enjoyed the work of such pseudonymous writers as Artemis Ward (Charles Farrar Browne), Yellow Bird (John Rollin Ridge), Dogberry (Prentice Mulford), Joaquin Miller (Cincinnatus Hiner Miller), Professor John Phoenix, and John P. Squibob (the last two both belonging to George Horatio Derby). Falling beyond the scope of the present project, this aspect of Gold Rush literary representation nevertheless deserves a fuller examination.

27. "Petrified Man" appeared in the *Territorial Enterprise* on 4 Oct. 1862; rpt. in *Early Tales and Sketches* 1: 159. "Silver Man" appeared in the *Golden Era* on 5 Feb. 1865; rpt. in Dwyer and Lingenfelter 178–84.

28. For the reception history of De Quille's hoaxes, see Lawrence Berkove's

headnotes in the collection *The Fighting Horse of the Stanislaus,* which reprints several of De Quille's most effective hoaxes. "Solar Armor," for instance, was reprinted in earnest by both *Scientific American* and the *London Daily Telegraph* (14).

29. In a number of articles for the *San Francisco Call,* Clemens (he was not writing as Mark Twain) inveighs against the assessment system (see *Clemens of the Call* 236–40). In one such piece, he charges sarcastically, "It is an idea entertained by some inconsiderate persons, that a mine should at some period of the world's history begin to pay its own expenses" (239).

30. De Quille, for instance, notes in his history of the Comstock Lode that throughout the 1860s and 1870s the Bullion Mine kept pace, in terms of rock excavated and shafts dug, with other large, seemingly more legitimate operations (*Big Bonanza* 160, 359, 386).

31. De Quille observes in *The Big Bonanza* that with respect to the amount of timber required to support a mining operation, "The Comstock lode may truthfully be said to be the tomb of the forests of the Sierra" (174). By way of historical contrast, I should note that he makes this assertion at the same moment in time that Muir begins his career in celebration of the untouched beauty of the Sierra.

32. For a discussion of how later nineteenth-century canonical realism, especially that of Henry James, conveys similarly an economic relationship between bodies and their representation on paper, see Seltzer.

33. See esp. Goldman's chapter 1, "Material Life on the Comstock Lode" 11–37. See also Elliot 123–51 passim. For insights into the role of photography, especially that of Timothy O'Sullivan, in the technologization of both Virginia City's natural environs and its miners, see Trachtenberg, *Reading American Photographs* 144–54.

34. From the *Territorial Enterprise,* 24 May 1864; reprinted in Twain, *Mark Twain of the Enterprise* 196–98. For Twain's apology, see *Letters* 1: 296.

35. Echoing Franklin Walker, Kowaleweski asserts that Gold Rush writing arises out of a situation in which "no *native* Californian wrote for publication during its frontier period. The writing and art of the 1850s were created by people translated from conditions of relative stability to social chaos" ("Imagining" 62–63). What this chapter attempts to argue, however, is that the forty-niners' particular chaos is not just "social" in nature—it is also material.

36. See, e.g., Steinbrink 104.

37. On the phenomenon of Harte's popularity, see Gary Scharnhorst's *Bret Harte,* esp. 40–65, and "Whatever Happened to Bret Harte?" A $10,000 contract with Fields, Osgood, publishers of the *Atlantic Monthly,* made Harte in 1871 the highest-paid author in America. For a discussion of the correlative career paths of Harte and Alfred Bierstadt, see Mitchell, *Westerns* 57–93.

38. Harte adds a further note of metareference when his narrator claims to own several of "Mistress Carmen's" paintings (81). In this manner he adds to the sense of truthfulness in his "veracious history" (36).

39. A selective (and largely recent) sampling of such critics includes Kowalewski, "Quoting the Wicked Wit of the West"; Steinbrink; Michelson 63–74; Florence; Scharnhorst, "Mark Twain, Bret Harte, and the Literary Construction of San Francisco"; Cox; Wonham 89–111; and Mitchell, "Verbally *Roughing It*." Most recently, Richard Lowry has quipped, "As Twain figures it [in *Roughing It*], authorial success, the creation of value, depends not on the painful digging for precious metal . . . but on one's ability to negotiate a world of signs" (73).

40. The text of this anecdote, as presented by Twain, is word for word the same every time he hears it: "I can tell you a most laughable thing indeed, if you would like to listen to it. Horace Greeley went over this road once. When he was leaving Carson City he told the driver, Hank Monk, that he had an engagement to lecture in Placerville, and was very anxious to go through quick. Hank Monk cracked his whip and started off at an awful pace. The coach bounced up and down in such a terrific way that it jolted the buttons all off of Horace's coat, and finally shot his head clean through the roof of the stage, and then he yelled at Hank Monk and begged him to go easier—said he warn't in as much of a hurry as he was awhile ago. But Hank Monk said, 'Keep your seat, Horace, and I'll get you there on time!'—and you bet you he did, too, what was left of him!" (131–36 passim). In 1894, the Midwinter International Exposition in San Francisco put the Hank Monk–Horace Greeley anecdote to an altogether different use, relying quite un-ironically on its value as a historical narrative. See chapter 4.

41. Indeed, upon returning to San Francisco a few days after the incident, Clemens incorporated the story of the hoax robbery into the lectures he continued to give. According to an advertisement in the *San Francisco Times,* Twain concluded his talk on the evening of 16 November with "the only true and reliable history of the late REVOLTING HIGHWAY ROBBERY, perpetrated upon the Lecturer, at dead of night, between the cities of Gold Hill and Virginia." See explanatory notes to *Roughing It* 745.

42. Referring to Twain's accomplishment in combining and adapting inherited modes of comic writing, Michelson observes that Twain "was extraordinary as a Southwest humorist" in that he "perfected the Southwestern *meta*-tale, the story of a story" (26). Such a formulation accurately describes both Twain's and Harte's corollary accomplishments regarding the mining tale—they turned it into a mining tale about the mining tale.

Chapter 2

1. These are the titles of articles written about Muir and published, respectively, in *Century Magazine* (see Barrus); the *San Francisco Daily Call* 28 Mar. 1897: 17; and *Sunset* Aug. 1914: 355–57.

2. Muir's most frequently quoted line about mountains, first published in an 1898 essay on wildness and National Parks, asserts that "Thousands of tired, nerve-shaken, over-civilized people are beginning to find that going to the mountains is going home" ("Wild Parks" 15).

3. Biographical details in this essay derive primarily from Wolfe. See also Turner. Wilkins focuses mainly on Muir's career as a conservationist and wilderness advocate. For extensive bibliographic data on Muir, see Kimes and Kimes.

4. Muir's "Studies in the Sierras, I–VII" appeared between May 1874 and January 1875; in 1950 they were collected and published as *John Muir's Studies in the Sierra*, ed. William E. Colby.

5. This 1874 departure for Shasta partially in the employ of the *Bulletin* is generally recognized by Muir's biographers and critics as the signifying moment of his assumption of a profession. See Cohen, *Pathless Way* 206; O'Grady 73; Turner 198–201; and Wolfe 171–79.

6. On Muir as an environmental writer see Branch; Cohen, "Muir's Public Voice," *Pathless Way*, "Brittle Thesis"; Fox; Nash 122–81; Oelschlaeger 172–204; O'Grady 47–86; Turner; Wilkins; and Wyatt, *Fall into Eden* 32–46. Regarding Muir's take on mining, the one notable exception is Cohen, who touches on Muir's use of a mining analogy to criticize the destruction wrought by "wildcat farming" (*Pathless Way* 226–27). Also, Stephen Fender argues briefly that Muir's writings derive in part from the work of Gold Rush journalists (184–86). Unlike the present study, though, Fender does not probe into the specifics of Muir's engagement with Gold Rush representations.

7. Briefly stated, the catastrophic theory held that Yosemite Valley had been formed by a sudden, cataclysmic subsidence in which a section of the mountain terrain dropped several thousand feet in elevation to create, almost instantaneously, the valley's floor and distinctive vertical rock faces. Muir, on the other hand, argued correctly that the formative process had been the slow grinding of rock and ice wrought by ancient glaciers (Fox 19–25).

8. The figure of nature as a book would prove to be a favorite of Muir's throughout his career. His very first article on Yosemite and his second publication ever, in fact, begins: "Two years ago, when picking flowers in the mountains back of Yosemite Valley, I found a book. It was blotted and storm-beaten; all its outer pages were mealy and crumbly, the paper seeming to dissolve like the snow beneath which it had been buried; but many of the inner pages were well preserved, and though all were more or less stained and torn, whole chapters were easily readable" ("Yosemite Glaciers" 1).

9. This particularly "wretched, woebegone" miner has arrived at his condition largely by virtue of drinking and gambling, forces that were blamed for contributing to a miner's destitution as frequently as bad luck in the diggings was. In either case, the literary type as described remains the same. For a recent analysis of the preponderance and profitability of both liquor and gaming institutions in the goldfields, see Rohrbough 146–50.

10. "Miggles" and "How Santa Claus Came to Simpson's Bar" first appeared, respectively, in the *Overland Monthly* in June 1869 and in the *Atlantic Monthly* in March 1872; the novella "Mrs. Skagg's Husband" was first issued in a collection published in 1873 by Boston's J. R. Osgood and Co. All three were widely re-

printed and eventually collected in *The Writings of Bret Harte,* Standard Library Edition. For full bibliographic details see Scharnhorst's *Bret Harte: A Bibliography.*

11. "Tuolumne, California," is not to be confused with the high Sierra locale known as Tuolumne Meadows in what is now Yosemite National Park and about which Muir frequently wrote. Twain's use of this name refers to the Jackass Hill/Angel's Camp mining region near present-day Tuttletown, in the foothills of Tuolumne County. See the explanatory notes to this passage in the 1993 edition of *Roughing It* for a brief but well-documented account of why Twain had to leave San Francisco and "hole up" in the mining country for several months (703–5); see also the notebooks Twain kept during his time in the Tuolumne goldfields, reproduced in *Mark Twain's Journals and Notebooks* (1: 63–90).

12. Not wholly without feeling for such a figure, Twain provides another glimpse of the abject, starving wraith in his highly sympathetic rendering of Blucher's story in chapter 59 of *Roughing It* (405–11).

13. Known in Muir's time as the Fresno Grove, this stand of sequoia trees was greatly reduced by logging in the 1880s. What remains is now known as the Nelder Grove, no doubt due in part to Muir's having focused public attention on the man once ensconced therein.

14. On Dowd's "discovery," see Willis; on the literary history associated with Murphy's Camp and Calaveras County, see Mace. The legend of Murieta was widely memorialized by John Rollin Ridge's *The Life and Adventures of Joaquín Murieta* (1854).

15. Muir's reference, after that to Harte, is to Joaquin Miller, poet, short-story writer, and self-styled frontier showman from San Francisco. The final reference to Hayes, however, is uncertain; I have thus far been unable to locate a Gold Rush sketch writer bearing this name who is contemporary with Muir.

16. For an account of Nevada's major mineral rushes, see Elliot 49–68, 90–151.

17. Speaking not of Harte but of Muir's engagement with Wordsworth, William Cronon describes Muir's landscape as a "domesticated sublime" devoid of the usual anxiety and terror (75).

18. See Rainey for a discussion of the development of a picturesque approach to tourism and landscape appreciation in late-nineteenth-century American print culture in general and the *Picturesque America* series in particular (Muir edited the California volume for this series). See also Hyde 107–46, 191–243; and Andrews, who provides an important study of the picturesque as it first developed in England.

19. Turner suggests in his biography of Muir that this passage shows Muir's unambiguous contempt for the dehumanizing mistreatment evident in the image of men chipping away "like navvies" at the ore (249). Turner's interpretation, however, requires that a great deal of irony be read into Muir's accompanying descriptions of the "orderly deliberation" of the enterprise and the haste-free handling of the materials, neither of which Turner mentions. Turner

also opts not to quote or even recognize Muir's choice of the term "workmen," preferring instead to revert to "miners" (248–49).

20. Married in 1880 to Louie Wanda Strentzel, Muir spent much of the 1880s working for his new in-laws as an orchard foreman and manager on their ranch near Martinez, California. He continued to write for the *Bulletin* through October 1881, reporting on his third trip to Alaska, and he published a two-part essay on "Bee-Pastures of California" in *Century Magazine* in June and July 1882. However, devoting himself to his new family and ranch, the usually prolix Muir published very little again until 1888, when *Picturesque California,* which he had both edited and written several chapters for, was issued by the J. Dewing Company of New York. According to Michael Cohen, this rather inauspicious and highly derivative initial attempt to recover his public voice arose largely as a consequence of Muir's reputation from the 1870s having limited any lingering appeal he may have had for publishers; the "picturesque" is predominantly what they remembered and expected of him. See Cohen, *Pathless Way* 240.

21. See Cohen's "John Muir's Public Voice" for a detailed discussion of how Muir's association with Johnson helped to shape this renewed public image. See also Fox 86–107.

22. Muir to Johnson, 3 Apr. 1894, in *The Life and Letters of John Muir* 2: 287; emphasis in original.

23. Originally published as "Flood-Storm in the Sierra."

24. The dating of the composition of *My First Summer* is of significance here, for the journals Muir kept during the summer of 1869 are no longer extant. However, sometime around 1887 Muir transcribed those journals into three notebooks, in all likelihood making changes and emendations as he did so (Cohen, *Pathless Way* 350). Furthermore, these notebooks, held in the John Muir Collection at the Holt-Atherton Library of the University of the Pacific and reproduced in the Microform Edition of *The John Muir Papers,* show extensive autograph revisions added sometime between 1887 and 1911 (the presumed date of initial transcription is that ascribed by the curators of the John Muir Collection and is used to determine the notebooks' chronological placement in the Microform Edition).

25. Cohen notes that "the structure of *First Summer* allowed both a young naturalist and an older creator of national parks to speak" (*Pathless Way* 351). In the case of Muir's note about mining's "light" impact "on the scenery," it is very much the older figure who speaks.

26. "Sierra Journal, Summer of 1869, v. 1" [ca. 1887], AMS notebook, p. 89, The John Muir Papers, Holt-Atherton Department of Special Collections, University of the Pacific Libraries, copyright 1984 Muir-Hanna Trust; reproduced in Limbaugh and Lewis, *The John Muir Papers,* Microform Edition, reel 31/00172. The manuscript of this heavily worked-over passage shows that the words "has been" were added in pencil at some later point, as were the sections "+ valley +" and "+ bare as if" and "alive" at one point struck through.

27. "Sierra Journal, Summer of 1869, v. III," AMS notebook, *John Muir Papers,* p. 141, reel 31/00531; and "Sierra Journal, Summer of 1869, v. III," TCCMS typescript, pp. 101–2, reel 31/00637-8.

28. See also Roorda 173–89 for an examination of the narratological and ethical dimensions of this rhetorical move.

Chapter 3

1. See Branch 144–45 n. 1 for a concise account of the various ways in which historians and critics have interpreted Muir's relation to Emerson and American romanticism. Particularly at issue has been the question of whether Muir's writings offer a continuation of or a challenge to Emersonian thought. In either case, Muir's debt to the author of *Nature* is undeniable. See also Wolfe; Cohen, *Pathless Way;* Oelschlaeger.

2. On Foote's illustrations see Armitage; and see L. A. Johnson for basic biographical and critical information. On Wallace Stegner's research into Foote's letters and his subsequent use of them in writing the character of Susan Burling Ward in his novel *Angle of Repose* (1971), see Walsh.

3. Similarly, Owen Wister claimed that Foote was the first writer to have "lifted to honor the cattle country and not to libel it" (qtd. in L. A. Johnson 157), that Foote's work had in fact been a formative influence on his own western stories (see Yates 11). On Field's extensive but virtually unknown writings about the West, see Scharnhorst's "Kate Field and the American West."

4. Foote's example also indicates clearly that literary realism in the West was neither exclusive nor reducible to the textual productions of California. However, given that her early apprentice work emerges from this locale, it does reaffirm the particular window onto western American literary realism that California affords and which serves as the focus of my argument in this book. Certainly much more work can be done to consider Foote's Colorado and Idaho mining tales in the context established by the present study.

5. Teague's chapter on "The Desert in the Magazines" provides a rough genealogy of how magazine representations moved from viewing deserts as either irrigable gardens or wastelands to the "cash crop" of aesthetics (91–125).

6. My thanks to Ray Boomhower of the Indiana Historical Society for providing details about the Western Association of Writers. Further information may be found in James Weygand's privately published history, *Winona Holiday.* For a contemporaneous critique of the association's overly regional emphasis, see Kate Chopin's "The Western Association of Writers."

7. Earlier in the week, Howells had himself written and published a review of Norris's new novel, a highly favorable reading that praises the author in part for what Howells implies is the accuracy of *McTeague*'s representations: "Polite readers of the sort who do not like to meet in fiction people of the sort they never meet in society will not have a good time in 'McTeague' " ("A Case in Point" 40).

8. Attempts to articulate the differing forms and functions of romance and realism in American literary history have a long and complex history. In addition to Glazener, recent forays into this field include the work of Brook Thomas, who in *American Literary Realism and the Failed Promise of Contract* characterizes the two modes as operating, respectively, on vertical and horizontal axes of reference and signification (8–12). Sundquist argues for seeing the two terms as practically interchangeable. For a discussion of the ways in which criticism, including that of Sundquist, has perhaps falsely maintained a schism between romance and realism, see Kaplan 1–14. See Bell's *The Development of American Romance* for a discussion of the terms as they were debated in antebellum literary circles. Finally, an earlier, highly influential argument can also be found in Chase.

9. Scharnhorst, "At War over Realism?" 300. Specific to Thompson's feelings about Howells, see Crissey, also Scharnhorst's "Maurice Thompson's Regional Critique."

10. For a fuller sense of the debate, see Cady, *The Realist at War;* Glazener; and the primary sources collected in Pizer. For a challenge to and modification of Cady's conclusions about Howells and regionalism, see especially Scharnhorst's research on Thompson.

11. With respect to the East, see Glazener 149–58 for an illuminating discussion of Agnes Repplier, who in her challenge of Howells became "one of the most influential framers and publicists of the ideas about reading that grounded the romantic revival" (149–50) in the late 1880s and 1890s.

12. Cf. Howells's comments on *McTeague* in note 7 above.

13. Newman is also reputed to have made his money selling leather across the West: "I lost money on wash-tubs, but I came out pretty square on leather" (86). For a fuller discussion of Newman's westernness as a significant component of the novel, see Saum. James's description of Newman could even be said to anticipate the vigorously Anglo-Saxon heroes of Owen Wister, particularly when he says of Newman that "exertion and action were as natural to him as respiration; a more completely healthy mortal had never trod the elastic soil of the West" (31).

14. Rowe, cited earlier, and Brooks, among others, have recently begun to argue for the formal and thematic elements of realism to be found in the ostensibly romantic ending of *The American*. Rowe considers James's expression of gender anxieties consistent with the fully realistic works of James's subsequent career, while Brooks argues that James, in the very last pages of the novel, finds his realist's topic and form in Newman's psychological state.

15. One contemporaneous position that suggestively mediates between the claims of romance and realism is that offered by Jack London in his description of his eponymous protagonist's fiction in the novel *Martin Eden:* "His work was realism, though he had endeavored to fuse with it the fancies and beauties of imagination. What he sought was an impassioned realism, shot through with human aspiration and faith. What he wanted was life as it was, with all its spirit-

groping and soul-reaching left in" (212). See also White's "The Saving Grace," discussed in the introduction above.

16. This point about literary culture during the late nineteenth century has been variously echoed and explored by Orvell, Shi, and Corkin, among others. Sounding a bit like Howells in explicitly making the connection to late-nineteenth-century prose from California, George Henderson succinctly writes: "Late-nineteenth-century authors strove to write fiction that had the aura of the true, the honest, the authentic" (112). For a suggestive and noteworthy modification, see the review essay by Dauber.

17. See McKeon for a thorough discussion of how "romance" and "realism" share their historical roots in debates over the novel's ability to represent, respectively, historical and present-day truths.

18. According to Norris, Twain is more humorist than fiction writer; Poe is great in everything but the novel and thus exempted; Hawthorne is concerned with English stories on American soil; and Cooper is too steeped in an English storytelling style; Henry James, by virtue of his self-imposed exile, is altogether too English; Longfellow, Lowell, Holmes, and Whittier are better understood as a New England school; Wharton and Garland are too regional; and Mary Wilkins (Norris's best bet for the future) is too susceptible to momentary public tastes for colonial romance (as in her novel *The Heart's Highway* [1900]) ("An American School" 108–9).

19. The books in which Howells treats his sense of westernness include *A Boy's Town* (1890), *My Year in a Log Cabin* (1893), *My Literary Passions* (1895), *Impressions and Experiences* (1896), *Literary Friends and Acquaintance* (1900), and *Years of My Youth* (1916). In large part these texts were compiled from essays and memoirs initially published in magazines such as *Harper's*. Subsequent biographers have also with varying degrees treated Howells as a onetime westerner. See esp. Cady; Lynn, *Howells;* and also Eble. Readings of Howells's literary use of the West include Bucco, Dean, Greenwald.

20. *A Modern Instance* served as the initial provocation for Thompson to question the integrity of Howells's westernness. The Indiana poet, who had hosted Howells when the latter came to Indiana to research the divorce court scenes, assailed the novel for not being true to its and its author's regional roots. See Scharnhorst, "Maurice Thompson's Regional Critique of William D. Howells."

21. Kenneth Lynn, among others, has suggested that Bartley Hubbard (B. H.) may have been modeled in part after Bret Harte (*Howells* 256–58). See also Bucco.

22. Martin Bucco points out that Lapham's discovery of his Vermont paint mine, which Howells places in 1855, coincides with the year in which the former forty-niner Matthew Kennedy discovered a real gold mine in Vermont (293).

23. See, e.g., Hyde, Rainey, and several of the essays collected in Cronon's *Uncommon Ground*.

24. Cf. Lynn, who suggests that Howells's westernness was perfectly tempered and complemented by four years in Venice (*Howells* 126).

25. See Bucco for an examination of the palpable presence of a nonspecific Texas throughout much of *Silas Lapham*.

26. Howells's narrator reserves judgment regarding Hubbard's untimely end for the reader, who must decide whether his death in Arizona is "consequence or penalty, as we choose to think it" (451).

27. Of the late nineteenth century in the United States, Trachtenberg writes: "Penetrating the West with government encouragement, the railroad and the telegraph opened the vast spaces to production. Following the lead of the railroads, commercial and industrial businesses conceived of themselves as having the entire national space at their disposal: from raw materials for processing goods to marketing" (*The Incorporation of America* 20).

Chapter 4

1. "Yellow back" westerns and adventure tales had exerted a tremendous cultural influence well before Wister. Recall, for instance, that as early as 1851 Dame Shirley complained that the men in the Rich Bar mining camp had been grossly misinformed about what to expect by having read "'yallow kivered' literature" (Clappe 18). The difference with *The Virginian* in 1902, however, is that it propelled the genre western to the publisher's A-list, achieving a sort of marketplace legitimacy that the genre had not previously enjoyed. See Cawelti, Klein, and also Bill Brown's important introduction to the dime-novel anthology *Reading the West*. On early-twentieth-century women writers of formula westerns, see Yates.

2. Donald Worster hails the passage of the Reclamation Act as the founding moment of a "hydraulic society" in the West, a bureaucratic and economic state of affairs that borders on oligarchy (64), a point echoed by Patricia Nelson Limerick (*Legacy* 87). Donald J. Pisani dissents from this view of an absolute and discernible shift effected by the act, but nonetheless agrees in seeing it as a key moment in western resource history, as evidenced by the dates given in his subtitle: "1848–1902." Of course, the availability of western water had been perceived throughout much of the nineteenth century as a problem of terrific and expensive proportions. John Wesley Powell's 1869 and 1872 explorations down the Colorado River had prompted him to caution Congress that only through massive irrigation projects could the West be made to sustain a population of any significance, an opinion shared with much less trepidation by the turn-of-the-century irrigation crusader William Ellsworth Smythe. Even the quintessential easterner Frederick Law Olmsted, in assuming in 1864 the position of manager of California's well-known Mariposa Mine, instantly recognized that profit in mining could only come at the expense of obtaining equally valuable water. He immediately wrote to his wife that "what the estate wants & must have if a million or two dollars would get it—is water" (109). What distinguished the passage of the Reclamation Act, however, is that with this legislation the federal government claimed the authority for building and managing massive federal projects such as Hoover Dam (initially called Boulder Dam), thereby setting into

motion the means by which the government would eventually become the primary force in western resource politics.

3. Harte's "Tennessee's Partner" was first published in the *Overland Monthly* in October 1869.

4. Both Miles Orvell and David Shi provide useful examinations of the extent to which post–Civil War American culture was, for the most part, concerned with referential verity and representational accuracy. The period of realism was, in many respects, a period of trying to capture and/or set the limits of the real. See Conn for a discussion of this phenomenon in the material culture of late-nineteenth-century museums. For a dissenting view of the positivist implications in Orvell and Shi, see Corkin.

5. See Nathan for an account of bohemian society in San Francisco.

6. From Chandler and Nathan: "The Firth Wheel was the Midwinter Fair's answer to—and imitation of—the Ferris Wheel. . . . Though smaller than the Ferris Wheel [by half], the builders cleverly placed it on a rise so that the Firth actually took riders to an altitude of 385 feet, 127 feet higher than the Chicago version" (18).

7. Steven Conn refers to the effect of such a collection as constituting an "object-based epistemology." Such assemblages of "stuff" were central to late-nineteenth-century America's efforts to understand, organize, and re-present the world as coherent knowledge (3–31).

8. To be sure, in speaking of Norris and Dreiser and Chopin, Michaels does posit that the "characteristic concerns of naturalism . . . [are] appropriation, legitimation, the need to end representation, and the desire to represent" (26). However, he concerns himself less with the cultural function of this set of conditions as he argues for seeing the structural stasis inherent in the paradox. But as the changing history of western literature would indicate, these representational issues are far from static.

9. A similar event involves the funeral for a lion tamer held in the fair circus's center ring during one of the shows; the tamer had been killed by a lion in that same ring one week earlier (Clary 75). See David Wyatt's *Five Fires* for a general discussion of California's ability to convert catastrophe into spectacle.

10. Michaels argues that on the level of ideology, writing and text are as prone to the logic of the gold standard as are currency and identity (169–70). My point here is not so much to disagree with Michaels but to suggest that Norris's response to the fair is somewhat determined by an explicitly textual, as opposed to material, set of representational concerns.

11. The leading Barbizon painters included Daubigny, Millet, and Corot. Among San Francisco's most popular practitioners of this style was William Keith, a close and longtime friend of Muir's.

12. Norris's self-professed stance as a writer interested in truthful, even realistic, representation is discussed in chapter 3.

13. Biographical details derive primarily from Franklin Walker's *Frank Norris: A Biography*, 157–60. On the question of Norris's whereabouts in 1897, see also McElrath, *Frank Norris Revisited* 35.

14. Émile Zola, Norris's most significant literary forebear and the influence Norris himself repeatedly singled out, is strangely absent from "Perverted Tales."

15. December 1898, in *The Letters of Frank Norris* 23.

16. It is instructive to note that one of the few actual shoot-outs in Harte's canon, the confrontation dramatized in "The Iliad of Sandy Bar," functions to satirize this type of scene as capably as does Norris's depiction.

17. For a discussion of the economic and geographic contexts of Norris's use of the Mussel Slough events, see Henderson 123–49.

18. Interestingly enough, for the sake of a unifying symbol Norris himself conspicuously places a live oak at both the geographic and figurative center of his novel's main action, a trivial but telling anomaly given that the live oak is a coastal species—it does not grow in the San Joaquin Valley where Norris places it.

19. See Benedict 51–53 for an interpretation of the Chicago Midway as a legitimating parody of the other exhibitions.

20. This and the following two excerpts all come from the full-text reproductions of reviews collected in McElrath and Knight, *Frank Norris: The Critical Reception*.

21. See Graham (85–97) and McElrath's "Edwin Markham in Frank Norris's *The Octopus*" for a discussion of Presley's rise to fame as a parody of Edwin Markham's 1899 poem "The Man with the Hoe."

22. The actual narrator, the voice that recounts listening to McBride's tales, is unnamed.

23. Scharnhorst suggests that the latter tale, in addition to its obvious send-up of the ending epitaph in Harte's "The Outcasts of Poker Flat," also parodies Wister's *The Virginian* ("Harte, Norris" 9).

24. Foote's *The Led-Horse Claim* appeared in 1883, *Ramona* in 1884. Milton categorizes *The Octopus* (1901), *The Virginian* (1902), and *The Land of Little Rain* (1903) as the three seminal texts of twentieth-century western literature (101–2). As I have developed my argument regarding the national and popular identification of "West" with California, I largely agree with this way of framing the point, although Foote's novels in particular deserve far greater attention to their place in the history of foundational western literature than space here allows.

25. See, e.g., Limerick's "Region and Reason."

26. When Howells suggested in 1881 that Foote alter the ending of "In Exile" to make it less sad, she extended the story beyond the California dry season and used the coming of the rains as the motivation for a happier resolution. See Foote, *Victorian Gentlewoman* 155, also 137.

Chapter 5

1. A brief mention of a miner named Tennessee (158), possibly an oblique reference to Harte's "Tennessee's Partner," indicates that Austin is nevertheless interested in engaging the genre of the mining story.

2. Glazener does not in fact mention nature writing as one of the genres of realism at issue in the *Atlantic*'s fight for authority. However, the longtime prominence of both Muir and Burroughs in the magazine's pages, as well as Burroughs's use of the *Atlantic* to initiate the "nature fakers" controversy, doubtlessly adds nature to the mix of subjects about which *Atlantic* readers learned to expect certain realist tendencies.

3. A number of Austin's contemporaries saw her as an accomplished and innovative realist, praising her often for the technical and thematic advances she had made over her predecessors. Francis Grierson wrote, "In Mary Austin I have found a kind of realism new to me, where natural forces, profound feeling which never approaches the sentimental, imagination controlled by a powerful reasoning intellect, all work together to produce one great haunting sensation in the mind of the reader" (qtd. on dust jacket of *The Land of Little Rain* [1950], intro. Van Doren). William Allan White, in a review of Austin's autobiography, observed, "Mrs. Austin arrived as an American novelist in the latter part of the first decade of the century. Her realism was regarded as rather advanced in that day; certainly she discusses matters that Mr. Howells would have avoided" (235). And Henry Nash Smith, in an appreciative 1931 essay on Austin written early in his career, argues in part that his colleague's writing is "above all things realistic" ("Feel" 23).

Recent assessments in this vein, however, have not been quite as numerous. One notable exception is Elizabeth Morrow, who discusses Austin's fiction as it fits into the realist style exemplified by the works of Howells and Henry James. Austin's most Jamesian prose and subject matter, if such a distinction will be allowed, can be found in two of her better New York–based novels, *A Woman of Genius* (1912) and *No. 26 Jayne St.* (1920). See also Witschi. The specific arguments about Austin's realism in the genre of nature writing, found in Buell et al., is the subject of this chapter.

4. In brief, Austin's first two chapters describe the conditions of aridity and the tiny trails animals make in the sand in their search for water. The first human encountered in the book is the lone "Pocket Hunter" of a chapter by that name, followed soon by "Jimville." After this, Austin presents a series of affirmative portraits of Native Americans well suited to desert life; of the sources, directions, and meanings of water resources; and, in conclusion, an explication of the utopian community of Las Uvas, in which harmony with the desert and with its people has ostensibly been achieved.

5. This comment comes from Buell's brief discussion of Austin's place in the tradition of American pastoral. Elsewhere in *The Environmental Imagination*, in a chapter on realism in the environmental text, Buell notes the way in which Austin's work, among others, "requires us to remake our image of the world in terms of a criterion of value intentionally dislocating in its focus on the intractably and minutely factical" (107). In other words, Austin in part succeeds in drawing attention to the "real" by picturing its distinctly unreal, grotesque aspects (106). While appreciative of Austin as a realist, such an assessment does

not yet fully come to terms with Austin's sense of realistic writing in relation to that of her period.

6. Austin met Howells in New York sometime in the 1910s; *Earth Horizon* offers no further details regarding the timing of the encounter. Concerning the topic of her conversation with Howells, Austin would in 1920 level a similar charge of combined ignorance and misogyny at Sinclair Lewis regarding his depiction of Carol Kennicott in *Main Street*. Austin to Lewis, 12 Dec. 1920, qtd. in Witschi 75.

7. McWilliams to Austin, 4 Dec. 1927, item no. AU3835, The Mary Austin Collection, The Henry E. Huntington Library, San Marino, California. This and all subsequent references to materials from the Austin Collection (hereafter HEH) are published by permission of The Huntington Library.

8. That Smith and Austin were colleagues is a detail that has thus far eluded Austin's biographers. In 1931 he was a new assistant professor of English at Southern Methodist University and an assistant editor of the *Southwest Review*, while she served on the journal's editorial board, the only woman to hold this position at the time. The Huntington Library's Mary Austin Collection contains well over thirty business and personal letters written by Smith to Austin.

9. On the novel, see Austin's "The American Form of the Novel" (1922) and "Regionalism in American Fiction" (1932); on poetry see especially *The American Rhythm* (1923); on the essay see "New York: Dictator of American Criticism" (1920) and "How I Learned to Read and Write" (1921), as well as the unpublished "[Notes on the Essay as a Literary Form]," HEH, AU413, discussed later in this essay; and on drama see, e.g., "Reorganization of the New Theatre" (1911) and "Gesture in the Primitive Drama" (1927). For a full sense of Austin's range, see her essays collected in *Beyond Borders*.

10. An inquiry into Austin's deployment of water as figure and trope suggests, at least in part, the sort of analysis of "fluid" feminist representations first advanced by Irigaray. Since the goal of this chapter, however, is to place Austin's early desert writing in its culturally specific intellectual context, I leave the theoretical implications of "fluidity" in better hands (see Grosz for a recent example). Significant feminist readings of Austin include Ammons 87–97; Graulich, "Afterword"; Jaycox; Pryse; Stineman; Stout; and Cynthia Taylor. The excellent essays in Graulich and Klimasmith variously engage both Austin's feminism and her status as cultural critic.

11. Adams was another colleague of Austin's, having coproduced a book on Taos, New Mexico, with her.

12. On Austin's abilities as an ironic satirist, see Witschi. The "study" of Austin to which Van Doren refers can be found in his *Contemporary American Novelists* 140–43.

13. This passage comes from an unpublished fragment found in the Huntington Library; cited in Graulich, "Afterword" 391.

14. See, e.g., Norwood xiii–xxii, 261–84; Buell, *Imagination* 25–27, 44–49.

15. The term "nature fakers" was coined by Theodore Roosevelt, who from

the White House became a very vocal and active ally of Burroughs's in the fight to define reality as it could—and should—be described by nature writing. See Lutts 101–38.

16. On Austin's awareness of her own market limitations as a woman writer, see Stineman, esp. 38–48; Graulich, *Western Trails;* and Langlois, "Austin's *A Woman of Genius*." For a discussion of Austin's repeated frustration over her publishers' lack of sensitivity to western writing and the potential for a western readership, see Langlois, "Austin and Houghton Mifflin."

17. Of related interest is also "Back to Nature" by Henry Seidel Canby, a friend of Austin's and a professor of English at Yale. On the early-twentieth-century rise of American literature as an institution of academic inquiry see especially Vanderbilt 153–410, Graff 98–144. See also Ammons 15–18 for a brief discussion of how the professionalization of literary study excluded women writers at the turn of the century.

18. In addition to Tracy's *American Naturists,* 1930 saw the publication of Foerster's New Humanism anthology *Humanism and America;* a responding set of essays collected in C. Hartely Grattan's *The Critique of Humanism: A Symposium;* the Southern Agrarian manifesto *I'll Take My Stand* (written by "Twelve Southerners"); and Vernon Parrington's unfinished third volume of *Main Currents in American Thought,* subtitled *The Beginnings of Critical Realism in America, 1860–1920*. See Vanderbilt 355–80.

19. See chapter 2 of Fritzell (37–88) for a much more comprehensive genealogy of, as the chapter title puts it, "The History and Criticism of Nature Writing." Though he briefly mentions the contributions of Halsey, Foerster, and Tracy, Fritzell emphasizes Joseph Wood Krutch's prologue to the 1950 anthology *Great American Nature Writing* as the instigator of a period in which "most serious readers of nature writing" begin to develop a far-reaching and coherent sense of the field and its history (40–41). I largely concur with Fritzell. However, the growth of an academic dimension to discussions of nature writing had a significant, discernible effect on Austin's career, and thus I point out the congruence of Austin's years of publication and the emergent recognition of a literary form with which she would be increasingly associated.

20. Edward Abbey does very much the same thing in his 1988 introduction to a Penguin edition of *The Land of Little Rain*. For an examination of the assumptions about gender and literary value in Abbey's dismissal of Austin, see Murphy 36–39.

21. See especially O'Grady 123–56.

22. Austin to Tracy, 24 July 1929, HEH, AU1249. After reading the typescript draft, Austin wrote to Tracy, "I don't know that I have ever had anything written about me which I have liked so much as what you say of THE FLOCK in the manuscript you sent me. I am so glad that you did not try to make my reputation as a naturist rest entirely on THE LAND OF LITTLE RAIN, which is good enough for a first book, but not so valuable as THE FLOCK" (14 Aug. 1929, HEH, AU5456). Since *The Flock* (1906) discusses very little with respect

to water, but rather focuses on the society of shepherds in eastern California, it falls outside the scope of the present study. However, it should be noted that as an example of Austin's nature writing, *The Flock* still seems largely underappreciated, Tracy's critical attention notwithstanding.

23. Austin to Tracy, 31 July 1929, HEH, AU1250.

24. Austin, "[Notes on the Essay as a Literary Form]," HEH, AU413, n.d., but internal evidence places it no earlier than 1927; underlining in original. The title given for this document is that assigned to it by the catalogers of The Mary Austin Collection at the Huntington Library. For the sake of clarity, typing errors in the manuscript have been silently corrected.

25. A series of gold strikes in Nevada between 1900 and 1904 (esp. at Tonopah) promised to transform the Owens Valley into a great center for commerce, as the valley offered the nearest and most accessible trade route for the delivery of much-needed supplies to these booming mining regions and, if the valley could maximize its water irrigation, for growing produce to feed the miners as well.

26. The phrase "proper destiny" is Austin's, which she uses in *The Land of Little Rain* during her discussion about irrigation ditches and the cultural role of western water (123).

27. In a 1927 essay on the Colorado River controversy for the *Southwest Review,* Austin will echo this assertion with a figurative twist by claiming once again that "the economic complex of Southern California has been built up, to an extent of which those involved in it are not always aware, by a process of scraping the jam off Peter's bread to spread Paul's" ("Colorado River Project" 114).

28. Plans to dam the Tuolomne River in the Hetch Hetchy Valley had been under consideration since 1901. Muir added his voice of dissent to the project in 1905.

29. Graulich's comment appears as a blurb on the back cover of a 1997 University of California Press paperback reprint. Similarly, Esther Stineman calls *The Ford* "an experimental social novel" (120). On *The Ford*'s engagement with conservationist politics, see Raine.

30. In *Earth Horizon,* an account somewhat sparing in its praise of influential writers, Austin discusses at length the example James had set for her. They presumably met for a private evening of conversation after a lecture he gave in Oakland, California, in 1898 (282–83).

31. For a more detailed discussion of Austin's understanding of and reworking of genre Western conventions, particularly in *Lost Borders,* see Jaycox.

32. For an argument about capitalist ideology in *The Ford,* see Henderson 204–8.

33. In a rather strange instance of historical extrapolation and embellishment, Marc Reisner's *Cadillac Desert* describes the conclusion of Austin's interview with Doyle's unnamed agent as follows: "After she had left, a subordinate came into his office and found him staring at the wall. 'By God,' Mulholland reportedly said, 'that woman is the only one with brains enough to see where

this is going'" (82). Imagining an auditor Doyle never mentions, probably to justify the provenance of the story, Reisner has taken Doyle's anecdotal report and, without citation, recast it as historical fact.

Of course, not everyone saw Mulholland as a villain. In the dedication to *The Winning of Barbara Worth,* Harold Bell Wright's best-selling 1911 novel about agriculture and water rights battles in the Imperial Valley, the author thanks Mulholland for his valuable and positive efforts on behalf of southern California's water resource needs. For a recent and insightful discussion of this novel, see Henderson 182–89.

34. Although they lie beyond the scope of the present study, Austin's post–*Little Rain* essays and book treatments of the 1920s debates over the Colorado River should be mentioned, if only to suggest further the career-long centrality of the resource to her work as a writer. Of particular interest are "The Colorado River: A Study of the River and the Canyon" in *Century Magazine;* "The Colorado River Controversy" in the *Nation;* "The Colorado River Project and the Culture of the Southwest" in the *Southwest Review;* and "The Future of the Southwest" in the *New Republic.* Additionally, see Austin's chapters on the river in *The Land of Journeys' Ending,* a book composed around the idea that narratives provide the only way of accurately knowing a land. Finally, for a discussion that treats southwestern water entirely as an economic basis for culture (as opposed to a piece of unalloyed nature), see "The Indivisible Utility."

35. Cf. Foote's "The Irrigating Ditch," which echoes the likes of Smythe and Powell in painting a brief but idealizing and progressive picture of the irrigation canal as the genesis of western society.

36. In what is undoubtedly a profound historical irony, Austin's house still stands at 253 Market Street in the town of Independence, protected as California State Historical Landmark no. 229. The invitation to the reader to come visit the "brown house under the willow-tree at the end of the village street" is etched on an accompanying plaque.

Chapter 6

1. See Glazener 150–57 for details of genre-founded Howells bashing as early as the late 1880s and 1890s.

2. On the more familiar antecedents to hard-boiled fiction, see Klein, who provides a helpful account of the popularity of such predecessors as true-crime tales, Pinkerton's adventure books, and other such mystery-oriented narratives (133–94). See also Cawelti.

3. The one possible exception to this observation is James Guetti, whose "Aggressive Reading: Detective Fiction and Realistic Narrative" (1982) correlates the aggressive behavior of Hammett's and Chandler's detectives with the aggressive reading practice that the notorious hard-boiled style demands of its readers. Guetti's formalist equation is this: the work required of the reader realistically echoes the actions and feelings of the detective, hence the hard-boiled

narrative is realistic in its effect. For a related yet strikingly dissimilar reading of aesthetic effect, see Fredric Jameson's "On Raymond Chandler." Jameson argues that the narrative forms of Chandler's novels function to surprise the reader with "the direct reality of death itself" (87).

4. The hard-boiled story form, moreover, serves as a key predecessor of the Hollywood film noir of both the 1940s and now, a point of influence frequently "challenged by film scholars" (Marling 237). However, studies such as those by Marling, Copjec, and Žižek have shown quite convincingly that beyond its generic, stylistic, and thematic ties to hard-boiled fiction, film noir's figurative and ideological matrix also derives in large part from the novels of writers such as Hammett, James M. Cain, and Chandler (Marling 237–69; Copjec; Žižek 48–66; also, see Krutnik 33–44).

5. See, e.g., Skenazy's *The New Wild West.*

6. In her essay "What Raymond Chandler Knew and Western Historians Forgot," Patricia Nelson Limerick nominates Chandler as the best writer that historians of the West should look to in order to "[ease] their field into the modern age." Simply put, he saw the West in very Turnerian ways, and he was a "hell of a writer" (29–30). Similarly, my own purpose is to view the genre of hard-boiled fiction not as the apotheosis of western realism—no single genre or text can be so—but rather as its clearest and fullest expression.

7. In the 1920s, a fascination with all things related to detectives and gangsters propelled into the mainstream of media production such material as was usually reserved for pulp magazines and books (the "yellow backs" that Frank Norris had derided in 1902). Perhaps most prominently, in 1925 the bootlegger Al Capone assumed control of the Chicago syndicate and, with the aid of the news media, began to promote his rise to power as the definitive American success story. He would become by the close of the decade a cultural icon whose impact was both material and textual: Capone could traffic with equal prosperity in liquor and celebrity (see Ruth 118–43). Hammett, among others, entered directly into this cultural matrix with his first published genre tales.

8. The connection between these two publications is much stronger than simply Hammett's authorship: *Black Mask* had been founded in 1920 by none other than H. L. Mencken and George Jean Nathan as a cash cow to support their other creation, the struggling but eminently more "respectable" literary magazine, the *Smart Set* (Nolan, *Black Mask Boys* 19–21).

9. Biographical details derive primarily from D. Johnson, *Dashiell Hammett: A Life* (1983). Also of note are Layman, *Shadow Man: The Life of Dashiell Hammett* (1981) and Nolan, *Dashiell Hammett: A Casebook* (1969).

10. Cf. John Burroughs's self-positioning as a knowledgeable and responsible reader/writer of nature writing, discussed in chapter 5.

11. S. S. Van Dine was the pseudonym of William Huntington Wright, a distinguished New York art critic and editor turned mystery novelist. His amateur sleuth, Philo Vance, is described by T. J. Binyon as "the American equivalent of Lord Peter Wimsey" (60), a detective of aristocratic breeding who, unlike the

police, can solve murders that occur among the upper classes through his intimate knowledge of the social codes of that set. During 1913 and 1914 Wright was editor of the *Smart Set*. See Loughery.

12. For a reconstruction of a 1920s and 1930s hard-boiled pulp magazine readership, see E. A. Smith, *Hard-Boiled*.

13. Attribution and full bibliographic citation for this unsigned review from the *Saturday Review of Literature* (1 Dec. 1928: 440) can be found in Layman, *Dashiell Hammett: A Descriptive Bibliography* 131.

14. The most comprehensive compilation of essays concerning the psychoanalytic interpretation of Poe's tale can be found in Muller and Richardson, *The Purloined Poe*. For an elaboration of Poe's debt to crime pamphlets, sensational reportage, and other popular cultural products involving crime, see Reynolds 241–48.

15. Cf. Dennis Porter, who notes that detective fiction is "an art . . . which discovers over and over again a hidden banality governed by familiar laws. . . . [T]he detective story has pursued the goal of perceptual refamiliarization" (245).

16. Written by Thomas Samuel Duke, *Celebrated Criminal Cases of America* was first published in 1910 by San Francisco's James H. Barry Company "with approval of the Honorable Board of police commissioners of San Francisco." *The Maltese Falcon* takes place in San Francisco. A case of real books in imaginary libraries?

17. Marcus Klein puts it succinctly: "Hammett wrote core, minimalist precisions, which by the stroke of the reduction itself would activate the ironies. . . . And it was Hammett (who as an attentive reader of Henry James and who would say later that it was to James that he owed his conception of literary style) who came to define both *Black Mask* and a genre" (181). Regarding Hammett as pioneer, although he is rightly credited by literary critics and historians as being among the earliest and most important influences on later hard-boiled mystery writers, the distinction of "first" in fact belongs to Carroll John Daly and his serial detective Race Williams. Daly's popularity as a *Black Mask* writer preceded Hammett's, and he also published the first recognizably hard-boiled novel, *The Snarl of the Beast,* in 1927 (Nolan, *Black Mask Boys* 35–43). Part of what distinguishes Hammett from Daly, however, is the former's repeated, explicit emphasis on "realism" as a formal requirement. For an informative analysis of Race Williams in the context of 1920s nativist debates, see McCann.

18. Chandler published several essays using this title. It first appeared in the *Atlantic* in 1944 and was revised slightly two years later for Howard Haycraft's critical collection *The Art of the Mystery Story*. This latter version was collected as the end piece of Chandler's 1950 collection of short stories also titled *The Simple Art of Murder*. Chandler's introduction to this latter book, an altogether different essay about the cultural merits of his early, pre–Phillip Marlowe short stories in *Black Mask,* first appeared in 1950 under the "Simple Art of Murder" title in *Saturday Review*. Needless to say, Chandler fancied the title.

19. As a young man in 1911, Chandler wrote for *Academy* magazine in England a defense of idealism in literature that praised genre realism for its attentions to a world other than that of the "fairyland" of romance but which disapproved of realism's alleged tendency to "rake over the rubbish-heaps of humanity in its close alleys and noisome slums to find fragments of broken moral crockery." Three and a half decades later, Chandler had obviously changed his mind about subject matter, as well as the choice of "realism" as a key term in his critical sensibility. See "Realism and Fairyland," rpt. in *Before Marlowe* 65–67.

20. Glazener offers the compelling argument that realism "might be more accurately identified as a reading formation than a body of texts or textual features" (14), a formulation well suited to the orientation toward reading exhibited by Hammett and Chandler.

21. A possible exception might be found in the work of Ross MacDonald, often hailed as the postwar inheritor of the hard-boiled mantle after Chandler and whose novels depict the overharvesting of timber and the pollution of the Pacific (*The Drowning Pool* [1950]), suburban sprawl and beach erosion (*The Zebra-Striped Hearse* [1962] and *The Chill* [1964]), an offshore oil spill near Los Angeles (*Sleeping Beauty* [1973]), and an out-of-control brush fire in the southern California foothills (*The Underground Man* [1971]). See Speir.

22. See, e.g., Flint's "A Cato of the Cruelties"; or more recently, Ruehlmann 76–90; D. Smith; and Skenazy, *The New Wild West* 28–44. Commenting on this aspect of Chandler, Stephen Knight argues that "much of Chandler's reputation as a realist depends on the idea that he perceived the socio-political sickness in American society. . . . [but] Socio-political perceptions about contemporary disorder come to act as only background to the genuinely felt personal threats" (153–54). According to Knight, Chandler fails in his critique by virtue of his continually deferring questions of class in favor of the survival of the lone detective, the isolated and ostensibly ethical self.

23. In the 1920s, E. L. Doheny (who built Los Angeles's first oil well in 1892) became one of the principal figures in the Teapot Dome Scandal, in which U.S. Navy reserve oil claims were illegally leased to private firms who in turn pumped up the oil and sold it (see Starr, *Material Dreams* 125–28). This scandal serves as the pivotal event in Upton Sinclair's highly polemical novel *Oil!* (1927).

24. Chandler's complex use of metaphor and simile has received a great deal of attention, the best and most recent such inquiry being Marling's *The American Roman Noir* (see esp. 209–16). See also Tanner, "The Function of Simile in Raymond Chandler's Novels."

25. Marling argues that this first sentence of *The Big Sleep* deliberately recalls and "overturns" the image of southern California as being all sunshine and oranges, an image promoted by the booster-like Arroyo culture fostered by Charles Lummis. In the latter category Marling includes Mary Austin's *The Land of Little Rain* (245).

26. In another, earlier essay entitled "On Raymond Chandler" (1970), Jameson writes that Chandler's repeated "demystification of violent death" (85) ul-

timately serves a diversionary purpose: "By diverting us with the ritual detective story of the detection of the criminal, and of his transformation into the Other, it [Chandler's writing] is able to bring us up short, without warning, against the reality of death itself, stale death, reaching out to remind the living of its own mouldering resting place" (87).

27. For an interpretation of the act of reading in *The Lady in the Lake* in relation to gender, see E. A. Smith, *Hard-Boiled* 109–14.

28. As Jameson puts it, Chandler's "landscape has already been itself fully humanized by the process of urban construction . . . [and the social system] has already endowed itself with spatial expression, so that the character types are already at least styles of architecture and gardening, and associated with specific neighborhoods or even ecologies (as Banham called them)" ("The Synoptic Chandler" 50).

29. According to the *Atlas of the New West,* "roughly 75 percent of people in eastern 'metropolitan' states like New York and New Jersey are urban dwellers, but fully 86 percent of Westerners live in cities" (Riebsame et al. 55). Given the *Atlas*'s somewhat curious exclusion of the highly urbanized state of California from its western demography, the figure of 86 percent becomes even more significant.

Works Cited

Allmendinger, Blake. *Ten Most Wanted: The New Western Literature*. New York: Routledge, 1998.

Alpers, Paul. *What Is Pastoral?* Chicago: U of Chicago P, 1996.

Alter, Judy. *Stewart Edward White*. Boise, ID: Boise State University, 1975.

Ammons, Elizabeth. *Conflicting Stories: American Women Writers at the Turn into the Twentieth Century*. New York: Oxford UP, 1991.

Andrews, Malcolm. *The Search for the Picturesque: Landscape Aesthetics and Tourism in Britain, 1760–1800*. Stanford: Stanford UP, 1989.

Armitage, Shelley. "The Illustrator as Writer: Mary Hallock Foote and the Myth of the West." Meldrum 151–74.

Austin, Mary. "The American Form of the Novel." *New Republic* 12 Apr. 1922: 3–4.

———. *The American Rhythm*. New York: Harcourt, 1923.

———. *Beyond Borders: The Selected Essays of Mary Austin*. Ed. and intro. Reuben J. Ellis. Carbondale: Southern Illinois UP, 1996.

———. "The Colorado River: A Study of the River and the Canyon." *Century* Aug. 1924: 462–70.

———. "The Colorado River Controversy." *Nation* 9 Nov. 1927: 510–12.

———. "The Colorado River Project and the Culture of the Southwest." *Southwest Review* 13.1 (1927): 110–15.

———. *Earth Horizon: An Autobiography*. 1932. Albuquerque: U of New Mexico P, 1991.

———. *The Flock*. Boston: Houghton Mifflin, 1906.

———. *The Ford*. Boston: Houghton Mifflin, 1917. Berkeley: U of California P, 1997.

———. "The Future of the Southwest." *New Republic* 8 Apr. 1925: 186.

———. "Gesture in the Primitive Drama." *Theatre Arts Magazine* Aug. 1927: 594–605.

———. "How I Learned to Read and Write." *My Maiden Effort*. Ed. Gelett Burgess. Garden City, NY: Pub. for the Authors' League of America by Doubleday, Page, 1921. 12–16.

———. "The Indivisible Utility." *Survey Graphic* 1 Dec. 1925: 301–6, 327.

———. *The Land of Journeys' Ending*. 1924. Tucson: U of Arizona P, 1983.

———. *The Land of Little Rain*. 1903. *Stories from the Country of Lost Borders*. Ed. Marjorie Pryse. New Brunswick, NJ: Rutgers UP, 1987. 1–149.

———. *Lost Borders*. 1909. *Stories from the Country of Lost Borders*. Ed. Marjorie Pryse. New Brunswick, NJ: Rutgers UP, 1987. 151–263.

———. "New York: Dictator of American Criticism." *Nation* 31 July 1920: 129–30.

———. "The Owens River Water Project." *San Francisco Chronicle* 3 Sept. 1905: 19.

———. "Regionalism in American Fiction." *English Journal* 21 (1932): 97–107.

———. "Reorganization of the New Theatre." *American Magazine* Nov. 1911: 101–4.

Babener, Liahna K. "Raymond Chandler's City of Lies." Fine 109–31.

Ballard, Rae Galbraith. "Mary Austin's Earth Horizon: The Imperfect Circle." Diss. Claremont Graduate School, 1977.

Banham, Rayner. *Los Angeles: The Architecture of Four Ecologies*. London: Penguin, 1971.

Barrus, Clara. "With John o' Birds and John o' Mountains in the Southwest." *Century* Aug. 1910: 521–28.

Bell, Michael Davitt. *The Development of American Romance: The Sacrifice of Relation*. Chicago: U of Chicago P, 1980.

———. *The Problem of American Realism: Studies in the Cultural History of a Literary Idea*. Chicago: U of Chicago P, 1993.

Benedict, Burton. "The Anthropology of World's Fairs." *The Anthropology of World's Fairs: San Francisco's Panama Pacific International Exposition of 1915*. Ed. Burton Benedict. Berkeley: The Lowie Museum of Anthropology; London and Berkeley: Scolar Press, 1983. 1–65.

Bicknell, Ralph E. "'Tennessee' and 'Partner.'" *Land of Sunshine* Nov. 1899: 325–29.

Binyon, T. J. *"Murder Will Out": The Detective in Fiction*. New York: Oxford UP, 1989.

Borthwick, John David. *Three Years in California*. 1857. Ed. Joseph A. Sullivan. Oakland, CA: BioBooks, 1948.

Borus, Daniel H. *Writing Realism: Howells, James, and Norris in the Mass Market*. Chapel Hill: U of North Carolina P, 1989.

Branch, Michael P. "'Angel Guiding Gently': The Yosemite Meeting of Ralph Waldo Emerson and John Muir, 1871." *Western American Literature* 32.2 (1997): 126–49.

Bredahl, A. Carl, Jr. *New Ground: Western American Narrative and the Literary Canon*. Chapel Hill: U of North Carolina P, 1989.

"Bret Harte's Lecture." *Springfield Daily Republican* 26 Nov. 1872: 8:1.

Brooks, Peter. "The Turn of *The American*." *New Essays on* The American. Ed. Martha Banta. Cambridge: Cambridge UP, 1987. 43–67.

Brown, Bill. *The Material Unconscious: American Amusement, Stephen Crane, and the Economies of Play*. Cambridge: Harvard UP, 1996.

——, ed. *Reading the West: An Anthology of Dime Westerns*. Boston: Bedford Books, 1997.

Bucco, Martin. "*The Rise of Silas Lapham:* The Western Dimension." *Western American Literature* 23.4 (1989): 291–310.

Buell, Lawrence. "Circling the Spheres: A Dialogue." *American Literature* 70.3 (1998): 465–90.

——. *The Environmental Imagination: Thoreau, Nature Writing, and the Formation of American Culture*. Cambridge: Belknap–Harvard UP, 1995.

Burroughs, John. "Real and Sham Natural History." *Atlantic Monthly* Mar. 1903: 298–309.

Butte, Edna Rosemary. "Stewart Edward White: His Life and Career." Diss. University of Southern California, 1960.

Cady, Edwin H. *The Realist at War: The Mature Years, 1885–1920, of William Dean Howells*. Syracuse: Syracuse UP, 1958.

——. *The Road to Realism: The Early Years 1837–1885 of William Dean Howells*. Syracuse: Syracuse UP, 1956.

Canby, Henry Seidel. "Back to Nature." *Yale Review* ns 6 (July 1917): 755–67.

Cassuto, David N. "Turning Wine into Water: Water as Privileged Signifier in *The Grapes of Wrath*." *Steinbeck and the Environment: Interdisciplinary Approaches*. Ed. Susan F. Beegle, Susan Shillinglaw, and Wesley N. Tiffney, Jr. Tuscaloosa: U of Alabama P, 1997. 55–75.

Caughey, John Walton. *Hubert Howe Bancroft: Historian of the West*. Berkeley: U of California P, 1946.

Cawelti, John G. *Adventure, Mystery, and Romance: Formula Stories as Art and Popular Culture*. Chicago: U of Chicago P, 1976.

——. *The Six-Gun Mystique*. Bowling Green, OH: Bowling Green U Popular P, 1971.

Chandler, Arthur, and Marvin R. Nathan. *The Fantastic Fair: The Story of the California Midwinter International Exposition*. St. Paul, MN: Pogo Press, 1993.

Chandler, Raymond. *Before Marlowe: Raymond Chandler's Early Prose and Poetry, 1908–1912*. Ed. Matthew J. Bruccoli. Columbia: U of South Carolina P, 1973.

——. *The Big Sleep*. 1939. Rpt. in *The Raymond Chandler Omnibus* 1–139.

——. *Farewell, My Lovely*. 1940. Rpt. in *The Raymond Chandler Omnibus* 141–315.

——. *The High Window*. 1942. Rpt. in *The Raymond Chandler Omnibus* 317–468.

——. *The Lady in the Lake*. 1943. Rpt. in *The Raymond Chandler Omnibus* 469–625.

——. *The Long Goodbye*. Boston: Houghton Mifflin, 1953.

——. *The Raymond Chandler Omnibus*. New York: Modern Library–Random House, 1975.

——. *Selected Letters of Raymond Chandler*. Ed. Frank MacShane. New York: Delta-Dell, 1987.

——. "The Simple Art of Murder." *The Art of the Mystery Story: A Collection of Critical Essays*. Ed. Howard Haycraft. New York: Simon & Schuster, 1946. 222–37.

——. "The Simple Art of Murder." *Atlantic Monthly* Dec. 1944: 53–59.

———. "The Simple Art of Murder." *Saturday Review of Literature* 15 Apr. 1950: 13–14.

Chase, Richard. *The American Novel and Its Tradition*. New York: Doubleday, 1957.

Chopin, Kate. "Development of the Literary West." *St. Louis Republic* 9 Dec. 1900. Rpt. in *American Literary Realism* 22.2 (1990): 69–75.

———. "The Western Association of Writers." *Critic* 7 July 1894: 15. Rpt. in *The Complete Works of Kate Chopin*. Ed. Per Seyersted. Vol. 2. Baton Rouge: Louisiana State UP, 1970. 691–92.

Civello, Paul. *American Literary Naturalism and Its Twentieth-Century Transformation: Frank Norris, Ernest Hemingway, Don DeLillo*. Athens: U of Georgia P, 1994.

Clappe, Louise Amelia Knapp Smith. *The Shirley Letters from the California Mines, 1851–1852*. Intro. Marlene Smith-Baranzini. Berkeley: Heyday Books, 1998.

Clary, Raymond. *The Making of Golden Gate Park: The Early Years, 1865–1906*. San Francisco: Don't Call It Frisco Press, 1984.

Clemens, Will M. "Bret Harte's Country." *Bookman* May 1901: 223–37.

Cohen, Michael. "A Brittle Thesis: A Ghost Dance: A Flower Opening." *The Wilderness Condition: Essays on Environment and Civilization*. Ed. Max Oelschlaeger. San Francisco: Sierra Club Books, 1992. 188–204.

———. "John Muir's Public Voice." *Western American Literature* 10.3 (1975): 177–87.

———. "Literary Theory and Nature Writing." *American Nature Writers*. Ed. John Elder. Vol. 2. New York: Scribner's, 1996. 1099–1113.

———. *The Pathless Way: John Muir and American Wilderness*. Madison: U of Wisconsin P, 1984.

Comer, Krista. *Landscapes of the New West: Gender and Geography in Contemporary Women's Writing*. Chapel Hill: U of North Carolina P, 1999.

"Comment on New Books." *Atlantic Monthly* Nov. 1894: 704–12.

Conn, Steven. *Museums and American Intellectual Life, 1876–1926*. Chicago: U of Chicago P, 1998.

Copjec, Joan. "The Phenomenal Nonphenomenal: Private Space in *Film Noir*." Copjec 167–97.

———, ed. *Shades of Noir: A Reader*. London: Verso, 1993.

Corkin, Stanley. *Realism and the Birth of the Modern United States: Cinema, Literature, and Culture*. Athens: U of Georgia P, 1996.

Cox, James M. *Mark Twain: The Fate of Humor*. Princeton: Princeton UP, 1966.

Crane, Stephen. "The Blue Hotel." *Collier's Weekly* 26 Nov. 1898: 14–16.

Crissey, Forrest. "With Maurice Thompson at Sherwood Place." *Saturday Evening Post* 22 Dec. 1900: 20–21.

Cronon, William. "The Trouble with Wilderness." *Uncommon Ground: Toward Reinventing Nature*. Ed. William Cronon. New York: Norton, 1995. 69–90.

Dauber, Kenneth. "Realistically Speaking: Authorship in the Late Nineteenth Century and Beyond." *American Literary History* 11.2 (1999): 378–90.

Davis, Mike. *City of Quartz: Excavating the Future in Los Angeles*. New York: Vintage Books-Random House, 1990.

Davis, Rebecca Harding. "Life in the Iron Mills." *Atlantic Monthly* Apr. 1861: 430–51.
Davis, Richard Harding. *The West from a Car-Window*. New York: Harper & Brothers, 1892.
Dean, James L. "The Wests of Howells and Crane." *American Literary Realism* 10.3 (1977): 254–66.
Delano, Alonzo. *Life on the Plains and Among the Diggings*. Auburn, NY: Miller, Orton & Mulligan, 1854.
——. *Pen-Knife Sketches, or Chips of the Old Block*. Sacramento: Union Office, 1853.
Denning, Michael. *Mechanic Accents: Dime Novels and Working-Class Culture in America*. London: Verso, 1987.
De Quille, Dan. "The Baby Crop." *Golden Era* 1 Jan. 1865. Rpt. in Dwyer 230–31.
——. *The Big Bonanza: An Authentic Account of the Discovery, History, and Working of the World-Renowned Comstock Lode of Nevada*. 1876. New York: Knopf, 1947.
——. *The Fighting Horse of the Stanislaus: Stories and Essays by Dan De Quille*. Ed. Lawrence I. Berkove. Iowa City: U of Iowa P, 1990.
Dexter, Ralph W. "Historical Aspects of the Calaveras Skull Controversy." *American Antiquity* 51.2 (1986): 365–69.
Dorst, John D. *Looking West*. Philadelphia: U of Pennsylvania P, 1999.
Doyle, Helen MacKnight. *Mary Austin, Woman of Genius*. New York: Gotham House, 1939.
Duckett, Margaret. *Mark Twain and Bret Harte*. Norman: U of Oklahoma P, 1964.
Duke, Thomas Samuel. *Celebrated Criminal Cases of America*. San Francisco: James H. Barry, 1910.
Dwyer, Richard A., and Richard E. Lingenfelter. *Dan De Quille, the Washoe Giant: A Biography and Anthology*. Reno: U of Nevada P, 1990.
Eble, Kenneth E. "The Western Idealism of William Dean Howells." *Western Humanities Review* 11 (Autumn 1957): 331–38.
Edel, Leon, ed. *Henry James Letters: Vol. 2, 1875–1883*. Cambridge: Belknap–Harvard UP, 1975.
Elliot, Russell R. *History of Nevada*. 1973. 2nd ed. Lincoln: U of Nebraska P, 1987.
Ellis, Reuben J. "'A Little Turn through the Country': Presley's Bicycle Ride in Frank Norris's *The Octopus*." *Journal of American Culture* 17.3 (1994): 17–22.
Emerson, Ralph Waldo. *Nature, Addresses and Lectures*. Boston: Houghton Mifflin, 1883.
Engberg, Robert, ed. *John Muir Summering in the Sierra*. Madison: U of Wisconsin P, 1984.
Erisman, Fred. "Western Fiction as an Ecological Parable." *Environmental Review* 6 (1978): 15–23.
Fatout, Paul. *Mark Twain in Virginia City*. Bloomington: Indiana UP, 1964.
Fender, Stephen. *Plotting the Golden West: American Literature and the Rhetoric of the California Trail*. Cambridge: Cambridge UP, 1981.
Field, Kate. "My Study and My Books." *Kate Field's Washington* 22 Jan. 1890: 69.
Fine, David, ed. *Los Angeles in Fiction: A Collection of Original Essays*. Albuquerque: U of New Mexico P, 1984.

Flint, R. W. "A Cato of the Cruelties." *Partisan Review* 14 (1947): 328–30. Rpt. in Van Dover 39–41.

Florence, Don. *Persona and Humor in Mark Twain's Early Writings*. Columbia: U of Missouri P, 1995.

Foerster, Norman, ed. *Humanism and America: Essays on the Outlook of Modern Civilisation*. New York: Farrar and Rinehart, 1930.

———. *Nature in American Literature: Studies in the Modern View of Nature*. New York: MacMillan, 1923.

Foote, Mary Hallock. "A California Mining Camp." *Scribner's Monthly* Feb. 1878: 480–93.

———. *The Chosen Valley*. Boston: Houghton Mifflin, 1892.

———. "How the Pump Stopped at the Morning Watch." *Century* July 1899: 469–72.

———. "In Exile." *Atlantic Monthly* Aug.–Sept. 1881: 184–92, 322–30.

———. "The Irrigating Ditch: Pictures of the Far West.—VII." *Century* June 1889: 298–300.

———. *The Led-Horse Claim*. Boston: Osgood, 1883.

———. "A Sea-port on the Pacific." *Scribner's Monthly* Aug. 1878: 449–60.

———. *A Victorian Gentlewoman in the Far West: The Reminiscences of Mary Hallock Foote*. [1922]. Ed. Rodman W. Paul. San Marino, CA: The Huntington Library, 1972.

Fox, Stephen. *The American Conservation Movement: John Muir and His Legacy*. Madison: U of Wisconsin P, 1981.

Fritzell, Peter A. *Nature Writing and America: Essays upon a Cultural Type*. Ames: Iowa State UP, 1990.

Glazener, Nancy. *Reading for Realism: The History of a U.S. Literary Institution, 1850–1910*. Durham, NC: Duke UP, 1997.

Glotfelty, Cheryll, and Harold Fromm, eds. *The Ecocriticism Reader: Landmarks in Literary Ecology*. Athens: U of Georgia P, 1996.

Goldman, Marion S. *Gold Diggers and Silver Miners: Prostitution and Social Life on the Comstock Lode*. Ann Arbor: U of Michigan P, 1981.

Graff, Gerald. *Professing Literature: An Institutional History*. Chicago: Chicago UP, 1987.

Graham, Donald. *The Fiction of Frank Norris: The Aesthetic Context*. Columbia: U of Missouri P, 1978.

Grattan, C. Hartley, ed. *The Critique of Humanism: A Symposium*. New York: Brewer and Warren, 1930.

Graulich, Melody. "Afterword: A Book You Could Walk Around In." Austin, *Earth Horizon* 373–94.

———, ed. *Western Trails: A Collection of Short Stories by Mary Austin*. Reno: U of Nevada P, 1987.

Graulich, Melody, and Elizabeth Klimasmith, eds. *Exploring Lost Borders: Critical Essays on Mary Austin*. Reno: U of Nevada P, 1999.

Greenwald, Fay T. "Kitty Ellison, Howells' Girl of the Democratic West." *Ameri-*

can Renaissance and American West: Proceedings of the Second University of Wyoming American Studies Conference. Ed. Christopher Durer et al. Laramie: University of Wyoming, Dept. of English, School of American Studies, and Dept. of Journalism and Telecommunication, 1982. 41–47.

Grosz, Elizabeth A. *Volatile Bodies: Toward a Corporeal Feminism*. Bloomington: Indiana UP, 1994.

Guetti, James. "Aggressive Reading: Detective Fiction and Realistic Narrative." *Raritan* 2.1 (1982): 133–54. Rpt. in Van Dover 139–44.

Halsey, Francis W. "The Rise of the Nature Writers." *American Monthly Review of Reviews* Nov. 1902: 567–71.

Hammett, Dashiell. "Bodies Piled Up." *Black Mask* 1 Dec. 1923. Rpt. in Nolan, *Black Mask Boys* 80–91.

——. "From the Memoirs of a Private Detective." *Smart Set* Mar. 1923. Rpt. in *The Smart Set Anthology*. Ed. Burton Rascoe and Groff Conklin. New York: Reynal & Hitchcock, 1934. 85–89.

——. *The Maltese Falcon*. New York: Knopf, 1930.

——. "Poor Scotland Yard!" *Saturday Review of Literature* 15 Jan. 1927: 510.

——. *Red Harvest*. 1929. Rpt. in *The Novels of Dashiell Hammett*. New York: Knopf, 1965. 1–142.

——. *The Thin Man*. New York: Knopf, 1934.

Harris, Sharon M. *Rebecca Harding Davis and American Realism*. Philadelphia: U of Pennsylvania P, 1991.

Harte, Bret. "Argonauts of '49." 1872. Rpt. in *Selected Stories and Sketches* 261–82.

——. *Bret Harte's California: Letters to the* Springfield Republican *and* Christian Register, *1866–67*. Ed. Gary Scharnhorst. Albuquerque: U of New Mexico P, 1990.

——. "The Iliad of Sandy Bar." *Overland Monthly* Nov. 1870: 479–85.

——. *Selected Stories and Sketches*. Ed. David Wyatt. New York: Oxford UP, 1995.

——. "The Society upon the Stanislaus." 1868. Rpt. in *Poems, and Two Men of Sandy Bar*. Vol. 12 of *The Writings of Bret Harte*. Standard Library Edition. 20 vols. Boston: Houghton Mifflin, 1896–1904. 132–33.

——. "The Story of a Mine." 1877. Rpt. in *The Story of a Mine, and Other Tales*. Vol. 3 of *The Writings of Bret Harte*. Standard Library Edition. 20 vols. Boston: Houghton Mifflin, 1896–1904. 1–122.

——. "To the Pliocene Skull (A Geological Address)." 1866. Rpt. in *Poems, and Two Men of Sandy Bar*. Vol. 12 of *The Writings of Bret Harte*. Standard Library Edition. 20 vols. Boston: Houghton Mifflin, 1896–1904. 280–81.

Henderson, George L. *California and the Fictions of Capital*. New York: Oxford, 1999.

Herndl, Carl George, and Stuart C. Brown, eds. *Green Culture: Environmental Rhetoric in Contemporary America*. Madison: U of Wisconsin P, 1996.

Highton, Jake. *Nevada Newspaper Days: A History of Journalism in the Silver State*. Stockton, CA: Heritage West Books, 1990.

Hittell, John S. *The Resources of California: Comprising Agriculture, Mining, Geogra-*

phy, Climate, Commerce, &c., and the Past and Future Development of the State. 2nd ed. San Francisco: A. Roman, 1866.

———. *The Resources of California, Comprising the Society, Climate, Salubrity, Scenery, Commerce, and Industry of the State*. 6th ed. San Francisco: A. Roman, 1877.

Hochman, Barbara. *The Art of Frank Norris, Storyteller*. Columbia: U of Missouri P, 1988.

Holliday, J. S. *Rush for Riches: Gold Fever and the Making of California*. Oakland: Oakland Museum of California; Berkeley: U of California P, 1999.

Horwitz, Howard. *By the Law of Nature: Form and Value in Nineteenth-Century America*. New York: Oxford UP, 1991.

Howard, June. *Form and History in American Literary Naturalism*. Chapel Hill: U of North Carolina P, 1985.

Howells, William Dean. "A Belated Guest." *Harper's New Monthly Magazine* Dec. 1903. Rpt. in *Literary Friends and Acquaintance* 242–55.

———. "A Case in Point." *Literature* 24 Mar. 1899: 241–42. Rpt. in McElrath and Knight 39–41.

———. *Criticism and Fiction*. 1891. Rpt. in *Selected Literary Criticism: Volume 2: 1886–1897*. Ed. Donald Pizer, Christoph K. Lohmann, David J. Nordloh, and Don L. Cook. Bloomington: Indiana UP, 1993. 293–354.

———. *A Hazard of New Fortunes*. 1890. New York: Meridian-Penguin USA, 1994.

———. *Indian Summer*. Boston: Ticknor and Co., 1886.

———. *Literary Friends and Acquaintance: A Personal Retrospect of American Authorship*. 1900. Rev. ed. 1910. Ed. David F. Hiatt and Edwin H. Cady. Bloomington: Indiana UP, 1968.

———. "Mark Twain, an Inquiry." *North American Review* Feb. 1901: 306–21. Rpt. in *Selected Literary Criticism: Volume III: 1898–1920*. Ed. Ronald Gottesman, Christoph K. Lohmann, and David J. Nordloh. Bloomington: Indiana UP, 1993. 37–49.

———. *A Modern Instance*. 1882. New York: Penguin, 1984.

———. *The Rise of Silas Lapham*. 1885. Ed. Don L. Cook. New York: Norton, 1982.

Hug, William J. "*McTeague* as Metafiction? Frank Norris' Parodies of Bret Harte and the Dime Novel." *Western American Literature* 26.3 (1991): 219–28.

Hutchings, James M. *The Miner's Ten Commandments*. San Francisco, 1853. *Western Americana: Frontier History of the Trans-Mississippi West, 1550–1990*. New Haven, CT: Research Publications, Inc., 1975. Reel 277, item 2735.

Hyde, Anne Farrar. *An American Vision: Far Western Landscape and National Culture, 1820–1920*. New York: New York UP, 1990.

The Idle and Industrious Miner: A Tale of California Life. Sacramento, 1854. Rpt. in *American West* 13 (May–June 1976): 39–45.

Irigaray, Luce. *This Sex Which Is Not One*. Trans. Catherine Porter with Carolyn Burke. Ithaca, NY: Cornell UP, 1985.

James, Henry. *The American*. 1877. Ed. James W. Tuttleton. New York: Norton, 1978.

——. *The Art of the Novel: Critical Prefaces*. Ed. Richard P. Blackmur. New York: Scribner's, 1947.

Jameson, Fredric. "On Raymond Chandler." *Southern Review* 6.3 (1970): 624–50. Rpt. in Van Dover 65–88.

——. *The Political Unconscious: Narrative as a Socially Symbolic Act*. Ithaca, NY: Cornell UP, 1981.

——. "The Synoptic Chandler." Copjec 33–56.

Jaycox, Faith. "Regeneration through Liberation: Mary Austin's 'The Walking Woman' and Western Narrative Formula." *Legacy: A Journal of Nineteenth-Century American Women* 6.1 (1989): 5–12.

Johnson, Diane. *Dashiell Hammett: A Life*. New York: Random House, 1983.

Johnson, Lee Ann. *Mary Hallock Foote*. Boston: Twayne, 1980.

Johnson, Theodore T. *Sights in the Gold Region, and Scenes by the Way*. New York: Baker and Scribner, 1849.

Kahrl, William L. *Water and Power: The Conflict Over Los Angeles' Water Supply in the Owens Valley*. Berkeley: U of California P, 1982.

Kaplan, Amy. *The Social Construction of American Realism*. Chicago: U of Chicago P, 1988.

Kelley, Robert L. *Gold vs. Grain: The Hydraulic Mining Controversy in California's Sacramento Valley*. New York: Arthur H. Clark, 1959.

Kelly, R. Gordon. *Mystery Fiction and Modern Life*. Jackson: UP of Mississippi, 1998.

Kimes, William F., and Maymie B. Kimes. *John Muir: A Reading Bibliography*. Fresno, CA: Panorama West Books, 1986.

Klein, Marcus. *Easterns, Westerns, and Private Eyes: American Matters, 1870–1900*. Madison: U of Wisconsin P, 1994.

Knight, Stephen. *Form and Ideology in Crime Fiction*. London: MacMillan, 1980.

Kolb, Harold H., Jr. "The Outcasts of Literary Flat: Bret Harte as Humorist." *American Literary Realism* 23.2 (1991): 52–63.

Kowalewski, Michael, ed. *Gold Rush: A Literary Exploration*. Berkeley: Heydey Books, 1997.

——. "Imagining the California Gold Rush: The Visual and Verbal Legacy." *California History* 71.1 (1992): 61–74.

——. "Quoting the Wicked Wit of the West: Frontier Reportage and Western Vernacular." *Reading the West: News Essays on the Literature of the American West*. Ed. Kowalewski. New York: Cambridge UP, 1996. 82–98.

——, ed. *Reading the West: News Essays on the Literature of the American West*. New York: Cambridge UP, 1996.

Kozlay, Charles Meeker, ed. *The Lectures of Bret Harte*. New York: Self-published, 1909.

Krutch, Joseph Wood. "Prologue." *Great American Nature Writing*. Ed. Krutch. New York: Sloan, 1950.

Krutnik, Frank. *In A Lonely Street: Film Noir, Genre, Masculinity*. London: Routledge, 1991.

Langlois, Karen S. "Mary Austin and Houghton Mifflin Company: A Case Study in the Marketing of a Western Writer." *Western American Literature* 23.1 (1988): 31–42.

———. "Mary Austin's *A Woman of Genius:* The Text, the Novel and the Problem of Male Publishers and Critics and Female Authors." *Journal of American Culture* 15.2 (1992): 79–86.

Layman, Richard. *Dashiell Hammett: A Descriptive Bibliography*. Pittsburgh: U of Pittsburgh P, 1979.

———. *Shadow Man: The Life of Dashiell Hammett*. New York: Harcourt, 1981.

Lillard, Richard G. "Contemporary Reaction to 'The Empire City Massacre.'" *American Literature* 16.3 (1944): 198–203.

Limbaugh, Ronald H., and Kirsten Lewis, eds. *The John Muir Papers, 1858–1957*. Microform Edition. Alexandria, VA: Chadwyck-Healey, 1986.

Limerick, Patricia Nelson. *The Legacy of Conquest: The Unbroken Past of the American West*. New York: Norton, 1987.

———. "Region and Reason." *All Over the Map: Rethinking American Regions*. Ed. Edward L. Ayers et al. Baltimore: Johns Hopkins UP, 1996. 83–104.

———. "What Raymond Chandler Knew and Western Historians Forgot." *Old West–New West: Centennial Essays*. Ed. Barbara Howard Meldrum. Moscow: U of Idaho P, 1993. 28–39.

Lockhart, Sandra. "*Legacy* Profile: Louise Amelia Knapp Smith Clappe (Dame Shirley) (1819–1906)." *Legacy* 8.2 (1991): 141–48.

London, Jack. *Martin Eden*. New York: Macmillan, 1909.

Loughery, John. *Alias S. S. Van Dine*. New York: Scribner's, 1992.

Love, Glen. "Revaluing Nature: Toward an Ecological Criticism." Glotfelty and Fromm 225–40.

Lowry, Richard S. *"Littery Man": Mark Twain and Modern Authorship*. New York: Oxford UP, 1996.

Lutts, Ralph H. *The Nature Fakers: Wildlife, Science, and Sentiment*. Golden, CO: Fulcrum, 1990.

Lynn, Kenneth S. *Mark Twain and Southwestern Humor*. Boston: Little, Brown, 1959.

———. *William Dean Howells: An American Life*. New York: Harcourt Brace Jovanovich, 1971.

Lyon, Thomas J., ed. *The Literary West: An Anthology of Western American Literature*. New York: Oxford UP, 1999.

Mace, O. Henry. *Between the Rivers: A History of Early Calaveras County, California*. San Andreas, CA : Calaveras Enterprise, 1991.

MacShane, Frank. *The Life of Raymond Chandler*. New York: Dutton, 1976.

Manes, Christopher. "Nature and Silence." Glotfelty and Fromm 15–29.

Marcy, General Randolph B., U.S.A. "Ramblings in the West." *Harper's New Monthly Magazine* Feb. 1888: 397–405.

Marling, William. *The American Roman Noir: Hammett, Cain, and Chandler*. Athens: U of Georgia P, 1995.

McCann, Sean. "Constructing Race Williams: The Klan and the Making of Hard-Boiled Crime Fiction." *American Quarterly* 49.4 (1997): 677–716.
McElrath, Joseph R., Jr. "Edwin Markham in Frank Norris's *The Octopus*." *Frank Norris Studies* 13 (Spring 1992): 10–11.
——. *Frank Norris Revisited*. New York: Twayne, 1992.
McElrath, Joseph R., Jr., and Katherine Knight, eds. *Frank Norris: The Critical Reception*. New York: Burt Franklin & Co., 1981.
McKeon, Michael. *The Origins of the English Novel, 1600–1740*. Baltimore: Johns Hopkins UP, 1987.
McWilliams, Carey. *California, the Great Exception*. New York: Current Books, 1949.
Meldrum, Barbara Howard, ed. *Under the Sun: Myth and Realism in Western American Literature*. Troy, NY: Whitson, 1985.
Merington, Marguerite, ed. *The Custer Story: The Life and Intimate Letters of General George A. Custer and His Wife Elizabeth*. New York: Devin-Adair, 1950.
Michaels, Walter Benn. *The Gold Standard and the Logic of Naturalism: American Literature at the Turn of the Century*. Berkeley: U of California P, 1987.
Michelson, Bruce. *Mark Twain on the Loose: A Comic Writer and the American Self*. Amherst: U of Massachusetts P, 1995.
Miller, D. A. *The Novel and the Police*. Berkeley: U of California P, 1988.
Milner, Clyde A., II, Carol A. O'Connor, and Martha A. Sandweiss, eds. *The Oxford History of the American West*. New York: Oxford UP, 1994.
Milton, John R. *The Novel of the American West*. Lincoln: U of Nebraska P, 1980.
Mitchell, Lee Clark. "Verbally *Roughing It:* The West of Words." *Nineteenth Century Literature* 44.1 (1989): 67–92.
——. *Westerns: Making the Man in Fiction and Film*. Chicago: Chicago UP, 1996.
Morrow, Elizabeth. "The Artist as Heroine and Anti-Heroine in Mary Austin's *A Woman of Genius* and Anne Douglas Sedgewick's *Tante*." *American Literary Realism* 22.2 (1990): 17–29.
Morrow, Patrick D. "Parody and Parable in Early Western Local Color Writing." *Journal of the West* 19.1 (1980): 9–16.
Muir, John. "Flood-Storm in the Sierra." *Overland Monthly* June 1875: 489–96.
——. "A Geologist's Winter Walk." *Overland Monthly* Apr. 1873: 355–58.
——. *John Muir's Studies in the Sierra*. Ed. William E. Colby. San Francisco: Sierra Club, 1950.
——. *The Life and Letters of John Muir*. Ed. William Frederic Badé. 2 vols. Boston: Houghton Mifflin, 1924.
——. *The Mountains of California*. New York: Century, 1894.
——. *My First Summer in the Sierra*. Boston: Houghton Mifflin, 1911.
——. "Nevada's Dead Towns." *Daily Evening Bulletin* 15 Jan. 1879: 1. Rpt. in *Steep Trails*. Ed. William Frederic Badè. Boston: Houghton Mifflin, 1918. 195–203.
——. "The New Sequoia Forests of California." *Harper's New Monthly Magazine* Nov. 1878: 813–27.

———. "Rambles of a Botanist Among the Plants and Climates of California." *Old and New* 5.6 (1872): 767–72.
———. "Salmon-Breeding." *Daily Evening Bulletin* 29 Oct. 1874: 1. Rpt. in Engberg 21–27.
———. "Sierra Journal, Summer of 1869, v. 1," AMS. *The John Muir Papers*. University of the Pacific, Sonoma, Calif. Rpt. in Limbaugh and Lewis, reel 31.
———. "Summering in the Sierra. A Bit of Forest Study by John Muir. The Royal Sequoia." *Daily Evening Bulletin* 21 Sept. 1875: 1. Rpt. in Engberg, 123–9.
———. "Summering in the Sierra. John Muir Discourses of the Ancient River Channels. Their Importance as Gold Fountains—Eccentric Characters." *Daily Evening Bulletin* 26 July 1876: 1.
———. "Twenty Hill Hollow." *Overland Monthly* July 1872: 80–86.
———. "Wild Parks and Forest Reservations of the West." *Atlantic Monthly* Jan. 1898: 15–28.
———. "Yosemite Glaciers." *New York Daily Tribune* 5 Dec. 1871: 8.
Muller, John P., and William J. Richardson, eds. *The Purloined Poe: Lacan, Derrida, and Psychoanalytic Reading*. Baltimore: Johns Hopkins UP, 1988.
Murphy, Patrick D. *Literature, Nature, and Other: Ecofeminist Critiques*. Albany: State U of New York P, 1995.
Nash, Roderick. *Wilderness and the American Mind*. New Haven: Yale UP, 1967.
Nathan, Marvin. "San Francisco's Fin de Siécle Bohemian Renaissance." *California History* 61.3 (1982): 196–209.
"The New Era in California." *Overland Monthly* Mar. 1874: 281–83.
Nolan, William F., ed. *The Black Mask Boys: Masters in the Hard-Boiled School of Detective Fiction*. New York: William Morrow & Co., 1985.
———. *Dashiell Hammett: A Casebook*. Santa Barbara, CA: McNally & Loftin, 1969.
Norris, Frank. "An American School of Fiction? A Denial." *Boston Evening Transcript* 22 Jan. 1902: 17. Rpt. in *The Literary Criticism of Frank Norris* 108–11.
———. "A Bargain with Peg-Leg." *Collier's Weekly* 1 Mar. 1902. Rpt. in *A Deal in Wheat, and Other Stories of the Old and New West*. New York: Doubleday, Page, 1903. 63–75.
———. "Dying Fires." *The Third Circle*. New York: John Lane Co., 1909. 215–33.
———. *The Letters of Frank Norris*. Ed. Franklin Walker. San Francisco: Book Club of California, 1956.
———. *The Literary Criticism of Frank Norris*. Ed. Donald Pizer. Austin: U of Texas P, 1964.
———. "'The Literature of the West': A Reply to W. R. Lighton." *Boston Evening Transcript* 8 Jan. 1902: 7. Rpt. in *The Literary Criticism of Frank Norris* 104–7.
———. *McTeague: A Story of San Francisco*. 1899. Ed. Donald Pizer. New York: Norton, 1997.
———. "A Neglected Epic." *World's Work* 5 (Dec. 1902): 2904–6. Rpt. in *The Literary Criticism of Frank Norris* 119–22.
———. *The Octopus: A Story of California*. 1901. New York: Penguin USA, 1986.

——. "The Passing of Cock-Eye Blacklock." *Century* July 1902. Rpt. in *A Deal in Wheat, and Other Stories of the Old and New West*. New York: Doubleday, Page & Co., 1903. 81–97.

——. "Perverted Tales." *Wave* 18 Dec. 1897: 5–7. Rpt. in *The Literary Criticism of Frank Norris* 169–82.

——. "A Plea for Romantic Fiction." *Boston Evening Transcript* 18 Dec. 1901: 14. Rpt. in *The Literary Criticism of Frank Norris* 75–78.

Norwood, Vera. *Made from This Earth: American Women and Nature*. Chapel Hill: U of North Carolina P, 1993.

Oelschlaeger, Max. *The Idea of Wilderness: From Prehistory to the Age of Ecology*. New Haven: Yale UP, 1991.

The Official Guide to the California Midwinter Exposition. San Francisco: George Spaulding & Co., 1894.

The Official History of the California Midwinter International Exposition. San Francisco: The Press of H. S. Crocker Company, 1894.

O'Grady, John P. *Pilgrims to the Wild: Everett Ruess, Henry David Thoreau, John Muir, Clarence King, Mary Austin*. Salt Lake City: U of Utah P, 1993.

Olmsted, Frederick Law. *The California Frontier, 1863–1865*. Ed. Victoria Post Ranney, Gerard J. Rauluk, and Carolyn F. Hoffman. Vol. 5 of *The Papers of Frederick Law Olmsted*. Baltimore: Johns Hopkins UP, 1990.

Olmsted, R. R., ed. *Scenes of Wonder and Curiosity: Hutchings' California Magazine, 1856–1861*. Berkeley: Howell-North, 1962.

Oravec, Christine. "John Muir, Yosemite, and the Sublime Response; A Study in the Rhetoric of Preservationism." *Quarterly Journal of Speech* 67.3 (1981): 245–58.

Orvell, Miles. *The Real Thing: Imitation and Authenticity in American Culture, 1880–1940*. Chapel Hill: U of North Carolina P, 1989.

Parrington, Vernon Louis. *The Beginnings of Critical Realism in America, 1860–1920*. 1930. Vol. 3 of *Main Currents in American Thought: An Interpretation of American Literature from the Beginnings to 1920*. New York: Harcourt, Brace, 1927–30.

Paul, Rodman. "In Search of 'Dame Shirley.'" *Pacific Historical Review* 33 (1964): 127–64.

Pearce, T. M., ed. *Literary America, 1903–1934: The Mary Austin Letters*. Westport, CT: Greenwood, 1979.

Pisani, Donald J. *To Reclaim a Divided West: Water, Law, and Public Policy, 1848–1902*. Albuquerque: U of New Mexico P, 1992.

Pizer, Donald, ed. *Documents of American Realism and Naturalism*. Carbondale and Edwardsville: Southern Illinois UP, 1998.

Porter, Dennis. *The Pursuit of Crime: Art and Ideology in Detective Fiction*. New Haven: Yale UP, 1981.

Pratt, Mary Louise. *Imperial Eyes: Travel Writing and Transculturation*. London: Routledge, 1992.

Pryse, Marjorie. "Introduction." Austin, *The Land of Little Rain* vii–xl.

Quinn, Arthur Hobson. *The Literature of the American People*. New York: Appleton-Century-Crofts, 1951.

Raine, Anne. "'The Man at the Sources': Gender, Capital, and the Conservationist Landscape in Mary Austin's *The Ford*." Graulich and Klimasmith 243–66.

Rainey, Sue. *Creating* Picturesque America: *Monument to the National and Cultural Landscape*. Nashville: Vanderbilt UP, 1994.

Rather, Lois. *Men Will Be Boys: The Story of E Clampus Vitus*. Oakland, CA: Rather Press, 1980.

Reisner, Marc. *Cadillac Desert: The American West and Its Disappearing Water*. New York: Penguin, 1986.

Reynolds, David S. *Beneath the American Renaissance: The Subversive Imagination in the Age of Emerson and Melville*. New York: Knopf, 1988.

Ridge, John Rollin. *The Life and Adventures of Joaquín Murieta, the Celebrated California Bandit*. 1854. Norman: U of Oklahoma P, 1955.

Riebsame, William E., et al., eds. *Atlas of the New West: Portrait of a Changing Region*. New York: Norton, 1997.

Robbins, William G. *Colony and Empire: The Capitalist Transformation of the American West*. Lawrence: U of Kansas P, 1994.

Robinson, Forrest G. *Having It Both Ways: Self-Subversion in Western Popular Classics*. Albuquerque: U of New Mexico P, 1993.

Rodriquez, Richard. "True West: Relocating the Horizon of the American Frontier." *Harper's Monthly Magazine* Sept. 1996: 37–46.

Rohrbough, Malcolm J. *Days of Gold: The California Gold Rush and the American Nation*. Berkeley: U of California P, 1997.

Roorda, Randall. *Dramas of Solitude: Narratives of Retreat in American Nature Writing*. Albany: State U of New York P, 1998.

Roper, Laura Wood. *FLO: A Biography of Frederick Law Olmsted*. Baltimore: Johns Hopkins UP, 1973.

Rosowski, Susan J. *Birthing a Nation: Gender, Creativity, and the West in American Literature*. Lincoln: U of Nebraska P, 1999.

"A Rough Novel." *Boston Evening Transcript* 22 Mar. 1899: 10. Rpt. in McElrath and Knight 38–39.

Rowe, John Carlos. *The Other Henry James*. Durham, NC: Duke UP, 1998.

Ruehlmann, William. *Saint with a Gun: The Unlawful American Private Eye*. New York: New York UP, 1974.

Ruth, David E. *Inventing the Public Enemy: The Gangster in American Culture, 1918–1934*. Chicago: U of Chicago P, 1996.

Rydell, Robert W. *All the World's a Fair: Visions of Empire at American International Expositions, 1876–1916*. Chicago: U of Chicago P, 1984.

Saum, Lewis O. "Henry James's Christopher Newman: 'The American' as Westerner." *Henry James Review* 15.1 (1994): 1–9.

Schama, Simon. *Landscape and Memory*. New York: Knopf, 1995.

Scharnhorst, Gary. *Bret Harte*. New York: Twayne, 1992.
——. *Bret Harte: A Bibliography*. Lanham, MD: Scarecrow Press, 1995.
——. "Harte, Norris, and 'The Hero of Tomato Can.'" *Frank Norris Studies* 15 (Spring 1993): 8–10.
——. "Kate Field and the American West." *Platte Valley Review* 28.3 (2000): 41–56.
——. "Mark Twain, Bret Harte, and the Literary Construction of San Francisco." *San Francisco in Fiction: Essays in a Regional Literature*. Ed. David Fine and Paul Skenazy. Albuquerque: U of New Mexico P, 1995. 21–31.
——. "Maurice Thompson's Regional Critique of William D. Howells." *American Literary Realism* 9.1 (1976): 57–63.
——. "'Ways That Are Dark': Appropriations of Bret Harte's 'Plain Language from Truthful James.'" *Nineteenth-Century Literature* 51.3 (1996): 377–99.
——. "Whatever Happened to Bret Harte?" *American Realism and the Canon*. Ed. Tom Quirk and Gary Scharnhorst. Newark: U of Delaware P, 1994. 201–11.
——. "William Dean Howells and Maurice Thompson: At War over Realism?" *Old Northwest: A Journal of Regional Life and Letters* 5.3 (1979): 291–302.
Seelye, John, ed. *Stories of the Old West: Tales of the Mining Camp, Cavalry Troop, and Cattle Ranch*. New York: Penguin, 1994.
Seltzer, Mark. "Physical Capital: *The American* and the Realist Body." *New Essays on The American*. Ed. Martha Banta. Cambridge: Cambridge UP, 1987. 131–67.
Shi, David. *Facing Facts: Realism in American Thought and Culture, 1850–1920*. New York: Oxford UP, 1995.
Sinclair, Upton. *Oil!* 1927. Berkeley: U of California P, 1996.
Skenazy, Paul. *The New Wild West: The Urban Mysteries of Dashiell Hammett and Raymond Chandler*. Boise: U of Idaho P, 1982.
Slotkin, Richard. *Gunfighter Nation: The Myth of the Frontier in Twentieth-Century America*. New York: Harper Perennial, 1993.
Slovic, Scott. *Seeking Awareness in American Nature Writing: Henry Thoreau, Annie Dillard, Edward Abbey, Wendell Berry, Barry Lopez*. Salt Lake City: U of Utah P, 1992.
Smith, David. "The Public Eye of Raymond Chandler." *Journal of American Studies* 14.3 (1980): 423–41.
Smith, Erin A. *Hard-Boiled: Working-Class Readers and Pulp Magazines*. Philadelphia: Temple UP, 2000.
Smith, Henry [Nash]. "The Feel of the Purposeful Earth: Mary Austin's Prophecy." *New Mexico Quarterly* 1.1 (1931): 17–33.
——. *Virgin Land: The American West as Symbol and Myth*. 1950. Cambridge: Harvard UP, 1970.
Speir, Jerry. "The Ultimate Seacoast: Ross Macdonald's California." Fine 133–44.
Starr, Kevin. *Americans and the California Dream, 1850–1915*. New York: Oxford UP, 1973.
——. *Inventing the Dream: California through the Progressive Era*. New York: Oxford UP, 1985.

——. *Material Dreams: Southern California through the 1920s*. New York: Oxford UP, 1990.

Stegner, Wallace, ed. *Selected American Prose: The Realistic Movement, 1841–1900*. New York: Rinehart & Co., 1958.

Steinbrink, Jeffrey. *Getting to Be Mark Twain*. Berkeley: U of California P, 1991.

Stevens, J. David. "'She War a woman': Family Roles, Gender, and Sexuality in Bret Harte's Western Fiction." *American Literature* 69.3 (1997): 571–93.

Stineman, Esther Lanigan. *Mary Austin: Song of a Maverick*. New Haven: Yale UP, 1989.

Stoneley, Peter. "Rewriting the Gold Rush: Twain, Harte, and Homosociality." *Journal of American Studies* 30.2 (1996): 189–209.

Stout, Janis P. "Mary Austin's Feminism: A Reassessment." *Studies in the Novel* 30.1 (1998): 77–101.

Sundquist, Eric. "The Country of the Blue." *American Realism: New Essays*. Ed. Eric Sundquist. Baltimore: Johns Hopkins UP, 1982. 3–27.

Tanner, Stephen L. "The Function of Simile in Raymond Chandler's Novels." *Studies in American Humor* 3.4 (1984–85): 337–46. Rpt. in Van Dover 167–75.

Tatum, Stephen. "Historical Realism and the American West: The Example of Charles Neider's *The Authentic Death of Hendry Jones*." Meldrum 31–48.

Taylor, Cynthia. "Claiming Female Space: Mary Austin's Western Landscape." *The Big Empty: Essays on Western Landscapes as Narrative*. Ed. Leonard Engel. Albuquerque: U of New Mexico P, 1994. 119–32.

Taylor, R. E., Louis A. Payen, and Peter J. Slota, Jr. "The Age of the Calaveras Skull: Dating the 'Piltdown Man' of the New World." *American Antiquity* 57.2 (1992): 269–75.

Teague, David W. *The Southwest in American Literature and Art: The Rise of a Desert Aesthetic*. Tucson: U of Arizona P, 1997.

Thomas, Brook. *American Literary Realism and the Failed Promise of Contract*. Berkeley: U of California P, 1997.

Tompkins, Jane. *West of Everything: The Inner Life of Westerns*. New York: Oxford UP, 1992.

Trachtenberg, Alan. *The Incorporation of America: Culture and Society in the Gilded Age*. New York: Hill and Wang, 1982.

——. *Reading American Photographs: Images as History, Mathew Brady to Walker Evans*. New York: Hill & Wang, 1989.

Tracy, Henry Chester. *American Naturists*. New York: Dutton, 1930.

Turner, Frederick. *Rediscovering America: John Muir in His Time and Ours*. New York: Viking, 1985.

Tuttle, Jennifer. "To Rest or To West? Charlotte Perkins Gilman, Owen Wister, and the Sexual Politics of Nervous Exhaustion." Western Literature Association 32nd Annual Meeting. Sheraton Old Town Hotel, Albuquerque, NM, 16 Oct. 1997.

Twain, Mark. "A Bloody Massacre Near Carson." *Territorial Enterprise* 28 Oct. 1863. Rpt. in *Early Tales and Sketches* 1: 325–26.

———. *Clemens of the Call: Mark Twain in San Francisco*. Ed. Edgar Marquess Branch. Berkeley: U of California UP, 1969.

———. *Contributions to* The Galaxy: *1868–1871*. Ed. Bruce R. McElderry, Jr. Gainesville, FL: Scholars' Facsimiles & Reprints, 1961.

———. *Early Tales and Sketches: Volume 1 (1851–1864)*. Ed. Edgar Marquess Branch and Robert H. Hirst. Berkeley: U of California P, 1979.

———. *The Mark Twain Letters: Volume 1, 1853–1866*. Ed. Edgar Marquess Branch, Michael B. Frank, and Kenneth M. Sanderson. Berkeley: U of California P, 1988.

———. *Mark Twain of the Enterprise: Newspaper Articles and Other Documents, 1862–1864*. Ed. Henry Nash Smith. Berkeley: U of California P, 1957.

———. *Mark Twain's Journals and Notebooks, Vol. 1 (1855–1873)*. Ed. Frederick Anderson, Michael B. Frank, and Kenneth M. Sanderson. Berkeley: U of California P, 1975.

———. *Roughing It*. 1872. Ed. Harriet Elinor Smith and Edgar Marquess Branch. Berkeley: U of California P, 1993.

———. "A Small Piece of Spite." *San Francisco Daily Morning Call* 6 Sept. 1864: 1. Rpt. in *Clemens of the Call* 235–36.

Twelve Southerners. *I'll Take My Stand: The South and the Agrarian Tradition*. New York: Harper & Brothers.

Vanderbilt, Kermit. *American Literature and the Academy: The Roots, Growth, and Maturity of a Profession*. Philadelphia: U of Pennsylvania P, 1986.

Van Doren, Carl. *Contemporary American Novelists, 1900–1920*. New York: Macmillan, 1923.

———. "Introduction." *The Land of Little Rain*. By Mary Austin. Boston: Houghton Mifflin, 1950. xi–xv.

Van Dover, J. K., ed. *The Critical Response to Raymond Chandler*. Westport, CT: Greenwood Press, 1995.

Walker, Franklin. *Frank Norris: A Biography*. New York: Doubleday, Doran & Co., 1932.

———. *San Francisco's Literary Frontier*. New York: Knopf, 1939.

Walsh, Mary Ellen Williams. "*Angle of Repose* and the Writings of Mary Hallock Foote: A Source Study." *Critical Essays on Wallace Stegner*. Ed. Anthony Arthur. Boston: G. K. Hall, 1982. 184–209.

Ward, Elizabeth, and Alain Silver, eds. *Raymond Chandler's Los Angeles*. Woodstock, NY: Overlook Press, 1987.

Warner, Charles Dudley. "Studies of the Great West." *Harper's New Monthly Magazine* Mar. 1888: 556–69.

Westbrook, Max. "The Authentic Western." *Western American Literature* 13.3 (1978): 213–25.

———. "Conservative, Liberal, and Western: Three Modes of American Realism." *South Dakota Review* 4.2 (1966): 3–19. Rpt. in *The Literature of the American West*. Ed. J. Golden Taylor. Boston: Houghton Mifflin, 1971. 9–22.

Weygand, James Lamar. *Winona Holiday: The Story of the Western Association of Writers*. Nappanee, IN: Private press of the author, 1948.

White, Stewart Edward. *The Claim Jumpers; A Romance*. New York: Grosset & Dunlap, 1901.

———. "The Saving Grace." *McClure's* Sept. 1899: 398–406. Rpt. in *Blazed Trail Stories, and Stories of the Wild Life*. New York: McClure, Phillips & Co., 1904. 198–221.

White, William Allen. "A Woman of Genius." *Saturday Review of Literature* 12 Nov. 1932: 235–36.

Wilkins, Thurman. *John Muir: Apostle of Nature*. Norman: U of Oklahoma P, 1995.

Will, Barbara. "The Nervous Origins of the American Western." *American Literature* 70.2 (1998): 293–316.

Willis, N. P. "The Mammoth Trees of California." *Hutchings' California Magazine* Mar. 1859: 191–203. Rpt. in R. R. Olmsted 205–17.

Wilson, Christopher P. *The Labor of Words: Literary Professionalism in the Progressive Era*. Athens: U of Georgia P, 1985.

———. *The Virginian: A Horseman of the Plains*. New York: Macmillan, 1902.

Witschi, Nicolas. "Sinclair Lewis, the Voice of Satire, and Mary Austin's Revolt from the Village." *American Literary Realism* 30.1 (1997): 75–90.

Wolfe, Linnie Marsh. *Son of the Wilderness: The Life of John Muir*. New York: Knopf, 1945.

Wonham, Henry B. *Mark Twain and the Art of the Tall Tale*. New York: Oxford UP, 1993.

Woods, Daniel B. *Sixteen Months at the Gold Diggings*. New York: Harper Bros., 1851.

Worster, Donald. *Rivers of Empire: Water, Aridity, and the Growth of the American West*. New York: Pantheon Books, 1986.

Wright, Harold Bell. *The Winning of Barbara Worth*. Chicago: Book Supply Co., 1911.

Wyatt, David. *The Fall into Eden: Landscape and Imagination in California*. Cambridge: Cambridge UP, 1986.

———. *Five Fires: Race, Catastrophe, and the Shaping of California*. Reading, MA: Addison-Wesley, 1997.

Yates, Norris. *Gender and Genre: An Introduction to Women Writers of Formula Westerns, 1900–1950*. Albuquerque: U of New Mexico P, 1995.

Žižek, Slavoj. *Looking Awry: An Introduction to Jacques Lacan through Popular Culture*. Cambridge: October–MIT Press, 1992.

Index